D1422421

Social and Stylistic Variation in Spoken French

Impact: Studies in language and society

IMPACT publishes monographs, collective volumes, and text books on topics in sociolinguistics and language pedagogy. The scope of the series is broad, with special emphasis on areas such as language planning and language policies; language conflict and language death; language standards and language change; dialectology; diglossia; discourse studies; language and social identity (gender, ethnicity, class, ideology); and history and methods of sociolinguistics

General editor

Annick De Houwer (University of Antwerp)

Advisory board

Volume 8

Social and Stylistic Variation in Spoken French: A comparative approach
by Nigel Armstrong

Social and Stylistic Variation
in Spoken French

A comparative approach

Nigel Armstrong
University of Leeds

db **John Benjamins Publishing Company**
Amsterdam/Philadelphia

∞ ™The paper used in this publication meets the minimum requirements of American National Standard for Information Sciences – Permanence of Paper for Printed Library Materials, ANSI z39.48-1984.

Library of Congress Cataloging-in-Publication Data

Armstrong, Nigel.
    Social and stylistic variation in spoken French : a comparative approach / Nigel Armstrong.
    p. cm. (Impact: Studies in language and society, ISSN 1385–7908 ; v. 8)
    Includes bibliographical references and indexes.
        1. French language--Variation. 2. French language--Spoken French. I. Title.
    II. Impact (Series : Amsterdam, Netherlands)

PC2074.7.A87   2001
306.44'0944--dc21   2001035022
ISBN 90 272 1839 0 (Eur.) / 1 58811 063 X (US) (Hb; alk. paper)

© 2001 – John Benjamins B.V.
No part of this book may be reproduced in any form, by print, photoprint, microfilm, or any other means, without written permission from the publisher.

John Benjamins Publishing Co. · P.O.Box 36224 · 1020 ME Amsterdam · The Netherlands
John Benjamins North America · P.O.Box 27519 · Philadelphia PA 19118-0519 · USA

Table of contents

Acknowledgments

I should like to express my thanks to the following for their help and encouragement in the preparation of this book, from its earliest stages as a PhD thesis to its drafting in article and then book-chapter form: Allan Bell, Aidan Coveney, Françoise Gadet, Anita Berit Hansen, Marie-Anne Hintze, Anthony Lodge, Ian Mackenzie, James Milroy, Lesley Milroy, Marie-Louise Moreau and Alan Smith. I am grateful equally to the dynasties of anonymous referees who commented upon the sections of the book that appeared first as journal articles or chapters in other volumes; and to the publisher's referees, who improved the book greatly by making many invaluable recommendations.

Special thanks are due to Zoë Boughton, who designed and carried out the perceptual study described in Chapter 2, and to Anita Berit Hansen, who provided the Paris results discussed in chapter 3.

Some chapters of this book have appeared as published journal articles or chapters in other volumes. A description and discussion of the perceptual study included in Chapter 2 was published, jointly with Zoë Boughton, as 'Identification and evaluation responses to a French accent: some results and issues of methodology', in *Revue PArole*, vol. 5/6. pp. 27–60, dated 1998 (published in 1999). Some sections of Chapters 2 and 3 were published as 'The socio-stylistic function of linguistic variation in contemporary standard French', in *Linguistic identities and policies in France and the French-speaking world*, D Marley, M.-A. Hintze, G. Parker (eds), pp. 131–48, London: AFLS/CILT, 1998. The earlier sections of Chapter 4 appeared in *Revue PArole*, vol. 3/4, pp. 191–216, 1997 (published in 1999) as 'A sociolinguistic perspective on variable grammar in French and English'. An earlier version of Chapter 6 appeared in *Zeitschrift für romanische Philologie*, vol. 114, 3, pp. 462–95 in 1998, entitled 'La variation sociolinguistique dans le lexique français'.

The author and publishers are grateful to Didier Erudition and to Max Niemeyer Verlag for permission reproduce this material; and to Editions du Seuil for permission to reproduce material from *La liaison avec et sans enchaînement. Phonologie tridimensionelle et usage du français*, by Pierre Encrevé, 1987.

CHAPTER 1

Introduction

1.1 Aim and scope of the present work

The aim of the present work is to examine the orientation of French speakers towards their standard or non-local language, as shown by their behaviour on different levels of linguistic analysis and in different speech styles. We discuss in a following section, and in several places in this book, the difficulties associated with applying terms such as 'standard', 'non-local', and 'levelled' to the French language. The research reported here is set within the variationist sociolinguistic paradigm developed by Labov, largely studying American English, since the 1960s, e.g. Labov (1966, 1972b), and adapted to other languages and language varieties: to British English, for example by Trudgill (1974) and Milroy (1987a); to Canadian French, for example by Sankoff and Cedergren (1976); and to Latin American Spanish, by Lavandera (1984).

The scope of this book is delimited by the variety, or set of sub-varieties, of French that are referred to by various terms, all more or less unsatisfactory: the Gallicisms 'metropolitan' or 'hexagonal' French include the southern varieties of French, concerning which we will say little here; a further term sometimes used, but which refers strictly to the Ile-de-France varieties, is 'Francien'. Similarly, the term 'standard French', although idiomatic in English, conveys a misleadingly limited sense of the social and stylistic compass of the language varieties that are the focus of attention here. These are subsumed under the variety normally thought of as 'French', the variety originating from the Ile de France, which has spread over the northern half of France to the detriment of almost all competing languages and Romance varieties; which is distinct in its pronunciation from, and bears a heteronomous relation to, the varieties of the Midi; and whose most prestigious form is the standard sub-variety, and is hence more or less by definition a benchmark against which all other varieties are measured. As we implied above, 'standard French' is not a monolithic language variety, but ranges from the 'frozen' sub-varieties appropriate to the most elevated speech styles, to the colloquial sub-varieties that most speakers use most of the time. In any event, the 'standard' accent is distributed very widely, both socially and geographically in the area of interest here (defined below), a fact whose implications we discuss at length here.

To summarise, the French variety of we examine here is what may be referred to, with some qualifications, by using the (now chiefly diachronic) term *langue d'oïl* or *oïl* French: the urban non-southern French of France, spoken in the area broadly north of the Garonne and the Massif Central, excluding the extreme peripheral areas of Alsace in the east, (arguably) the Lille-Roubaix-Tourcoing conurbation in the north, and the Breton-speaking west of Brittany. The *oïl* variety is of course distributed in these latter areas as a prestige lect, but we explain below the theoretical reasons for excluding them. Regarding the stylistic dimension, by the term 'standard' we do not intend to imply a highly formal style; the language data discussed here were recorded in the course of sociolinguistic interviews intended to elicit an approximation to an everyday 'consultative' style (cf. Joos 1961). In addition we will examine some quite informal language data in Chapters 2 and 3. Thus defined, our object of study lines up quite closely with an intuitive perception of 'French'; use of this term, unless specified otherwise, should be understood henceforward in the sense described above. For clarity we shall occasionally refer to '*oïl* French'.

Despite its demographic and cultural importance French has been rather little studied using Labovian methods. The numerical importance of French is considerable: some nine million speakers live in the Parisian region alone; and the northern half of the country, which is rather densely populated and highly industrialised, at least relative to the Midi, comprises at least half of the French population; especially if the Lyon conurbation, which linguistically appears to be in the *oïl* area, is included. The interest of studying French lies in the attempt to establish whether or not its socio-stylistic patterns bear fundamental similarities to languages that are comparable in being spoken in countries that have a fairly similar social, economic and industrial organisation; that is Western industrial societies.

We will say rather little here about the other major French varieties. Canadian French has been studied in some depth by the variationist researchers mentioned above as well as many others, with the result that in contrast to *oïl* French, a good deal is known of social-linguistic variation in the Canadian varieties.

The research issues examined in this book are the following: phonological, grammatical and lexical variation in French, considered from the point of view of the sociolinguistic functions that French speakers exercise in their variable language use on these levels of linguistic analysis. The quantitative analysis of these functions implies in turn a further issue: an examination of the relationship between social and stylistic variation. We devote furthermore a chapter to liaison, an unusual area of variation that deserves separate study on account of the fact that it receives input from several linguistic levels and has an idiosyncratic social-stylistic distribution.

The relationship between social-stylistic variation is of course central to the Labovian programme, which is concerned primarily to understand how linguistic change is actuated and diffused by studying patterns of, and interactions between, synchronic linguistic variation along the social and stylistic dimensions of language use. The present work is concerned similarly with the examination of these patterns of variation, but has as its principal aim not the relation between variation and change, but rather the analysis of sociolinguistic patterning in French with a view to examining the distinctive effects on the social-stylistic relationship in this language of the considerable standardisation and levelling pressures that have been exerted (and continue to be exerted) upon speakers of the French language. More plainly, the aim in this book is to examine whether variationist methods and theories, which have been developed to a large extent on the basis of British and American English, 'work' or can be applied successfully to French. In what follows, comparison will be made above all with the British varieties of English, partly because a substantial volume of successful variationist research has been carried on them, and partly because the present author feels confident in referring to this work with a native speaker's intuitive knowledge. In the rest of this chapter we examine in some detail the methods and theories referred to above, and the concepts that underpin them. We have made use above of certain terms that are of central significance in variationist analysis: 'standard language'; 'standardisation'; 'speech style'; 'social variation'. In the rest of this chapter, these terms will be defined and discussed. The account of the social-stylistic relation that we consider here is perhaps the most theoretically robust so far proposed: Bell's (1984) 'audience design' theory. We set out in detail below the theories of social-stylistic variation in phonology and grammar to which the present work makes reference; as stated above these theories are formulated largely on the basis of research findings in English, as well as in Canadian French and Latin American Spanish. In a subsequent section we sketch, in relation to a cross-linguistic perspective suggested by Hudson (1996), the contrasting sociolinguistic situations in English and in French.

1.2   Levelling and standardisation

The connotations of the term 'standard language', even for scholars of linguistics, have the potential to evoke notions of 'correctness'. Therefore we largely avoid the term henceforward, referring to the variety of French of interest here as 'levelled'. We discuss this distinction briefly, before discussing the substantive research issues that are the principal focus here.

The pronunciation of the variety of French of interest here can be described as being relatively 'levelled' and/or 'standardised'. We use the term 'levelling' to refer to the diminution of linguistic differences between language varieties as a result of acts of accommodation taking place relatively 'horizontally' or non-hierarchically, at the level of peer groups and essentially as a result of social and geographical mobility. Levelling can be broadly opposed in principle to language standardisation, the process of the suppression of linguistic variation in response to institutional, 'top–down' initiatives, perhaps most notably through pressures exerted by the educational system, as well as by the examples of the written and electronic press. In practice of course, at the level of the individual speaker these processes are inseparable, since speakers who participate in a levelling process that they perceive to be relatively non-coercive will also be responsive to institutional pressures. Correspondingly, the asymmetrical relation between the standard and non-standard sets of varieties of French implies a degree of upward convergence belied by the term 'levelling', rather than more truly mutual accommodation processes such as those reported recently by several researchers in more than one country, for instance Hinskens (1992); Kerswill and Williams (2000).

The phenomenon of dialect levelling is currently the focus of considerable interest in UK English; for instance, Foulkes and Docherty (1999b: 1–24) suggest that many changes current in these varieties of English can be thought of in connexion with social processes that are reducing regional accent differences. Foulkes and Docherty state (p. 13) that 'levelling differs from standardisation (or dedialectalisation) in that speakers do not automatically abandon their local forms in preference for the standard'. What appears to be happening in the UK is that highly localised accent features are in recession, in favour of more widely distributed regional norms. Very broadly, this is taking place over two large areas: in the south of the UK, the south-eastern variety popularly known as 'Estuary English' is spreading north and west, while in the north, localised features are giving way to a widely distributed northern English. At the same time, certain features of 'Estuary English' are spreading throughout the nation.

This process is pertinent to the current *oïl* French situation, firstly because a comparable situation appears already to have been consolidated over the *oïl* area, with Parisian French having successfully spread over this area to the detriment of regional varieties of French; secondly, the French situation is distinctive because it is arguable that standardising rather than levelling pressures have been more largely responsible for this state of affairs. This is in contrast to what is in progress in other countries, where as Foulkes and Docherty point out that in recent years (1999b: 2) 'urban dialectology has been touched [...] perhaps most of all by upheavals in the social structure of the communities under scrutiny'. These upheavals essentially concern the dissolution of close-tie networks under the pressure exerted by the need for increasing social and geographical mobility. These pressures are also at work in France, of course. We shall have more to say about the standardising–levelling distinction in subsequent chapters, but in the mean time note that we hope in the present book to throw light on this current debate by discussing the French situation.

1.3   Variationist sociolinguistics

The subject of this study is therefore sociolinguistic variation in a corpus of contemporary spoken French, looked at largely within a Labovian, 'variationist' framework of analysis. As such it is addressed both to scholars of French, and of sociolinguistics generally. For this reason we gloss French examples in what follows. Within this context it need hardly be said that the variationist approach seeks, through the quantitative study of synchronic linguistic variation, to uncover the principles, both social and linguistic, that govern the actuation and diffusion of diachronic language change. Nevertheless we set out these principles in order to situate them in relation to the aims of this book. For the purposes of clear exposition we can distinguish (although the two are of course inextricably linked) between differences of goal and method.

Milroy's (1987b: 96) definition of the goal of the Labovian programme provides a useful way in: 'Labov's main concern [is] to obtain insights into processes of linguistic change and to challenge linguistic theories which modelled language as a static entity, identifying *homogeneity* with *structure*' [emphasis in original]. The Labovian variationist method, by analysing variable language data using quantitative methods, attempts to formulate general principles of linguistic variation and change. Sociolinguistics is of course a broad discipline, extending on the one hand to the 'socio' end which draws heavily upon the insights of sociology and may regard linguistic variation as a form of social behaviour like any other; and on the other hand to the end which emphasises the linguistic aspects of sociolinguistic variation, tending to abstract away from the individual speaker in order to focus on variation and change in the language through the examination of the 'sociolinguistic patterns' that speaker groups exhibit.

The present study is situated, so far as method is concerned, towards the 'system-oriented', quantifying-linguistic end of sociolinguistics, rather than the 'speaker-oriented' discursive-social end. But the principal goal of the research reported here differs from that mentioned above, namely the formulation and testing of general principles of linguistic variation and change. We now look at variationist goals and methods in more detail.

We said above that the variationist method tends to focus on the linguistic behaviour of groups of speakers. It will be obvious that the linguist working in this paradigm sees speaker groups as being constituted, for research purposes, according to the social or 'demographic' attributes of the speakers concerned: those attributes that have been shown in many studies, starting of course with Labov, to be important in influencing linguistic behaviour.

Although a few early studies foreshadowed Labov's pioneering work on linguistic variation, Labov was the first to show the structured nature of linguistic variation and change, and to bring to light systematic correlations between speakers' demographic attributes (principally social class, age, sex and ethnicity) and their orientation to the standard language. He did this by developing a methodology that allowed him to study linguistic change and how it penetrates linguistic contexts, as well as spreading socially. An essential element of this methodology involves the study of stylistic variation; that is, linguistic variation which responds broadly to the formal–informal dimension of a speech situation (we use the term 'style' where some linguists have 'register', reserving the latter term to refer to the dimension of linguistic variation that responds to topic: the register of law, of medicine and so forth).

The methodology developed by Labov has in effect placed the situational variable of speech style centrally in variationist theory. The reason for this is that Labov accords to a speaker's vernacular, or most informal speech style, a primary importance; it is in the more unguarded styles that the actuation and diffusion of linguistic change appears to take place. Furthermore, the regular structural patterns evident in the vernacular tend to be obscured in more formal styles; whence the emphasis in the Labovian programme of the development of methods designed to gain access to the least formal speech styles.

However, the 'classic' sociolinguistic interview aims also at capturing, if not the whole range, then a least a reasonable spread of a speaker's stylistic repertoire. This involves the recording of more formal speech styles: formal spoken as well as several reading styles. Again, numerous findings demonstrate that speakers show their awareness of the relation between social and stylistic variation by using, in more formal speech situations, linguistic forms which are correspondingly closer to the standard variety available to them; conversely, speakers approximate to vernacular forms in less formal styles. This is intuitively obvious, although again Labov was the first scholar clearly to articulate and systematise this principle.

More importantly however, from the Labovian viewpoint we can consider the study of speech style as a methodological procedure which seeks to infer mechanisms of linguistic variation and change by interpreting patterns of association, between on the one hand stylistic (intraspeaker) variation, and on the other hand variation on the social (interspeaker) levels of age, sex, class etc. This indirect, inferential method is required given that linguistic change cannot be observed directly in a systematic way. Through the use of inferential procedures therefore, certain patterns of interaction can be interpreted as being indicative of change in progress, others of stability; others of temporary change; yet others of incipient change. We discuss some of these patterns more fully in Chapter 2.

In contrast to this variation–change relationship, the present study has as its principal aim the examination of patterns of social-stylistic variation in French with a view to examining the effects on the social-stylistic relationship of the high degree of standardisation that the French language has undergone. We aim to do this by examining the currently prevalent model of social-stylistic variation in the light of the results that have emerged from a Labovian analysis of a corpus of spoken French. We do however devote some space in Chapter 4 to a discussion of the relation between patterns of variation and change, with the aim of elucidating the patterns characteristic of French variable grammar.

The relation that obtains between social and stylistic variation is thus a central theoretical element of the present work. This relation is of course of interest across languages generally, but we focus here on UK English and in particular on French, given the interest inherent in examining the rather highly standardised languages of two nations that are fairly closely comparable in their present social and industrial organisation; even if their respective linguistic histories differ rather sharply.

1.4   Social and stylistic functions of sociolinguistic variation

Numerous studies of British and American English have shown that in these two sets of varieties, variable pronunciation differentiates speaker groups in highly systematic ways, notably along the social dimensions of age, sex, class and ethnicity. A theoretically well-motivated and powerful way of regarding these patterns of variation is in terms of speakers' perceptions of the relationship of vernacular language varieties to the standard or standards. This is because the vernacular–standard relationship propels both social and stylistic variation. Many findings demonstrate that, in English at least, speakers have hitherto shown their awareness of the relation between social and stylistic variation by using in formal speech styles linguistic forms that are closer to the standard variety; conversely, speakers approximate to vernacular forms in less formal styles. Thus speakers can be regarded as signalling their localisation in what Hudson (1996:207) has called a 'multi-dimensional [social] space' by situating themselves, on the one hand in relation to values (perhaps principally educatedness) associated with the supra-regional standard language variety available to them; and on the other, to the localised vernaculars associated with solidarity-based, 'home-team' values. This orientation is in its turn expressed in the interaction between social and stylistic variation.

As noted above, perhaps the most systematic and well-grounded account of the relationship between social and stylistic variation is the theory of audience design formulated by Bell (1984). We will have occasion to discuss Bell's theory in some detail in later chapters, but briefly, Bell developed this theory with the aim of constructing a coherent account of social-stylistic variation in spoken language. The major postulate which is relevant here is that it is the 'audience', in the sense of a speaker's addressee(s), that is/are primarily responsible for causing the speaker to 'design' a stretch of language in response to the social characteristics of the audience, by pitching the language at a certain point on the formal–informal style continuum. This account seems to fit the British English sociolinguistic situation more closely than the functional view, propounded most notably by Finegan and Biber (1994), according to which the relation between social and style variation is broadly explicable by reference to the fact that middle-class speakers have greater occasion to use, and therefore greater access to, a wider range of 'elaborated' speech styles than working-class speakers. This view fails to take into account the linguistically arbitrary nature of much socially conditioned phonological variation in English; Bell (1995) has a more recent critical evaluation of Finegan and Biber's account of style variation.

Bell (1984) suggests further that social or interspeaker variation is primary in the way in which complex societies are organised. These undergo division into groups, some of which enjoy more prestige than others; the language of prestige groups comes to be highly prized. Thus speakers perceive the prestige standard to be the language variety most appropriate to more formal speech situations. Bell's theory was formulated in response to an earlier suggestion (Labov 1972b: 99) that the principal factor which determines the degree of (in)formality in speech is the degree of self-monitoring, or attention paid to speech production, exercised by the speaker. Bell argues that self-monitoring is a lower-order, mechanical factor which intervenes between choice of style and language production. Bell applied the insights of the accommodation theory of social psychology (cf. Giles and St Clair 1979) to a wide range of sociolinguistic data, concluding (i) that a speaker's choice of speech style is conditioned by the social status of the addressee(s) (social status taken in a broad definition and including at least age, sex and social class); and (ii) that speech style and social status are related in that formal speech events call for the use of prestigious language varieties. A central assumption is that speakers wish to accommodate or converge their speech to resemble that of their addressee, in order to enhance co-operation and win approval; but speakers may of course prefer to diverge their speech so as to mark social distance. In this sense style variation derives from social variation; the important point of this argument for our purposes is the quantitative relation between social and style variation. Bell (1984: 153) asserts that the primacy of social variation entails that interspeaker variation will always exceed style or (in Bell's phrase) intraspeaker variation in quantitative terms.

In summary, phono-stylistic variation in English and other languages has been shown to be mediated largely through the probabilistic use of arbitrary linguistic variants, and appears to be motivated, as Bell suggests, by orientation to addressee. A number of researchers (Johnston 1983; Newbrook 1986) have however reported patterns of social-stylistic variation which run contrary to the numerical social-style relation described above, suggesting that certain linguistic situations disfavour the classic pattern described by Bell. This latter pattern tends to be found where standard and vernacular phonologies are similar, but breaks down in 'dialect divergent' situations, where the standard and the vernacular are structurally very dissimilar. The classic pattern may also break down where a language's phonology has been greatly levelled, as in the case of French. In the following section we discuss the *oïl* French situation in more detail.

1.5   Variation in French and English; and across languages generally

As was mentioned above, Bell has suggested that the inherent primacy of social variation necessarily entails that interspeaker variation will always exceed intraspeaker variation quantitatively. This is perhaps principally because no one speaker or speaker group will command the entire stylistic spectrum as reflected in the range of socially conditioned linguistic variation, from the lowest to the highest ranked social group (in social-class terms). Bell's assertion is of course predicated upon the assumption that speakers inevitably employ phonological variation to express social affiliation. The thesis we aim to examine in this book is that where the phonology of a language has undergone rather radical level-ling, the quantitative social-stylistic relation described by Bell may show some unusual effects. Specifically, the situation referred to by Bell as 'hyperstyle' variation, where the degree of style variation is greater than variation along the social dimension(s), may be widespread in French on account of social factors as well as linguistic ones. Bell described hyperstyle variation as essentially anomalous, but where a language has a phonology that shows rather small degrees of phonological variation along the interspeaker dimensions, degrees of stylistic variation may be *relatively* large (the adverb is crucial).

A further corollary to this hypothesis is that social-stylistic variation in French may have been displaced to the grammatical and lexical levels. It has been pointed out by several scholars (Hudson 1996: 45; Chambers 1995: 51–2) that grammatical variation is less likely to be quantitative than variation in the sound system (for reasons discussed in the following paragraph), but one can question the view that variation on this linguistic level is by its nature virtually always qualitative; this view may reflect a strong bias towards English in the existing data. Certainly, the findings available (e.g. Wolfram 1969; Cheshire 1982) suggest that grammatical variation in English shows a quasi-qualitative pattern, with the variable use of some grammatical features present in working-class speech, but almost totally avoided by middle-class speakers.

A rather dissimilar situation in French is suggested by the somewhat fragmentary variationist data available, represented for instance by findings reported in Valdman (1982) and Coveney (1996). These findings suggest a sociolinguistic distribution of certain French grammatical variables that resemble phonological variables in their non-polarised patterning. Thus it may be that a language such as French, whose phonology has been successfully levelled, may not conform to the tendency to suppress grammatical variation; this tendency is suggested by Hudson (1996: 44–8) as a general one across languages. This issue is the subject of Chapter 4.

One principal aim of the present work is therefore to analyse a number of sociolinguistic patterns in various corpora of spoken French, with a view to considering the significance of the non-conformity of these patterns to the 'classic' ones described in the sociolinguistic literature and systematised by Bell into a theory of social-stylistic variation at the phonological level. At the same time we consider some issues of sociolinguistic methodology that have a bearing on these patterns of variation in phonology.

We also present some results from French with the more extended aim of investigating the way in which variation functions on linguistic levels other than phonology and grammar. A further aim in this connexion is to examine the implications for sociolinguistic theory and methodology of the attempt to analyse variation on linguistic levels that have not commonly been the object of study from a variationist optic.

1.6   Structure of this book

This monograph is organised as follows: Chapter 2 describes and discusses the patterns of phonological variation most frequently found in the sociolinguistic literature. Subsequently, the results of a recent evaluative survey of French social-regional pronunciation are described, and their implications for the way in which variable pronunciation functions in French are examined. Chapter 3 describes the corpora of spoken French that are the basis of the present study, and analyses some patterns of phonological variation in the corpora in order to examine the distinctive character of variation in French on this linguistic level. In Chapter 4 we discuss the socio-stylistic distribution of some grammatical variables in English and especially French, suggesting that the distinctiveness of the French situation is as described above, namely that French variable grammar functions in a 'quantitative' way that recalls the phonological level in other languages. A concluding section examines some results and issues connected with a variationist cross-stylistic examination of the French variable *ne* in the corpus of spoken French that is largely the focus of interest here. In Chapter 5 we consider the linguistic and socio-stylistic character of French variable liaison, using variationist results, and we examine the cross-linguistic distinctiveness of this area of variation. Chapter 6 discusses some results, as well as some of the issues of theory and method, issuing from an attempt to apply the variationist method to the lexicon of French. Chapter 7 summarises the findings and conclusions presented in this book, and suggests further lines of enquiry.

CHAPTER 2

Patterns of phonological variation

2.1 Introduction

The aim of this chapter is to provide a broad overarching account of the theoretical issues that relate to the socio-stylistic functions of phonological variation, principally in French although substantial reference will be made to English also. These issues will be discussed using illustrative data from the two languages. In the following chapter we examine in greater detail the factors that in French influence the relationship between social (interspeaker) and stylistic (intraspeaker) variation, using more copious French language data. In what follows we use these terms, coined by Bell (1984), since 'social' variation, unless narrowly defined, can be thought of as comprising style variation, and since usage varies among linguists between 'style' and 'register' variation (cf. Biber and Finegan 1994).

Among the consistent findings which have emerged from the quantitative work carried out on variable language data in the Labovian paradigm over the last 35 years or so, those concerning variation on the levels of phonology and grammar are now numerous enough, certainly in English, to permit consideration of certain fundamental issues in variation theory which are the themes of the present book: the relation between interspeaker and intraspeaker variation; and the relative importance for the expression of different aspects of a speaker's social identity of variability, principally on the phonological and grammatical levels.

One of the central achievements of Labovian methodology has been to show, in a clearly accountable way, initially in English and then in many other languages, that socially-conditioned language variation is motivated by the wish of speakers to perform, through the use of variable linguistic structures, symbolic 'acts of identity' or of belonging to various micro- and macro-social groupings (age, sex, class, ethnicity, social network, etc.). At the same time, on the level of individual, face-to-face interaction, intraspeaker variation is propelled by the psychosocial motivations that lead speakers to modify their speech in response to the social identity of their interlocutor, again through the use of variable linguistic items and structures. Socio-stylistic variation in pronunciation is mediated in highly systematic ways, through the probabilistic use (in English at least) of phonological variants that are often linguistically arbitrary (not explicable in ease-of-articulation terms) and regionally marked. Conversely, grammatical variation in English often appears to show a quasi-categorical pattern, with middle-class speakers almost totally avoiding certain stigmatised forms. We concentrate in this and the following chapter on patterns of phonological variation, examining grammatical variation in Chapter 4.

Many studies of British and American English have reported a characteristic pattern of association between social class and intraspeaker variation, such that for a given phonological sociolinguistic variable, most if not all social class groups, as well as differentiating themselves from each other by their treatment of the variable, show a similar pattern of behaviour across speech styles; standard variants are associated with formal styles, non-standard with informal. This type of variable therefore shows social class as well as style differentiation, and continues often to be referred to as a marker variable (cf. Chambers and Trudgill 1998: 70). This pattern of advertence in formal speech styles to standard linguistic forms may in turn, for some variables, indicate change in progress. As Eckert (1989: 248) expresses the situation: 'Labov's original (1966) findings in New York City clearly lined up socio-economic class, style, sound change, prestige, and evaluation on a single axis'. This means that in more formal styles, speakers approximate more closely to the standard language, which is often an older state of the language, is used by higher-ranking social groups, enjoys more overt prestige, and is therefore the object of positive evaluation judgments. We discuss the marker variable in further detail below.

Sociolinguistic findings on languages other than English are less copious, but we present below some findings from French that cast an interesting and suggestive light on the differences in the social functions that phonological variation appears to fulfil in English and French; considering, as indicated above, in more detail the various factors that influence socio-stylistic variation in French in the next chapter.

As we implied above, any examination of interspeaker variation in phonology must also necessarily consider a set of theoretical postulates that seek to explain intraspeaker variation, given the close, indeed indissoluble relation between these two extra-linguistic axes of variation. As an integral part of the discussion, the theory of the relationship between social and stylistic variation we will examine here is that formulated by Bell (1984). We have already referred to Bell's notion of audience design in some detail in Chapter 1; for convenience, we reiterate the postulates of Bell's theory that are relevant to the present data and argumentation as follows:

i.   It is the 'audience', in the sense of the hearer(s) or reader(s) of a stretch of language, who are primarily responsible for causing the speaker or writer to 'design' the stretch of language in question in response to the social characteristics of the audience, by pitching the language at a certain point on the formal–informal style continuum. There are of course several factors which provide an input into the choice of speech style: topic, setting, degree of formality (itself probably determined above all by the degree of intimacy subsisting between the colocutors), degree of self-monitoring or attention paid to speech production, channel (face-to-face interaction, telephone, radio broadcast etc.), the tone or tenor of the interaction (whether solemn, facetious, sarcastic), etc. Several of these factors are of course closely interrelated. One of Bell's aims was to provide a principled account of stylistic variation capable of systematising rather unordered taxonomies such as that given above. Bell's account implies a hierarchical view that stresses the primacy of the audience in conditioning intraspeaker variation, with other situational variables standing in a relation of dependency to the primary variable.

ii.   The second major postulate that concerns us here is the quantitative relation that obtains between the interspeaker and intraspeaker axes of variation. Bell (1984: 153) asserts that the primacy of interspeaker variation entails that variation along this dimension will always exceed intraspeaker variation in quantitative terms. From this perspective, stylistic variation effectively reproduces social variation, although within narrower parameters. This seems plausible since no single speaker or speaker group will command the entire range of linguistic variables that are socially sensitive in a given speech community, so that interspeaker variation will always exceed intraspeaker variation in the speech of a single speaker or group that is socially homogeneous.

This latter assertion has been abundantly demonstrated on the quantitative levels of linguistic behaviour, at least in British and American English (see for example Labov 1966, 1972b; Trudgill 1974); we shall see below that different patterns may be observed in French. In this and the following chapter we therefore examine the socio-stylistic role of phonological variation in the light of evidence drawn from patterns of variable phonology found in various corpora of spoken English and French. Specifically, we consider whether it is possible to propose a general model of the social function of variable phonology, even to the rather limited extent of generalising across two highly standardised languages spoken in countries which are fairly closely comparable in their present social and industrial organisation; even if their respective histories with respect to language standardisation contrast considerably. We also consider whether Bell's suggestions concerning the relation between social and stylistic variation are valid, at least in the sense that Bell intended, across the two languages.

This chapter is organised as follows: firstly we examine some well-known patterns of phonological variation in English, with a view to determining their relation to socio-stylistic variation. We then survey phonological variation in northern French with the same object, subsequently examining some indirect findings relating to this issue and considering the implications of the fact that social-regional phonological variation in the variety of French of interest here appears to have been rather successfully levelled out, at least in comparison with the situation in Great Britain. In a final section we summarise our suggestions regarding the differences between phono-stylistic variation in English and French.

2.2   Patterns of phonological variation in English

The literature on sociolinguistic variation in English is very substantial, and space is lacking here to conduct a comprehensive survey of phonological variation reported in English. We will therefore discuss the distinction between the two much discussed characteristic patterns of variation seen in the classes of phonological variation termed 'markers' and 'indicators', since these categories imply a definition of the phonological variable in terms of the relation between interspeaker and intraspeaker variation.

2.2.1   The marker variable: Social-linguistic factors

Markers tend to show steep differentiation patterns, as well as an interaction between the effect of speech style and other social variables, typically class. An example discussed by Trudgill (1974) is the widely quoted Norwich (ng) variable (walking ~ walkin'), which shows variation along, and interaction between, the axes of social class and speech style. Table 1 below shows this class-style interaction.

The abbreviations used in Table 1 are as follows: MMC = middle middle-class (professional and managerial); LMC = lower middle-class (junior non-manual); UWC = upper working-class (skilled manual); MWC = middle working-class (LWC = lower working class (unskilled manual); WLS = word-list style; RPS = reading-passage style; FS = formal style; CS = casual style. Familiarity with these speech styles is assumed; the distinction between scripted and unscripted speech styles will in any event be discussed in several places below. These abbreviations, which are common in the literature, are used throughout this work. The broader middle-class/working-class distinction is referred to as MC/WC. Other abbreviations are explained when first used.

Table 1. Variation in Norwich (ng) by class and style (Trudgill 1974: 92)

	WLS	RPS	FS	CS
MMC	000	000	003	028
LMC	000	010	015	042
UWC	005	015	074	087
MWC	023	044	088	095
LWC	029	066	098	100

Table 1 shows informants in Norwich assigned to the MMC category displaying zero or near-zero realisation of the non-standard variant in all styles except the most casual, while speakers assigned to the MWC and LWC categories (respectively, manual and unskilled working-class) show high realisation rates of non-standard [n]. These results are percentage scores; '000' indicates zero realisation of the non-standard variant. This pattern is closer to the sharper, near-qualitative pattern alleged to be characteristic of grammatical variation (Romaine 1984: 86; Chambers 1995: 241). The effect of speech style on treatment of (ng) is considerable for all speaker groups except MMC. Chambers and Trudgill (1998: 70–4) attempt to explain the style-class interaction typical of marker variables by suggesting that speakers are more aware of their sociolinguistic value, for various reasons; for example, they propose that the (ng) variable has marker status because the standard variant is clearly marked in spelling. Its apparent absence in speech can therefore suggest a low level of education in the speaker, even though the relationship between the two variants can perhaps be expressed as an arbitrary alternation (between a dental and a velar nasal) rather than in terms of presence/absence. Further analogous variables in Norwich English discussed by Chambers and Trudgill are (h) and (t), where again only the standard variants (/h/ and /t/) are indicated in spelling (non-standard variants are Ø and /ʔ/). As Chambers and Trudgill express the situation (p. 72): 'the low prestige variants of the three Norwich variables [i.e. (h), the glottal stop and (ng)] — zero, [ʔ] and [n] — can be, and often are, characterised as "dropping your *h*s, *t*s and *g*s"'.

This quotation highlights a twofold aspect of the disapproval to which marker variables such as (ng) are subject. On the one hand there is perceived divergence from the spelling, and on the other the non-standard variant, perceived as the result of 'dropping' the standard variant, may be seen as a 'lazy' or 'sloppy' pronunciation feature. Thus 'walking' varies in Norwich and other cities between standard [wɔːkɪŋ] and non-standard [wɔːkɪn] or [wɔːkn̩]. As with (h) and the glottal stop, it is unclear whether the non-standard variant results from an ease-of-articulation process; this seems plausible as the non-standard variant of (ng) has less linguistic substance, and at least one scholar has referred to the [n] variant as resulting from 'laxing' (Preston 1991:35). Similarly, h-dropping has as its output less linguistic substance, and thus may plausibly be thought of in terms of articulatory economy. By contrast, Chambers (1995:234–5) argues that glottalling of /p,t,k/ cannot be thought of in terms of articulatory economy. However this may be, it remains puzzling that some ease-of-articulation processes which also result in divergence from the spelling do not attract strong disapproval: one difference may be that these latter are subject to stringent linguistic constraints, which when violated do indeed result in stigmatised forms. Chambers (1995:236) mentions the example of the reduction of word-final consonant clusters in English, which (broadly) in MC casual speech can reduce from three to two ('west side' > 'wes' side'), but not from two to one ('west end' > *'wes' end'). The classic formulation of this problem is due to Kroch (1978:18–19), who from a linguistic perspective suggests that speakers can exploit two strategies for adopting prestigious features: they can resist connected-speech processes (CSPs) such as consonant-cluster simplification, vowel centralisation and schwa deletion; and they can adopt linguistic features from outside the immediate speech community. As suggested above, in this optic the (ng) variable is potentially the object of negative evaluation from several points of view: the standard variant is stable; distributed nationally (this is of course a defining characteristic of standard variants); it is marked in the spelling or so perceived; and the non-standard variant is motivated by articulatory economy, or so perceived.

Having considered some of the possible social-linguistic factors influencing the social-class variation characteristic of the marker, we now turn to an examination of some influences bearing upon the intraspeaker axis of variation shown in Table 1.

2.2.2   The social-class–style relationship in marker variables

Bell (1984) drew on the findings of all available sociolinguistic studies between 1966 and 1982 in order to formulate, among other things, a hypothesis aiming to elucidate the relationship between social and stylistic variation. We are concerned here with considering whether factors in addition to the social attributes of the addressee, which Bell asserts to be the primary factor motivating 'audience design', need to be considered as having an input into the interaction between social and style variation.

Bell (1984: 152–3) asserts that the relation between social and stylistic variation is a derivative one: 'style variation [...] derives from and mirrors "social" variation'. In any society above a given level of complexity, division of labour becomes necessary, and social groups come to be (perceived as being) ranked hierarchically, some occupational groups enjoying more overt prestige, deriving from a perceivedly greater access to power and wealth than others. The social behaviour (including of course non-linguistic as well as linguistic) of the more highly-ranked groups, who are in a position to define the standard language and behaviour generally, comes to be highly prized by all social groups; the next step is that the social behaviour of the higher groups is associated with more formal situations. Thus, the more formal the speech situation, the more prestigious will be the speech variety used, just as for instance more prestigious forms of dress are worn on formal occasions: the tailcoat may on the one hand be worn by members of all social classes at weddings, and on the other forms part of daily dress only at prestigious establishments such as certain British 'public schools' (endowed fee-paying boarding schools).

As mentioned previously, Bell argues further from the assumption that interspeaker variation drives intraspeaker variation to an explanation of the patterns very often seen in the literature, where interspeaker variation always exceeds intraspeaker variation in quantitative terms, with two classes of exceptions; in Bell's phrase (1984: 152–3), style 'mirrors' or reflects social variation, and 'as is the habit of mirrors, the reflection is less distinct than the original'. As mentioned above, the explanation for this may be formulated in terms of the social networks of everyday interactions: no single speaker or speaker group will command with full confidence the entire range of linguistic variables that are socially sensitive in a given speech community, since no single speaker or group will interact at all regularly with representatives of all members of the community. Therefore the stylistic compass of a speaker or speaker group will be circumscribed by their range of social interactants.

The two exceptional categories of the social-style quantitative relation referred to above are firstly, the well-known case of lower-middle-class hyper-correction, where LMC speakers produce forms which are further from the vernacular than the groups above them, i.e. MMC or UMC. This pattern, held to be often indicative of change in progress, may be considered as belonging in a sub-category of the often-observed 'marker' variable, where an interaction is observable between a style effect and that of another extra-linguistic parameter, typically social class.

The second aberrant pattern is what Bell terms 'hyperstyle' variation, where style variation exceeds social variation for all speaker groups. Bell argues that this is a truly exceptional category, asserting it to be characteristic (a) either of societies where there is very marked discontinuity between reading and speaking styles, such that the standard sociolinguistic interview fails to repro-duce variation between spontaneous speaking styles (the example given is of Tehrani Persian, reported by Jahangiri (1980) and Jahangiri and Hudson (1982) among others); and (b) where there is a 'generally unusual behaviour of [...] linguistic variables' (Woods' (1979) research on Ottawa English is also cited). Bell mentions that he is aware of only these two cases of hyperstyle variation. In the following chapter we discuss some French language data that also show this hyperstyle pattern, and speculate whether the phenomenon is so marginal, and therefore so irrelevant to the thrust of Bell's argument, as may be thought.

Here however we consider some issues of methodology that bear upon this numerical social-stylistic relationship. The relation shown in Table 1 conforms to the pattern that Bell suggests as typical of the marker variable: the maximum range of interspeaker variation is in the formal style, between 98% use of [n] for LWC speakers against 3% for MMC. This is a difference of 95%. Along the intraspeaker dimension the widest range is for UWC speakers, who have 87% [n] in formal style against 5% in word list style, a range of 82%. The question at issue here is whether in societies having the social structures described above, these structures will inevitably entail this numerical social-style relation in variable language use; or indeed whether this relation applies to all languages. Preston (1991) applied a VARBRUL analysis to the factors governing variation in Trudgill's results on (ng), as well as variationist findings from several other languages. Preston concluded that the maximum range of social variation constitutes an 'envelope' within which stylistic variation is inherently delimited; his VARBRUL results showed further that social variation is in turn delimited within the envelope of the linguistic constraints governing variation. Those constraining variation in (ng) would relate for instance to the phonetic nature of the following segment; the lexical frequency of the ing word; and whether the ing word is a full or auxiliary verb form. We do not wish to take issue here with Preston's statistical methods, but discuss below some methodological factors that may be thought of as influencing the ratio between interspeaker and intraspeaker variation typically seen in the literature.

The influence of elicitation methods in producing this ratio has been mentioned by several scholars: Wheeler (1995) suggests that the low degrees of style shift reported in the literature (low relative to interspeaker variation) may be 'an artefact of the standard Labovian method', i.e. of the classic socio-linguistic interview on the one hand, which may not capture a speaker's entire stylistic range, and on the other the sampling methods employed, which aim to represent the entire social range of the speech community being studied. Against this it must be pointed out that Trudgill's elicitation methods succeeded in capturing a very wide range of variation in the use of (ng) for some speaker groups, notably UWC speakers who as mentioned above had a range of variable use close to 100%. It can be suggested in connexion with other speaker groups, notably the MMC speakers who show a narrow range of intraspeaker variation (and who therefore compress intraspeaker variation and at the same time widen interspeaker variation in all styles) that the interview methods used did not elicit the most casual styles of which the MMC speaker were capable.

Several scholars have levelled criticisms at the proposition that intraspeaker variation as shown in the results that issue from the standard sociolinguistic interview can be thought of in terms of audience design. Thus Milroy (1987b: 173) points out that 'the contrast between spontaneous speech and reading styles is a simulation, for experimental purposes, of differences in the amount of attention paid to speech which crop up in natural interaction'. Such simulations do not of course necessarily capture accurately the differences between percent-ages of non-standard forms used across two or more spontaneous speech styles; this is partly because the definition, and therefore quantification, of the difference between formal and casual styles depends on the linguist's judgment, at least if the addressee is the linguist in both styles. As to differences between speaking and reading styles, Hudson (1996: 200) has the following criticism of the standard elicitation methods: '[...] it is hard to see how audience design applies to the difference between spontaneous speech and reading [...]'. The answer of course is that audience design does not apply directly to the differ-ence between spontaneous and scripted speech styles; the use of reading styles, as Milroy suggests, presupposes an exploitation of the mechanism of attention paid to speech (self-monitoring) as a substitute for the psychosocial factors grouped under the 'audience design' heading that govern intraspeaker variation in more spontaneous interactions. Bell (1984: 147–50) emphatically rejects the notion that self-monitoring plays a primary role in intraspeaker variation, maintaining instead that the degree of attention paid to speech is a mechanism intervening between speaker and hearer in the audience-design process. The question at issue here is whether the simulacra that issue from these experiments can be thought of as sufficiently representative of genuine intraspeaker variation to from the basis of generalisations such as Bell's, concerning the quantitative relation between inter- and intraspeaker variation. One difficulty associated with the deployment of reading styles in this connexion can be raised by varying attitudes across speech communities to the act of reading aloud, as Hudson points out (ibid.): 'one of the facts that emerged from Milroy's Belfast work was that speakers did not use more standard pronunciations when reading [...], as Trudgill's Norwich speakers and Labov's New Yorkers had done'. As stated above in connexion with Table 1 however, the criticism of the Norwich results that might be alleged concerns the casual rather than formal language data gathered. We discuss this issue further below in relation to the French variables in question.

2.2.3   The indicator variable

The previous sub-sections were devoted to a discussion of marker variables. One implication of the foregoing may be that vocalic variables, whose representation in spelling (at least in English) is less direct, or more complex, may have in general sociolinguistic value more directly related to regional origin than to social class; at least in the sense that English orthography does not systematically favour the standard vowel system over non-standard systems. An extreme example is that discussed by Labov (1994: 347), where a northern speaker of UK English wishing to acquire the distinction between the set of words exemplified by the pair 'putt' and 'put' and differentiated in southern/standard English by two distinct back vowels, respectively [ʌ] and [ʊ], cannot rely on spelling as a guide. Thus, the guidance provided by the spelling of 'putt' and 'put' contradicts that suggested by 'puss' (standard realisation [pʊs]) and 'pus' ([pʌs]).

The *putt/put* distinction is a notorious shibboleth, but perhaps commoner examples are represented by the vocalic variable (a:), again reported in Trudgill's Norwich study. Trudgill describes Norwich (a:) as an indicator variable, which shows a considerable degree of differentiation along the dimensions of class and sex, but rather little style variation.

Table 2. variation in Norwich (a:) by class and style
(adapted from Trudgill 1974:98)

	WLS	RPS	FS	CS
MMC	028	035	042	090
LMC	075	080	097	111
UWC	132	136	160	181
MWC	140	146	177	195
LWC	163	177	188	195

The standard variant of (a:) is a long low-back unrounded vowel, as in standard British English 'cart' [kɑːt], while the non-standard Norwich variant is front: [kaːt]. The scores shown above are index, not percentage realisations, and potentially range from 0 to 200, as Trudgill quantified an intermediate variant between the localised, frontmost [aː] variant and non-localised back [ɑː].

As with the (ng) variable, one might adduce several extra-linguistic factors as determining the lesser sociolinguistic value of this variable, reflected in its non-involvement in style variation. The lexical split between front and back 'a' is complex and not reflected particularly accurately in English orthography, although of course an orthographic 'r' after 'a' always indicates a long back vowel in southern/standard English. As to socio-geographical factors, it may be that Norwich (a:) constitutes principally a regional variable; the (a:) variable, unlike (ng) or the glottal stop, is highly localised, found also in Cardiff (Mees 1990) and the north-west of the UK, but it is not a nationally recognised shibboleth or perceived stereotypically as used by lower-class speakers. It may be that variables which are perceived as having local connotation, rather than as principally lower class, are viewed less unfavourably, because they are associated with 'home team' values, perhaps especially in cities, such as Norwich, Cardiff or Liverpool, which possess distinctive local characteristics and are the object of positive evaluation by non-locals.

It would be possible to multiply examples from English of variables whose behaviour is similar to the two types described above. Whether markers or indicators, many if not most variables in English appear to show large degrees of differentiation along the most studied social dimensions; notably social class. Those which show what Chambers and Trudgill call 'sharp stratification' (1998:70) seem to bear some resemblance to syntactic variables in that some speaker groups show quasi-categorical behaviour in their treatment of the variables. As mentioned above, this may be partly because use of the standard variant is perceived as being associated with a high level of education, or at least with a positive attitude towards the values represented by the education system: Laks's (1983) formulation that refers to a speaker's 'social trajectory' is perhaps the least normative way of expressing this association.

However this may be, it appears that patterns of phonological variation in English and other languages endorse Bell's view (1984: 152–3) of the relationship between social and stylistic variation: as was mentioned above, Bell asserts that the relation is a derivative one, stylistic variation deriving from social. Whether or not this is the case (Finegan and Biber (1994: 315–47) argue the opposite view), it is clearly true that social and stylistic variation in English are closely associated insofar as speakers sense that formal styles call for prestige language, at all linguistic levels. The further point highlighted by the results discussed above is that the linguistic nature of the variables in question, as well as their representation in spelling, may influence their socio-stylistic patterning.

In the next section we look at patterns of phonological variation in French, with the object of comparing certain socio-stylistic phonological patterns found in this language with those reported in English.

2.3   Patterns of phonological variation in French

The sociolinguistic literature on French is substantial: Blanche-Benveniste and Jeanjean (1987: 201–209) list 47 corpora of spoken French, although not all of these were collected with a view to sociolinguistic enquiry. Most work on French in the variationist paradigm has focused on the Canadian variety, and the very large corpora collected by Sankoff and Cedergren in 1971 (Sankoff and Cedergren 1971) and Poplack in 1984 (Poplack 1989), respectively in Montreal and Ottawa-Hull, have been much studied with a view to analysing variability. However, it seems legitimate to state that the majority of Labovian variationist research in French, both metropolitan and Canadian, has been concerned with grammatical rather than phonological variation. Thus, Blanche-Benveniste and Jeanjean (pp. 189–200) also categorise research on spoken French by area of linguistic inquiry; out of 14 categories, 12 are concerned with syntax and morphology. Research into phonological variation in metropolitan French has been developed principally within a functionalist perspective, perhaps most notably by Martinet (1945, 1962, 1974) and Walter (1976, 1982). Lavandera (1981: 129–228), in a long article discussing sociolinguistics in the Romance languages, points out that a long-established tradition exists in Romance philology which '[relates] linguistic facts to social, economic or political facts' (p. 130). At the same time, Lavandera notes 'the indifference toward the American model [which] can be found in France' (p. 157).

This relative neglect of phonological variation in French, at least in the quantitative Labovian framework, may perhaps reflect an intuitive awareness of the lesser sociolinguistic importance of variable phonology in French. It is a matter of common (impressionistic) observation that social-regional differences of pronunciation are less strongly marked in France (leaving aside the major north-south dialect division) than for example in the UK. In the following section we present some attitudinal evidence reinforcing these impressions. Lodge (1993:256), debating whether the current linguistic situation in France can be described as diglossic, cites several examples of the 'numerous' phonological reductions which result in L forms, but also remarks that the 'syntactic differences between H and L styles in French are particularly strongly marked', and further that 'it is probably in the lexicon that style-shifting in French is indicated most obviously'. We examine this latter issue in Chapter 6, but here we again reiterate the point that these differences in French, phonological, syntactic and lexical, are social, not regional-social. A number of studies concerned with phonological variation have reported patterns of variation in metropolitan and especially Canadian French that can be related to some extent to those familiar in the Anglo-American literature, with the vital qualification just articulated.

The phonology of French has given rise to a great deal of research in the generative paradigm, notably on liaison, schwa and the nasal vowels. But in comparison with the volume of theoretical research published, the sociolinguistic literature on *oïl* French phonology is not enormous. What is notable concerning the *oïl* French phonemic inventory is its relative stability. Of the twelve oral and four nasal vowels generally referred to in pronunciation manuals (Lodge et al. 1997, Chapter 5), those listed below (2–7) appear to be involved in variation, but rather little change appears to be in progress. Recent urban variationist results (discussed below) indicate that change is affecting, or has affected, schwa phrase-finally (item 5); the back mid-vowel [ɔ] (item 7); and the front nasal vowels [ɛ̃] and [œ̃]. The French consonantal system seems similarly stable, with the exception of the weak consonants /l/ and /r/ (item 1 below), and of variable liaison. This latter area of variation responds, at least in part, to morpho-syntactic input and in any event seems not to be localised regionally, at least in France; although different patterns have been reported in Montreal French. We discuss variable liaison more fully in a separate chapter.

Gadet (1997:71–9) discusses elision operating on other relatively weak consonants such as /v/ and /b/; again, these processes seem to be areas of variation
rather than change. It is notable from the list below that two items concern
schwa, a vowel that is variable across several languages. If accurate, this is a
situation of considerable stability, and where processes of simplification, chain
shift and merger are at work. This is of course in contrast with the UK English
situation, where processes of variation and change involve alternation between
variants that by and large cannot be thought in terms of natural or functional
processes. In what follows we take rather little account of national surveys of
French such as that of Martinet (1945), Carton et al. (1983), Walter (1982) or
Léon (1993), which, despite their undoubted descriptive and analytical merits,
have not shared the urban dialectological perspective that we adopt here.
French phonological variables recently reported in this perspective are listed
below, and then discussed in more detail:

1.   Deletion of the liquid consonants /r/ and /l/, especially word-finally, as in
genre 'type, kind'; *ronfle* 'snore'. Non-standard realisation of *genre* [ʒɑ̃ː];
standard realisation [ʒɑ̃ːʁ]. Non-standard realisation of *ronfle* [ʁɔ̃f]; standard
realisation [ʁɔ̃fl].

2.   Deletion of schwa between two consonants, as in: *la semaine* 'the week'.
Non-standard realisation [lasmɛn]; standard realisation [lasəmɛn]. This area of
variation is rather complex, and involves schwa deletion in syllable-initial,
-medial and -final position in polysyllabic words, as well as in the monosyllabic
words containing schwa. Armstrong and Unsworth (1999:133–7) give a
summary of the current situation.

3.   Alternation between, or neutralisation of, oral mid-vowel contrasts. The
French oral mid-vowels are [e] and [ɛ], as in *thé* 'tea' and *taie* 'pillowcase'; [ø]
and [œ], as in *peu* 'little' and *peur* 'fear'; and [o] and [ɔ], as in *paume* 'palm' and
pomme 'apple'. Non-standard realisations can involve alternations between
high-mid and low-mid vowels, as well as intermediate realisations, as in *café*
(standard form [kafe]) realised [kafɛ] or [kafẹ]. As can be seen from these
examples, the phonemic status of mid-vowel contrasts is dependent on the
vowel-pairs in question and their distribution in closed or open syllables. In
particular, the [ø] ~ [œ] contrast famously depends on two minimal pairs, *veule*
'lackadaisical' [vøl] ~ *veulent* 'want' (6th-person present) [vœl]; and *jeûne* 'fast,
abstain from food' (3rd-person present) [ʒøn] ~ *jeune* 'young' [ʒœn]. This low
functional yield is of course of relevance if one considers that communicative
factors are an important constraint on variation. Vowel harmony is also in

question here; for instance, the sequence of mid-vowels in *intérêt* 'interest' is standardly [ɛ̃teʁɛt], but often levels to [ɛ̃teʁet] or [ɛ̃tḛʁḛt].

4. Neutralisation of, and variation between, nasal vowel contrasts. Front nasal vowels [ɛ̃] and [œ̃]: non-standard realisation of *quelqu'un* 'someone' [kɛlkɛ̃]; standard realisation [kɛlkœ̃]. However, it is more accurate to speak of the merged realisation as intermediate between [ɛ̃] and [œ̃], in the form of [œ̃] or [ɛ̃] with unrounded or neutral lip position. This is a change which appears now to be largely complete, at least in the Paris region and probably beyond. The back nasal vowels are [ɑ̃] and [ɔ̃]: non-standard realisation of *élément* 'element' [elemɔ̃]; standard realisation [elemɑ̃].

5. Insertion of schwa word-finally: so-called 'schwa-tagging'. This takes place both orthographically and intrusively. Non-standard realisation of *c'était Pierre* 'it was Peter' [setɛpjɛʁə]; standard realisation [setɛpjɛʁ] (orthographic example). Non-standard realisation of *bonjour* 'hello' [bɔ̃ʒuʁə]; standard realisation [bɔ̃ʒuʁ] (intrusive example).

6. Variation between front and back (a), as in *pas* 'not'. Non-standard realisation of *pas* [pɑ] or [pɔ]; standard realisation [pa].

7. Centralisation/fronting of [ɔ] in the direction of [œ] as in: *joli* 'pretty'. Non-standard realisation [ʒœli]; standard realisation [ʒɔli]

As mentioned above, this list does not aim to be exhaustive. Léon (1993:225) lists further features that characterise regional French, such as diphthongised and denasalised vowels, pronunciation of *h aspiré* (defined and discussed in Chapter 5 on liaison), and devoicing of final consonants, that he suggests 'do not shock and can even add charm to an accent'. Many if not most of these features are distributed in rural and non-*oïl* dialects, and hence do not lie within the present terms of reference.

We now discuss items 1–7 listed above from the point of view of their socio-geographical distribution in *oïl* French, and of their linguistically motivated character. Studies of the deletion of schwa and of /l/ and /r/ and of the levelling of the mid-vowels (see Armstrong 1993 for a review of these) are perhaps most frequent in the quantitative paradigm applied to French variable phonology. Although, as stated above, evidence is not copious, some researchers have reported relatively sharp differentiation patterns similar to those found in English; for example, Laks (1977), in a network study of a group of six Parisian working-class adolescent males who were relatively similar in respect of their social class (L/MWC), reported a correlation between deletion of /r/ in word-final syllables (as in item 1 above) and 'social trajectory' as evidenced by adherence to non-mainstream behaviour such as petty crime and truancy on the one hand, and assimilation to school and work on the other. Deletion rates varied between 45% and 100% for individual speakers. Another researcher who studied spoken French in Tours, Ashby (1984), reported rather modest degrees of variation between social groups in deletion of /l/ in the French clitic pronouns and definite articles. The greatest degree of variation reported was between an elision rate of 50% (for all linguistic contexts aggregated) for older MC females and almost 90% for younger males irrespective of social class.

One interesting aspect of these results is that although the variable use of features such as the liquid consonants and schwa is undoubtedly socially sensitive in French, there appears to be an absence of dramatic contrasts between the very high elision rates reported by Laks, who recorded his informants in informal style in the course of relatively long-term participant observation, and those of Ashby, whose elicitation methods were closer to the classic sociolinguistic interview developed by Labov. In other words, even the rather formal interviews that Ashby conducted did not elicit the type of pattern commonly seen in English, where MC speakers show almost total avoidance of non-standard phonological variants. This suggests that the social-stylistic relationship found in English variable phonology may be less salient in French, and is perhaps complemented by variable grammar and lexis to a greater extent than obtains in other languages. A further crucial point here is the apparent absence of regional localisation in socially diagnostic speech, as suggested by the fact that similar findings have been reported for variables such as /l/, /r/ and schwa in quite widely separated locations: Tours (Ashby 1984), Paris (Laks 1983); Lorraine (Armstrong 1996).

Another important point concerns the linguistic properties of the French phonological variables that are socially diagnostic. These are largely natural; by this we mean features that are subject to elision and neutralisation phenomena. As stated above, the phonetic variables subject to elision that have been studied using variationist methods in French are principally /l/, /r/ and schwa. Elision and neutralisation occur across languages generally, of course, for reasons associated with the phonetic and metrical characteristics of the segments concerned; but it may be that these phenomena constitute the principal resource in variable pronunciation that French speakers have available. Neutralisation in French chiefly concerns vowel oppositions; notably the mid-vowels, both nasal and oral. Neutralisation of the front nasal mid-vowels [ɛ̃] and [œ̃] has a straightforward functional explanation (few minimal pairs are involved) and is widespread across northern France, while it is unclear whether variation between the front vowels and the two back vowels ([ɔ̃] and [ɑ̃]) is explicable from a functional point of view. Hansen (1998:11–12) summarises the situation as follows: the merger between [ɛ̃] and [œ̃], which is now largely complete in *oïl* French, may perhaps be in the process of being followed by the merger of [ɔ̃] and [ɑ̃], even though hundreds of minimal pairs depend on this latter opposition. But as Hansen points out, a simplification of the French nasal vowel system from four into a pair widely separated in phonetic space ([ɛ̃] and [ɔ̃]) could also be accounted for broadly in functional terms. A further line of reasoning points to a three-vowel system involved in a chain shift, with merged [ɛ̃] backing towards [ɑ̃], which in turn backs and raises towards [ɔ̃]. The consequent raising of the latter vowel then results in a third phoneme, [õ], which has been attested in some sociolects, albeit largely impressionistically. However, the phonetic and sociolinguistic data regarding these various alternations are by no means straightforward: Hansen's substantial book (1998) is devoted entirely to the phenomenon, discusses contradictory findings and arguments, and draws no simple conclusions concerning the linguistic, regional or social significance of variation in the nasal vowels (apart from the [ɛ̃] ~ [œ̃] merger). We must confess ignorance of how this area of variation can be classified in terms of the arbitrary–natural, and local–national distinctions we are discussing here.

The situation regarding the oral mid-vowels seems a little clearer; the most recent report (Landick 1995) suggests a process of simplification that sees the high-mid / low-mid set of six vowel contrasts reducing in unguarded speech to a set of three intermediate mid-vowels. Again, a functional explanation seems adequate here, as rather few minimal pairs that are respected in everyday speech are threatened. Landick's results concerning male Parisian MC and WC speakers show no sharp differentiating patterns. Again, the geographical spread of this merging process is unclear.

It may be therefore that phonological variation that is both arbitrary and regional has rather limited salience in northern French, although relatively few variationist findings are available to confirm or confute this proposition. Arbitrary phonological variation is present chiefly in the French vocalic system; as listed above, one linguistic change of this kind which appears to be in progress in the variety of French of interest here is the fronting or centralisation of the back mid-vowel [ɔ], to [œ] as the frontmost realisation, as in *joli* realised as [ʒœli] where the standard realisation is [ʒɔli] (Landick 1995). Landick's results show rather little use of the non-standard variant, and little social differentiation. A further example of perhaps arbitrary vocalic variation, which of course endorses one's impressionistic knowledge, is provided by Dannequin (1977: 145), cited in Romaine (1984: 189–90), who reports an exchange between three French schoolgirls, in which two girls correct the third for her pronunciation of *oui* non-standardly as [wɛ] rather than standard [wi]. As with the majority of variables in French phonology, the current social-stylistic value of the vowel alternation in oui is unclear, ([wɛ] is heard quite often in public speech) and once again the alternation appears not to be localised.

A further seemingly arbitrary phenomenon is the recent and apparently increasing tendency to 'schwa-tagging', i.e. the insertion in northern, perhaps principally Parisian French of a word-final schwa after a single phonetic consonant and before a pause, such that *c'était Pierre* is variably realised by some speakers as [setepjɛʁ(ə)]. (The conventional brackets indicate variable realisation of schwa in this and the following transcription). Furthermore, schwa-tagging may take place either where there is an orthographic schwa, as in *c'était Pierre*, or intrusively where the spelling indicates no vowel, as in *au revoir* pronounced [ɔʁvwaʁ(ə)]. This phenomenon has been analysed from a variationist viewpoint by Hansen (1997). It is unclear whether variation between front [a] and back [ɑ] continues to convey social significance in everyday speech, although this sociolinguistic opposition has often been mentioned in the literature (but cf. Pooley 1996: 128–34 for a recent account of the [a] ~ [ɑ] alternation in Lille French, what he refers to as 'regional French', which seems to lie outside our purview).

To anticipate the arguments that follow, the phonological variables observed in 'levelled' French that have been subjected to variationist quantification (principally schwa- and liquid-deletion) give a paradoxical picture. On the one hand, these connected-speech processes might be thought of as being akin to certain English processes in connected speech that appear to have limited socio-stylistic value, such as the simplification of final consonant clusters. On the other hand, as we will argue below, the highly normative linguistic traditions in France that weigh upon speakers' behaviour seems to be in tension with the 'natural' character of certain of the linguistic variables that are available. We have therefore a speech community sharing evaluative norms that are rather different from those commonly studied in countries where the variationist method has been conspicuously successful. In the following sections and in Chapter 3 we present some findings that support this view, and discuss the implications arising from it.

2.4 French speakers' reactions to a 'levelled' accent: An evaluative test

The aim of the study described in this section is to explore the observation discussed above: namely, that the pronunciation of the urban varieties of French, leaving aside the north-south split, is what could be termed homogeneous, levelled or perhaps 'standardised'. If this were true, it would of course be difficult for French speakers to judge one another's social-regional origins on the basis of their accent alone. This is in sharp contrast, notably to the urban British English situation, where regional accent generally marks social class rather clearly. This observation regarding French is by no means new: Nicolson (1955: 267) suggested that 'One can detect by the accent of Frenchmen [...] from what provinces they originate, but not to what social class they belong; in England, the several layers of society are as it were labelled by intonation.' Impressionistic remarks such as this tend to neglect the crucial element that in English the social and regional components of accent are indissociable. Regarding the association between the social and regional components of French accents, the findings reported by Bauvois (1996), on the success with which Belgian French speakers identify one another's regional or urban origin as marked by their accent, appear to be most closely comparable to the research reported here.

The long-term aim of the project reported here (Armstrong and Boughton 1999) is to gather and analyse adequate empirical data on two regional varieties of standard French, those of Nancy and Rennes, with a view to testing through a variationist analysis of language recordings the hypothesis discussed above concerning the uniformity of French pronunciation. However, the intermediate result we discuss concerns the evaluative axis of variation rather than the behavioural. From the point of view of linguistic variation and change, this axis is integral to the sociolinguistic nexus that interrelates the extra-linguistic factors influencing variable language. We again cite Eckert (1989: 248): 'Labov's original (1966) findings in New York City clearly lined up socio-economic class, style, sound change, prestige, and evaluation on a single axis'. One aspect of the evaluative dimension is that at a first encounter, a listener attempts to identify a speaker's social characteristics by analysing (among other features) their language, as Trudgill's (1995: 1–2) train-compartment example is designed to illustrate. A further step is one of evaluation: listeners form a normative judgment on the basis of their identification. This process is of course observable in its most striking form at a first meeting, when listeners must attempt this identification-evaluation process in the absence of truly verifiable social information about the speaker in question. It is perhaps for this reason, as suggested by Bradac (1990:387), that most social-psychological investigation into accent evaluation has been carried out in precisely this area, i.e. the evaluation by listeners of the speech of locutors unknown to them.

Thus the data we examine here are French speakers' identifications and evaluative judgments of the accent features in the tape-recorded speech of a speaker sample with whose social characteristics they are unacquainted. The present project bears resemblances to the well known 'matched-guise' experiment reported in Giles and Powesland (1975:28–34), with the principal contrast that the differentiation in the present source language data is genuine, not constructed as in the study conducted by Giles. Giles (1970) presented a recording purportedly of thirteen speakers of different British English and foreign accents to a panel of 117 school-age listeners for evaluation according to certain personal characteristics. The thirteen speakers were in fact one; this speaker produced the different accents or 'guises', and the guises were 'matched' in the sense that variables such as voice quality, pitch and intonation were held constant. The panel of listeners consistently rated the RP accent highly on power-related qualities such as intelligence and competence, but low on attributes associated with solidarity such as friendliness and reliability. Highly localised social-regional accents were rated conversely, that is broadly low for power qualities but high for solidarity.

2.4.1   The speaker samples

The linguistic and evaluative data discussed below derive from sociolinguistic fieldwork conducted in 1997–8 in two medium-sized provincial centres in the *oïl* area of northern France. Among other considerations described below, these cities were chosen with a view to avoiding interference from southern French or non-French regional-language features (e.g. Occitan, Breton, Flemish, Alsatian). The two research sites chosen were Nancy, which is well within the Francophone Lorraine region of eastern France, and Rennes, in the eastern, non-Breton-speaking part of Brittany. Rennes and Nancy are therefore both located in areas with *oïl* substrata, referred to as *gallo* and *lorrain roman* respectively. These locations were suitable principally because they are sufficiently distant from one another geographically for any regional language features to be localised to each city. They are both commercial and administrative centres with large universities. The two cities are also more or less equidistant from Paris: Rennes is some 190 miles from the capital (300 km), Nancy about 170 miles (275 km). The significance of these geographical and linguistic considerations is that the intention of the current project is broadly to match the research strategy of Trudgill's Norwich survey (1974) in selecting provincial cities with a view to examining the orientation of speakers toward supra-local and localised language varieties. The difference is of course that Trudgill examined productive, not behavioural language data. Nevertheless Rennes (pop. 240,000 in the conurbation) and Nancy (310,000) are comparable to Norwich in that they are both regional centres possessing distinctive local characteristics, while at the same time maintaining close commercial and cultural links with the national capital: both cities are some three hours from Paris by train. Rennes and Nancy present therefore the theoretical and method-ological advantage of having available only one standard variety and a closely related, structurally comparable vernacular. We assume that all speakers have available a range of varieties situated on this continuum. In short the two cities are closely comparable in a way that Nancy and Toulouse, for example, are not. This research aim coincides with our intention broadly to limit the scope of this book to *oïl* French. For this reason also, we do not discuss here studies (e.g. Paltridge and Giles 1984) that have reported evaluative tests concerning the comparison of *oïl* and non-*oïl* accents. Limiting the number of speakers in each speaker group or 'cell' to four, the sample gathered in each location was of the size and structure shown in Table 3.

Table 3. Speaker sample recorded at each research site

Age	Male		Female	
	WC	MC	WC	MC
16–25	4 YWCM	4 YMCM	4 YWCF	4 YMCF
40–60	4 OWCM	4 OMCM	4 OWCF	4 OMCF

Key: YWCM = Younger Working-Class Male, YMCM = Younger Middle-Class Male; OWCM = Older Working-Class Male; OMCM = Older Middle-Class Male; YWCF = Younger Working-Class Female; YMCF = Younger Middle-Class Female; OWCF = Older Working-Class Female; OMCF = Older Middle-Class Female

2.4.2   The listening test

The principal difference between the interviews conducted in the two cities was the addition of a listening-based evaluative exercise at the end of the Rennes interviews. The results of this exercise are the focus of the research reported here. Since a full sample of recordings had already been gathered in Nancy, it was decided to include this exercise in the Rennes interviews in order to gather perceptual and evaluative information on the Nancy data from native speakers. It was hoped that this would confirm some of the impressions already formed by the field researcher (Boughton) with respect to the markedness or otherwise of the Nancy accent, and its social distribution.

A cassette was therefore produced of recordings of eight different Nancy informants, one representative from each cell of the sample. Approximately one minute of the recording of each of these speakers was copied onto the cassette, in a random order, as follows: OWCM; YMCF; OMCM; YWCF; YMCM; OMCF; YWCM; OWCF. The speakers were chosen as representatives of their respective cells in the sample because they provided the most clearly recorded and relatively uninterrupted stretches of speech; and because they were unambiguous representatives of their social-class group.

The Rennes informants were asked to listen to each of the eight voices, and after each voice, the tape was paused and they were asked a number of questions. We discuss here the responses to the following questions:

A. In your opinion, does the person speaking have an accent?
    Possible answers: yes; no; don't know. Further question: If yes, what kind of accent: regional; social; urban; rural; etc.?

B. Is the person more likely to be working-class or middle-class?
    Possible answers: working-class; middle-class; don't know. Further question: why?

C. i.   Can you identify the person's region of origin?
         Possible answers: yes; no. Further question: if yes, where?
    ii. Do you have any idea of which city it might be?
         Possible answers: yes; no. Further question: which city?

This exercise formed part of the Rennes interviews wherever possible; essentially when informants had enough time. At the end of the field visits to Rennes, the requested information had been collected from 40 respondents in all. These respondents were male and female, younger and older, middle-class and working-class, reflecting the structure of the speaker sample. Space precludes a discussion of the interactions between the social characteristics of the Rennes informant sample and their responses to the questions listed above; however, previous research (e.g. Harms 1961) shows that high- and low-status listeners are equally capable of estimating the social-class provenance of a speaker on the basis of speech alone.

Before discussing results we note some limitations of this study: (i) Clearly, it is confined to the variety of French that is the object of interest to the present work; this variety, although demographically important (comprising at least half the French population) also excludes many, principally southern French speakers. Manifestly, several researchers, for example Martinet (1945); Walter (1982); Carton et al. (1983), have demonstrated the fact of social-regional variation over France as a whole; our concern, as stated above, is with a major but limited area of the country. Therefore generalisations formulated below with reference to 'French' should be understood with this caveat in mind. (ii) Our generalisations concerning the supposed uniformity of French pronunciation are based on perceptual, not productive data, and are correspondingly indirect. (iii) The perceptual judgments were formed on the basis of the speech of a sub-sample of only eight informants. (iv) The Nancy speaker sample was controlled for to a rather narrow MC–WC division; a broader social-class compass might have shown a greater degree of perceived social-regional variation than that discussed below. (v) Similarly to the corpora reported in the following chapter, the style of the speech recorded in the Nancy and Rennes interviews was elicited in the course of tape-recorded sessions from virtual strangers by an English advanced non-native speaker of French (Boughton), and hence it would be imprudent to claim that a speech style closely approaching the vernacular had been captured. (vi) The eight stretches of speech were not controlled for subject matter, and the Rennes informants could therefore have formed judgments based on linguistic features other than accent.

It is not clear from the literature what linguistic features might have aided the Rennes informants in their identification of urban Lorraine speech; national accent surveys such as Carton et al. (1983: 19–22) concentrate on features of rural speech. These authors, in discussing dialectal features of Lorraine, distinguish between francophone and germanophone Lorraine, asserting that germanophone Lorraine is confined to the north-east of the region, specifically to the north-eastern part of the Moselle *département* or administrative district, the most northerly and easterly of the four *départements* that make up Lorraine. Nancy is situated well to the west of this region. Carton asserts that the isogloss bundle between the two dialectal areas is of considerable antiquity and is clear-cut.

The section devoted to Lorraine reports on the speech of a woodcutter, and the principal features noted are denasalisation of vowels that are standardly nasal, as in *quand même* 'even so' realised [kamɛm] (standard [kãmɛm]); lengthening and backing of [a] in word-final syllables before a fricative, as in *village* 'village' pronounced [vilaːʒ] (standard [vilaʒ]); diphthonged vowels in stressed syllables, as in *ferré* 'steel-tipped' pronounced [feʁeʲ] (standard [feʁe]); long stressed oral and nasal vowels in penultimate position, for instance in *vingt* and *bonnes* in the phrases *vingt ans* 'twenty years' [vɛ̃ːtã] and *bonnes chaussures* 'good shoes' [bɔnʃoːsyʁ]. Standardly, vowels in this position are short and unstressed: [vɛ̃tã], [bɔnʃosyʁ]. No recent urban-dialectological information appears to be available on urban Lorraine French.

2.4.3   Results

2.4.3.1   *Replies to question A*
Figure 1 shows the number of Rennes informants who answered 'yes' to the question: 'In your opinion, does the person speaking on the tape have an accent?'. Numbers of affirmative replies given by the Rennes sample (N = 40) are shown on the vertical dimension of the graph, against each of the Nancy speakers who were the object of the evaluation test, ranged along the horizontal axis in order of decreasing perceived markedness of accent from left to right. It should be emphasised that an affirmative reply to this question implied that the speaker was perceived to have an accent associated with one or more of several independent social variables; a given accent might be reported in the subsequent discussions as being closely linked to socio-economic status, region, town/country or age. This reflects the fact that the question was intentionally

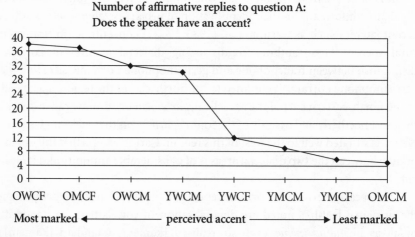

Figure 1. Rennes speakers' affirmative replies to question A: does the person speaking on the tape have an accent?

framed rather loosely, so as not to prompt a response linking regional origin with social class. It should also be mentioned that some Rennes informants explicitly made reference to language features other than pronunciation, i.e. syntactic and lexical features, in justifying their evaluations. Clearly, non-linguists are not accustomed to distinguishing sharply between the various levels of linguistic analysis, and are liable to interpret the term 'accent' rather flexibly.

Bearing in mind these qualifications and leaving aside until 2.4.3.2 below interactions between age, gender and class, Figure 1 shows a broad positive correlation between perceived markedness of accent and social class of speaker; with two notable exceptions, those perceived to have a marked accent are working-class, while those not so perceived are middle-class. The two strikingly unexpected results show CL, the OMCF speaker, perceived as having a more marked non-standard accent than either of the working-class men, or the younger WC female. The further surprising result is the very sharp disjunction between the younger WC male and younger WC female; the latter is grouped emphatically with the remaining three MC speakers. These four latter speakers have a 'markedness score' quite dramatically below the four ranged on the left of the graph. While the speakers judged to have a marked accent have scores ranging from 38 to 30 affirmative responses (average 34.2), those not so judged score between twelve and five (average eight). Given that this first question is such a general one, we suspend until the presentation of results shown below in Figure 2 (relation between perceived accent and perceived social class) a consideration of the question of the extent to which these results line up with the expectations that the findings of rural and urban dialectology produce.

As mentioned above, the most anomalous result concerns the older MC female speaker, CL. One might be justified (cf. 2.4.3.2 below) in assuming that a representative of this speaker group would be the least likely to be considered as having an accent, regional or otherwise. However, in this instance, 37 of the 40 Rennes respondents thought that she did indeed have an accent, although this was most often described, vaguely and inaccurately, clearly, as regional and rural. Regarding her socioeconomic history, it is perhaps pertinent that although this speaker had been in white-collar employment throughout her professional life (as a secretary) and was married to a retired bank-clerk, her family background was working-class, her parents were from Nancy and she herself had never left the city for any prolonged period; indeed, she still lived in an area very close to where she lived as a child. She was aware of having an accent (of which she was ashamed), but stated that it used to be much broader than it is now and has gradually lessened over the years. As stated previously, the eight Nancy informants were chosen by reason of their being, in the fieldworker's judgment, quite clearly representative of their social class, rather than on account of their accent.

The result of this sampling method is in CL's case rather difficult to interpret. In terms of a Linguistic Market Index (LMI) analysis of her occupation (Milroy 1987b: 99–100; Sankoff and Laberge 1978), CL would have been interpreted quite clearly as an MC speaker. The LMI is a social-class index, based on a Marxist class analysis and designed to provide a more sophisticated measure than those more commonly used of the relation, on the one hand between the orientation of speakers towards the standard language and on the other their occupation. Social-class indices largely used by Anglo-American sociolinguists are defined primarily by reference to models of social class based fairly directly on occupational category, among other descriptors. In contrast, the LMI is designed to handle the not infrequently indirect relation between the remuneration levels of certain occupational groups who are numerically important in demographic terms (teachers, secretaries, service employees), and the 'importance of the legitimized language in the socioeconomic life of the speaker' (Sankoff and Laberge 1978: 241). More plainly, the LMI aims to provide a closer fit between income level and ability or obligation to control the standard language; for our present purposes it can be viewed broadly as a social-class index. On the other hand, the LMI (or any other) index fails to capture CL's past social trajectory and her present social-network structure. In retrospect, a sampling method based on linguistic as well as social criteria might have prevented this apparently anomalous result, always assuming a sufficient level of competence on the fieldworker's part.

Regarding identification, seven informants remarked explicitly on a linguistic feature which appears to have betrayed to them CL's degree of localisation: long stressed oral and nasal vowels in penultimate position, for instance in *vingt* and *bonnes* in the phrases *vingt ans* and *bonnes chaussures*, as mentioned previously. However, only four of the Rennes informants mentioned eastern France as a possible location, and none mentioned Lorraine explicitly. One guessed at Canada, another Switzerland, yet another at Brittany (360 miles or 580 km from Nancy); most suggested a rural accent, while only four informants positively suggested an urban accent. The closest guess was: 'a bit like east or north-east; from a town'. It is worth mentioning further that the pronunciation feature that alerted the Rennes informants to CL's regional origin, occurred 45 seconds into the one-minute recording; we may contrast this with the much greater sociolinguistic frequency and salience in other languages, perhaps most notably British English, of variable pronunciation features. Harms, reporting the results of an early test (1961: 168) that sought to elicit from a panel of listeners judgments of American English speakers' social status on the basis of their speech alone, reported that most of the listeners required only 10–15 seconds to estimate the social provenance of fellow-speakers' accents, which clearly is a good deal less than the 45 seconds that elapsed before the salient accent feature in CL's speech occurred. Similarly, the evaluative test conducted by Bauvois (1996) allowed informants only 20 seconds of speech upon which to form their judgments.

2.4.3.2 Replies to Question B

Figure 2 shows, superimposed upon the information shown in Figure 1, the number of respondents who answered 'working-class' to the question, 'is the person more likely to be working-class or middle-class?'. Thus the order of speakers is the same as shown in Figure 1, that is from perceivedly most marked accent to least. The purpose of organising the two dimensions of information in this way is to show the degree of correlation between them. We can see that the correlation that holds for the Rennes informants between perceived markedness of accent and perceived working-class membership is fairly strong, though by no means perfect; clearly a very high degree of correlation would show the two lines in the graph following an identical or near-identical configuration. As it is there are some considerable mismatches between these two lines,

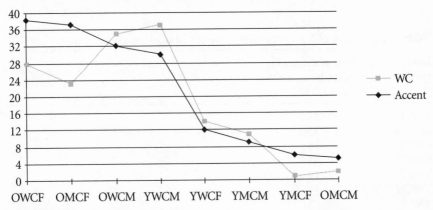

Relationship between perceived accent and perceived social-class

WC
Accent

OWCF OMCF OWCM YWCM YWCF YMCM YMCF OMCM

Figure 2. Relation between perceived markedness of accent and responses to question B (perceived social-class origin)

principally on the left-hand, largely WC side of the graph. Figure 2 shows two especially interesting results; firstly, three MC speakers and the young WC female are strongly perceived to have neither an accent nor, more narrowly, a WC accent. Secondly, of the four left-hand speakers who rate highly as having an accent, only two (both male) rate equally highly or more highly as having a WC accent, while the other two (both female) rate considerably less highly. One obvious conclusion to be drawn from this second result is that for the Rennes informants, the term 'accent' is not necessarily co-referential with 'working-class accent', and many qualitative comments, gathered from the informants and mentioned selectively above with respect to the OMCF confirm this. The most frequent evaluations of the OMCF's speech were 'regional accent', 'rural accent' and 'country-town accent'.

To address the question to what extent the results shown in Figure 2 square with any expectations prompted by a survey of the findings of dialectology and sociolinguistics, we need to consider the issue of the interactions between the social variables of interest here: age, gender and class. The findings reported in the rural and urban dialectological literature show overwhelmingly that more 'conservative' speakers (older, female, higher social class) are the guardians of the high-value language variety of a speech community. Conversely, the custodians of the vernacular are male and working-class: the role of age may be less important, as we suggest below. This broad proposition would produce a ranking of the Nancy speakers in descending order of perceived vernacular or localised accent as follows: OMCF or OMCM as least localised and perhaps YWCM or OWCM as most. Table 4 below shows the Nancy speakers ranked in descending order of the Rennes informants' evaluations of their degree of

Table 4. Rank order of Nancy speakers by perceived working-class accent

Nancy speaker	Number of Rennes informant who agreed on WC accent, / 40
YWCM	37
OWCM	35
OWCF	28
OMCF	23
YWCF	14
YMCM	11
YMCF	2
OMCM	1

working-class accent. Thus the same information is shown in Table 4 as in the superimposed line in Figure 2, but not organised as a function of the information shown in Figure 1.

We mentioned above that WC males might be expected to rank highest on this test, and MC females lowest. Table 4 shows this broadly to be the case, with the most notable exception of CL (OMCF), discussed above. It is unclear however whether any kind of consistent ranking is to be expected between the WC and MC extremes. This area of uncertainty is indicated in boldface in Table 4. Uncertainty is present because accent differentiation is not static but dynamic; we cite Eckert further (1989:248) in expanded form:

> Labov's original (1966) findings in New York City clearly lined up socioeconomic class, style, sound change, prestige, and evaluation on a single axis. The hierarchical socioeconomic continuum is also a continuum of linguistic change, wherein extent of historical change correlates inversely with socioeconomic status.

The image of a single axis appears less suitable if we consider, firstly, that prestige is not a uniplex social characteristic; secondly, that incoming sound changes can be from above or below, and hence be the object of different types of evaluation; and thirdly, that different social groups can be responsible for promoting language change. A good deal of recent research has highlighted the role of younger women in promoting sound changes, lining up with the findings of many traditional, geographical dialect studies that show conservative rural dialects to be largely the preserve of 'NORMs': non-mobile older rural males (Chambers and Trudgill 1998:29–30). Variationist urban sociolinguists have often interpreted differences in male and female patterns of linguistic behaviour in terms of their respective orientation to rather ill-defined constructs such as 'prestige' or 'standard' language varieties. It is only relatively recently that findings from English, for example L. Milroy (1992); J. Milroy et al. (1994); and French (Hansen 1997, 1998), Armstrong and Unsworth (1999) have brought into sharper focus a pattern of urban dialectology that is comparable to the NORM pattern referred to above: urban males, both young and old, also appear to resist the introduction of non-localised (and often 'non-standard') innovative linguistic variants, while females promote them. At the same time, female speakers appear to use higher frequencies of stable standard variants. Regarding the contemporary urban sociolinguistic situation, Labov (1990) suggests the two following principles governing the sociolinguistic gender pattern:

I   In stable sociolinguistic stratification, men use a higher frequency of non-standard forms than women.

II   In the majority of linguistic changes, women use a higher frequency of the incoming forms than men.

There seems to be a contradiction between these two principles, caused by the ambiguity inherent in the terms 'standard' and 'non-standard'. Supra-local, incoming forms are often non-standard, while localised, socially sensitive variants are non-standard virtually by definition. (Some localised, non-standard vocalic variants in English are identical to those found in RP, the regionless prestige variety. An example is the vowel in 'our', pronounced [ɑ:] both in RP and also widely distributed in WC English except in the northern varieties. These examples seem not to be very numerous, however.) One would therefore expect men to be the agents of most linguistic change according to this schema. One possible way of resolving this paradox is to replace in principle I 'non-standard' by 'local'; principle I then accounts for the female tendency to avoid localised, non-standard forms. At the same time this commutation is in conformity with principle II: females often promote the introduction to local communities of supra-local (and often non-standard) forms; a subsequent stage is perhaps a conferring on the variables of standard status, by virtue of their having been promoted by females. This argument seems to hold if we assume, as indeed does Labov in principle II, that linguistic change generally proceeds through the introduction to a speech community of forms that hitherto were largely foreign to it (but see Trudgill (1999b: 124–40) for a recent discussion of endogenous elements involved in language change).

Bearing these considerations in mind, we can suggest that a consistent ranking of perceived or actual working-class or vernacular accent is difficult to conceptualise in any given speaker group controlled for class, age and sex. In particular, it is the intermediate ordering between the 'extreme' speakers, perhaps OWCM and OMCF, which presents difficulties. This is because prestige (whether overt or covert) as mediated through accent will vary across communities as a function of the changes currently working within them, and of the social groups promoting these changes. Judging by recent findings in French (mentioned above), these social groups will typically be young, female and intermediate in the social-class continuum, and these groups may be promoting innovative variants from above or below. In view of the number of these factors and the complex way in which they interact with each other, we reiterate that the ordering shown in Table 4, leaving aside the anomalous position of CL that has already been discussed, is approximately in line with expectations in view of the fluidity of these. In view of these considerations we can say that the Rennes informants identified the Nancy speakers' social-class provenance fairly accurately. What remains to be examined is the issue of the accent features upon which French speaker-listeners focus in order to do this. We discuss this in a concluding section, when we consider the interactions between the various results presented here.

We now consider the relation between perceived WC accent and the responses of the Rennes informants to question C (ii) listed in 2.4.2 above, i.e. their success in identifying the Nancy speakers' regional origin.

2.4.3.3   *Replies to question C (ii)*

Figure 3 shows, juxtaposed with the social-class information given in Figure 2, the numbers of correct responses to question C (ii) shown above in 4.2. Speakers were initially asked: C (i) 'Can you identify the speaker's regional origin?' If they replied affirmatively, they were then asked: C (ii) 'Where do you think the speaker comes from?'.

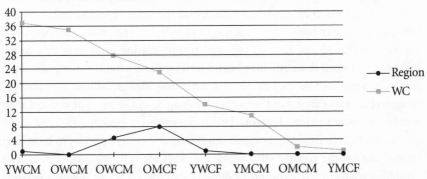

Figure 3. Relation between Nancy speakers' perceived social class and correctly perceived regional origin

It should be noted that answers counted as correct and shown negatively in Figure 3 were subject to a generous interpretation: thus 'correct' answers were those that mentioned northern or north-eastern France. If we showed only those responses mentioning Nancy or Lorraine, the numbers of correct responses would be negligible. Figure 3 shows very clearly that even for those

Nancy speakers who were perceived to have a strongly marked accent, rather few Rennes respondents were able to say where they might be from with precision. Thus the YWCM speaker, whose perceived WC-accent score was 92.5% or 39/40, rated one rather vaguely 'correct' responses in relation to his regional origin; 13 of the 40 Rennes informants hazarded the guess that he came from Rennes or Brittany. Figure 3 suggests therefore that for a sample of Rennes informants at least, the very close relation between social-class accent and regional accent characteristic of the UK is quite largely attenuated.

Against the foregoing we must consider the extent to which the openness of questions C (i) and (ii) were responsible for inducing error. Despite their surface structure the questions: (i) 'Can you identify the person's region of origin?' and (ii) 'Do you have any idea of which city it might be?' are *wh*-questions equivalent to: 'What is the speaker's region of origin?'. A speaker who treated the questions according to their surface *yes/no* form would be regarded as uncooperative. The questions are obviously very open ones, and may have led to some more or less random guessing by the Rennes informants in the absence of any cues provided by the researcher. Clearly an either/or question of the type: 'Is the speaker from (for instance) Paris or Nancy?' would have provided a tighter framework and indeed a 50–50 chance of a correct answer. A more sophisticated test still would have involved a sample of speakers from Paris (in the present example) and Nancy on the same tape. We feel nevertheless that the rather high rate of failure in identifying regional origin shown in Figure 3 is due to the lack of regional pronunciation cues available to the informants, rather than any bias introduced by the elicitation methods; this is partly in view of the higher success rates for identifications reported for comparable tests carried out on other languages, in the present context most notably Belgian French (Bauvois 1996). Surprisingly perhaps in view of the distinctive British English situation, no systematic study appears to have been carried out on the success with which speakers identify regional provenance. Trudgill's well-known pyramid (1995: 29) schematising the relation between social class and regional origin does imply the ability on the part of UK English speaker-listeners to identify, if not the regional provenance of a locutor, at least the presence of a localised accent.

At an impressionistic level, one of the factors frequently cited as influential in promoting the salience of the regional component of UK English socio-regional accents is the role of the broadcast media in raising the general consciousness of certain accents, perhaps most notably through the national broadcasting of several very popular daily television drama serials set in large conurbations such as London, Liverpool, Newcastle upon Tyne and Manchester, as well as rural Yorkshire. It is true further that familiarity with an accent or sub-accent distributed within a broad dialect area promotes a sensitivity to certain of its features that is unavailable to those who are not in close geographical contact with the accent, in the measure that features which seem subtle or even undetectable to some listeners will appear quite gross to others. Thus speakers within a broad accent region will be sensitive to small degrees of accent variation within the region, in contrast to speakers from outside it. At the national level the vast majority of speakers of British English are no doubt broadly aware of the major urban accents of the UK; a further factor that is influential is the size of the major British urban centres relative to the French situation. All of the cities mentioned above, as well as several others, have populations above one million in the conurbation. This is in contrast with the 'hypercephalic' French situation, where apart from the Paris conurbation (population 9m), of the 25 largest cities only six in France as a whole have a population over 500,000 (Dauncey 1999: 105); only one of these, Nantes, is squarely in the oil area: the other is Lyon, in the transitional *franco-provençal* area. At the same time, France has approximately twice the land mass as the UK for about the same population. The French situation, leaving aside the large Parisian region, is one of relatively small and widely separated cities, in contrast to the more concentrated UK distribution. In this perspective we can suggest that speakers from two relatively small British cities with a low national prominence may well have difficulty in identifying geographically one another's accent with any precision; a pertinent example is perhaps Derby in central England and Norwich in the east central area, both medium-sized cities of some 200,000 inhabitants in the conurbation. This is all the more true since although Derby and Norwich are not very distant from each other (some 120 miles or 190 km), no major communication routes link them. Indeed, they are divided by one of what Labov (1966: 499) refers to as 'troughs in the network of communications' which he suggests often coincide with dialect boundaries.

These considerations relate to Nancy and Rennes in that, as mentioned above, the two French cities are relatively small in UK terms (310,000 and 240,000 in the conurbation respectively) and no nationally broadcast television drama serials are based in the cities. Further, the fairly small size of these two conurbations implies that the speech of their inhabitants may well not be very widely diffused through processes other than electronic broadcast media; most notably through the widespread mobility of the cities' inhabitants. However, the principal factor that appears to differentiate the Derby–Norwich and Nancy–

Rennes cases is linguistic: it does indeed appear that rather subtle accent features differentiate the speech of Nancy and Rennes, and these are useful as cues to identification only to those speakers situated in relatively close proximity to the cities. By contrast, it seems highly likely that listeners from Derby could identify a Norwich accent as considerably different from their own, without however necessarily being able to locate the accent with a high degree of accuracy.

What emerges from the foregoing is that the ability to identify a regional accent depends on the salience of its phonological features on the one hand, and on the social salience of the accent on the other. It seems likely in turn that the salience of the phonological features of an accent depends on the number of features that differ from the listener's accent; as well as the extent to which they differ, measured in terms of phonetic space, complexity, etc.; to these factors may be added others such as phonological contrast caused by differences between dialects (cf. Trudgill 1986: 13–21). We can summarise this situation in tabular form as shown in Table 5.

Table 5. Relation between accent features and listener's identifications

Accent features		Listener's correct identification
linguistically different	socially salient	
+	+	+
+	−	−
−	+	+
−	−	−

Table 5 indicates in schematic form the influence of two aspects of regional accents upon listeners' correct identifications: the degree to which an accent is perceived as different from the hearer's; and what we have called the social salience of the accent, in other words the degree to which the accent is familiar to the hearer. The first line of the table indicates that if an accent is perceived both as having markedly different features to that of the listener and is also familiar, the listener will be able to identify it correctly. So much seems fairly obvious, and the first three lines of the table simply express in schematic form one's intuition: the regional provenance of an accent needs to be previously known to a listener if an accurate identification is to be made. The second line of the table expresses the Derby–Norwich example discussed above, and the third line expresses a situation where an accent is perceived as similar to the listener's, and is salient by virtue of its speakers' being situated in the locality (in contrast to line one, where an accent is markedly different from the hearer's but salient by virtue of having a high national profile).

Lines one–three of the table have a relation between perceived difference and social salience that differs from that shown in the fourth line. In lines one–three there is simple juxtaposition of perceived difference and social salience; a listener may or may not perceive an accent as being different, and at the same time is or is not aware of the accent, either by virtue of its having been diffused nationally, or of its being located in proximity to the hearer. The output, shown in the right-hand column, will depend on the presence or absence of social salience, which, for obvious reasons, is the more powerful factor. By contrast, line four, which expresses the Rennes–Nancy situation, shows a different relation between perceived difference and social salience; the relation is not one of juxtaposition, but of mutual dependence. Thus it may well be that the Rennes informants failed to identify the Nancy speakers' accents because they are not socially salient (the situation indicated in line two) but the reverse relation seems equally likely: the Nancy accent lacks social salience for the Rennes informants because the differentiating accent features necessary for the achievement of social salience are not present to any marked extent. In this sense the Rennes — Nancy situation resembles that expressed in line three, to the extent that any differentiating accent features between Nancy and Rennes appear to be subtle; with the difference that the Nancy accent lacks social salience for the Rennes informants by virtue of the small size of the cities and their location 600 km apart. The most convincing element in the Rennes informants' responses in favour of this argument is their tendency to identify the Nancy informants as having a Breton or Rennes accent: this suggests strongly an overwhelming absence of differentiating accent features that might have helped the Rennes informants' judgments. No parallel case in British English appears to exist.

A further issue of methodology corresponds to the openness of question C (ii). The results concerning social-class identification shown in Figure 2 and Table 4 could be argued to have been induced, in part at least, by the either/or character of question B: Is the person more likely to be working-class or middle-class? Clearly a person responding to this question has a 50–50 chance of answering correctly. The results shown in Table 4 are nevertheless impressively accurate, and it is of course not possible to determine the extent to which chance played a part in producing them. Question B could have been framed in a more open way, for example: 'What social class do you think the speaker belongs to?'. However, it seems likely that asked this question, the Rennes informants would in any event have replied for the most part in either/or terms, since the broadest social class division is very commonly perceived as a middle-class–working-class bipartition.

Figure 4 shows the responses of the Rennes informants to question C (ii), organised by number of informants and region identified.

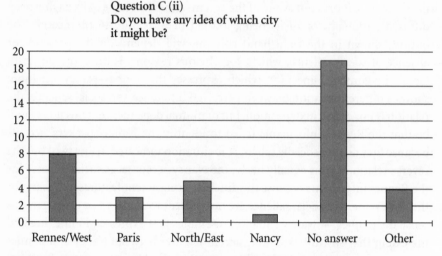

Figure 4. Numbers of responses to question C (ii), by perceived regional origin

Figure 4 shows a different organisation of the numbers of the Rennes inform-ants' guesses at question C (ii), the regional origin of the Nancy speakers; clearly, no information concerning any individual Nancy speaker is shown in Figure 4, in contrast to Figure 3. What is striking is that only one out the forty Rennes informants' responses were 'correct' in the narrow terms discussed above, compared to the 19 professions of ignorance and the remaining more or less inaccurate responses. In total, it can be seen that six of the respondents guessed more or less accurately: five identified the north/east region and one Nancy. We discuss fully the inferences that may be drawn from these results in a concluding section, but we may say here that the Rennes informants' rather high rate of incorrect judgments of the Nancy speakers' regional (as opposed to social-class) origin are all the more impressive, as a judgment of regional origin based on features other than accent is difficult to conceive for French. This is because regional (again, as opposed to social-class) differences in syntax and lexis are not more clearly marked in French than pronunciation, so that accent features are almost the sole cue aiding regional identification. A further point of interest here is the 'annexationism' (Bauvois 1996) shown by the Rennes informants, i.e. their tendency (eight speakers) to identify the accent as their own, perhaps by concentrating on any linguistic features that they perceived as being characteristic of the Rennes accent and ignoring others.

2.5 Summary and discussion: Summary of results

We may summarise the results shown in Figures 1–4 and Table 4 as follows. In this summary we leave aside the fact that the Rennes informants may have concentrated on features other than pronunciation when asked to evaluate the accents of the Nancy speakers.

i.   Figure 1 shows that the speech of the Nancy speakers triggers in the Rennes informants a fairly accurate association between the Nancy speakers' social attributes (age, sex, class) and their 'accent', defined perhaps generally as the accent's degree of regionality or localisation, although with the crucial qualification (see (iii) below) that the Rennes informants' success in estimating accurate regional localisation is rather low.

ii.   Table 4 shows quite a high degree of success on the part of the Rennes informants in estimating the Nancy speakers' social class, and Figure 2 shows further that the social-class judgments line up fairly closely not only with (a) the Nancy speakers' actual social class but also (b) with their perceived degree of accent localisation, as in (i) above.

iii.   Figures 3 and 4 show perhaps the most interesting results to issue from this study. What is of interest here is the gross mismatch between on the one hand the Rennes informants' relative success in identifying the Nancy speakers' social class judging by their speech, and on the other their lack of success in identifying the Nancy speakers' regional origin using the same cues. This goes against Nicolson's (1955) suggestion referred to above; it also contradicts more recent observations made by Francophone scholars of linguistics. For example, Walter (1988:159) suggests that middle-class speakers are differentiated from one another geographically by their speech, but not socially from working class speakers; thus the speech of a banker and a bank clerk from Paris will be more similar to each other than will the speech of a banker from Paris and one from Strasbourg (Alsace) or Toulouse (southern France). However, these examples do not compare like with like, given that Strasbourg and Toulouse are not

located in the *oïl* area. Furthermore, to the extent that our results are comparable with Walter's example, they show that the French *oïl* speaker sample
considered here is indeed socially differentiated by their speech, while the
regional element of sociolinguistic differentiation appears to have been dislocated from the social-class component.

2.6   Discussion: Phonological variation in French

Clearly, the results summarised in (i)–(iii) raise the following question: if, as the
results presented above strongly suggest, French speaker-listeners can identify
the social class of speakers solely on the basis of their speech, what accent
features do they focus on in order to do this? One answer suggested by the
results shown above is negative: they do not rely on the linguistically arbitrary
accent features that in British English link a speaker's degree of regional
localisation to his/her social class. This is apparent from the notable failure of
the Rennes informants to identify the Nancy speakers' regional provenance.
These English variables can be linguistically arbitrary in a further sense, namely
that their socially symbolic value can vary from one location to another, as
shown in Table 6 below.

Table 6. Percentage use of post-vocalic /r/ in New York City (US) and Reading (UK)
(Trudgill 1975:35)

Social class	New York City	Reading
UMC	32	0
LMC	20	28
UWC	12	44
LWC	0	49

The results shown above derive respectively from research reported by Labov
(1966:234–43) and Trudgill (1975:104) The pattern in Table 6 brings out very
clearly the fact that speakers can employ linguistically entirely arbitrary phonological items in a way that is highly charged socially: thus rhoticity is used by
overtly prestigious speaker groups in New York City, while almost exactly the
opposite pattern obtains in Reading. This principle of linguistic arbitrariness is
taken as axiomatic in sociolinguistics, but, as has been mentioned previously, it
may be that more 'natural' pronunciation features are responsible for indicating

social-class provenance in France, without at the same time indicating regional origin; precisely because these features are shared by the entire speech community. As stated previously, this absence of regional localisation in socially diagnostic speech is suggested by the fact that similar findings have been reported for certain French variables in quite widely separated locations: Tours (Ashby 1984), Paris (Laks 1983); Lorraine (Armstrong 1996).

The obvious inference is that the kind of arbitrary phonological variation characteristic of American and British English may has been levelled out of French, and that the phenomena discussed above largely represent the available residue. If these elision and neutralisation phenomena are the principal socially diagnostic pronunciation elements available to the French speech community in question, then it appears that French speakers are able to signal to one another their social status in terms of class, but not of regionality; or at least to a much lesser extent. We now propose some general conclusions that emerge from the foregoing.

2.7   General conclusions emerging from the perceptual test

i.   The first conclusion is that local accents in France continue to be perceived often as rural. To the extent that these perceptual results reflect behaviour, they oblige us to qualify Rickard's (1993: 243) suggestion that: 'What we in fact have today is no longer a situation of standard versus rural dialects, but instead class-based differences arising from the spread of Parisian French.' Regarding the second element of this statement, the spread of Parisian French is unsurprising in view of the political, cultural, economic and demographic dominance exerted by the Paris region over the rest France; Walter (1988: 160) suggests the terms 'Parisian by adoption' and 'provincial Parisian' to designate speakers of what we have referred to here as 'levelled French'.

However, the rather unexpected result reported here and contradicting Rickard's observation, shows that to the extent that class-based differences are perceived as being associated with a localised accent, this localisation is more often perceived as rural than urban. Of the four Nancy speakers strongly perceived by the Rennes informants as having a marked accent and as being working-class (Figures 1 and 2 above), the perceptions expressed by the Rennes informants in terms of rural or urban provenance were as shown in Table 7 below.

Table 7 shows observed frequencies (i.e. fractions, not percentages) of the

Table 7. Rennes informants' perception of Nancy speakers with marked accent as rural or urban

Nancy speaker	Perceived as rural	Perceived as urban
YWCM	10/34	8/34
OWCM	15/31	2/34
OWCF	11/29	6/29
OMCF	15/34	2/34

Rennes informants who explicitly commented on the 'marked' Nancy speakers' accents as either rural or urban. Not all informants commented in each case, which is why the denominators are not the same. The replies do not total across the table because vague replies such as 'regional' have been excluded; thus for the older WC female for example, 12/29 of the Rennes informants who commented explicitly, mentioned neither rural nor urban as a possible provenance. It is perhaps significant that the younger WC male, whose perceived social-class score was 37/40 (Table 4 above), also attracted a relatively large number of comments linking his accent to an urban origin. More specifically, four of the eight Rennes informants who mentioned a perceived urban accent suggested *banlieue* as the possible provenance for this speaker. This term is often translated as 'suburbs', and to the extent that the *banlieues* are typically large, recent (post-war) and low-quality housing developments located at some distance from the city centre, the term 'suburb' is denotationally not grossly inaccurate. Alpin (1993:47) has the following definition of the *banlieue*: 'the outer suburbs of a city, [...] the *banlieue* is a product of expansion in this century and the last one. It is sometimes used as a term to suggest unplanned sprawl and a cultural wasteland'.

Within this broad definition, two broad types of *banlieues* can be distinguished: *petite* and *grande*. The *grande banlieue* shows similarities with the British and American conception of a middle-class residential area, located at some distance from the city centre. The demand for a slower and more rural pace of life, the desire to avoid urban malaise, as well as the rise in city-centre property prices, are factors influencing this 'counter-urbanisation'. The *petites banlieues*, the zones directly in contact with the town centres, originate from distinct villages or towns that have been assimilated by the progressive development of the centres. The population of a *petite banlieue* is generally composed of the lower classes; similarities with the British and American inner cities can be found in a high rate of unemployment, a concentration of ethnic minorities and low-quality housing stock. Thus the term 'inner-city' captures more accurately the English connotation of *petite banlieue* in the measure that the term evokes inadequate housing, high rates of crime and unemployment, and a large immigrant population. To refine Alpin's definition, it may be noted that it is in a sense the over-planned (or simply ill-planned) character of the *petite banlieue* areas, built on a production-line basis in often hasty response to the rapid urban population growth in the post-war years, without suitable transport or leisure facilities, that has caused these areas to be associated with social malaise. Insofar as a distinctive French urban working-class accent, often referred to as an *accent de banlieue*, can be said to be exist, it may be young WC males who are its guardians, again with the crucial qualification that an *accent de banlieue* appears to imply little or no element of geographical localisation within the *oïl* area. Gadet (1998a), in an article devoted to a discussion of the French of the Parisian *banlieues* (she uses the term *cités*, translatable as 'housing estates/projects') refers to changes occurring in this variety of French in such a way as to imply that they are not localised to the Parisian area.

Concerning the extent to which the Rennes speakers perceive the 'marked' Nancy speakers as having a rural accent, we may hypothesise that the societal correlate to these perceptions is the relative recency and abruptness of the social mobilisation of the French rural population in the interests of industrialisation: Lodge (1993:222) points out that it was only in 1931 that the French urban population began to outnumber the rural: the comparable date for the UK is 1851 (Hobsbawm 1977:23). However, this 'explanation' seems to presuppose a knowledge of their recent demography on the part of French speakers, and merely raises the question why French speakers have difficulty in identifying the regional origin of unfamiliar accents, whether they perceive these marked accents as being of an urban, rural, inner-city or country-town provenance. The results shown in Table 7 are rather difficult to explain with precision, but previous research has shown that speakers' perceptions of a linguistic situation frequently lag behind the reality (e.g. Juillard, Moreau, Ndao and Thiam (1994:56–8) for Wolof). A further issue raised by this result is the comparative success reported by Bauvois (1996) of Belgian WC informants in identifying the regional provenance of speakers in a similar listening test; this suggests that the urban/rural population balance may have evolved differently in Belgium relative to the French situation. Belgium is a rather small country geographically, and more densely populated than France, factors that must aid accent identification.

We discuss in some detail in 2.8 below some of the socio-economic elements that have contributed to the current levelled French situation, but briefly we can suggest tentatively that as a result of the lateness of the social mobilisation that took place in France, urban accents have for the most part simply not had time to develop. As an aside, it is interesting to speculate whether they now will in view of the levelling processes that appear to be diminishing social-regional differences in comparable languages; British English, for example (Williams and Kerswill 1999). Against this of course must be set the tendency towards increasing divergence between Black and White English varieties reported in several US cities, notably Philadelphia (Labov and Harris 1986). It seems likely that divergent processes such as these are the linguistic results of economic and ethnic, and hence social, polarisation, and as remarked above, conditions are such in some *banlieues* that the varieties of French spoken there may continue to diverge sharply from the variety that is the focus of interest here.

To return to the rural/urban issue mentioned above, we suggested that French urban accents have not had time to develop. Clearly however, there is no *a priori* reason why an accent cannot develop in a fairly small town as a consequence of in-migration from its hinterland; on the contrary, this appears very plausibly to be the normal state of affairs. Trudgill (1986) has examined in some detail the processes that occur in situations where dialects come into contact. The process discussed by Trudgill that is chiefly relevant here is levelling; the suppression of linguistic differences by speakers of different language varieties, in response to the need for mutual accommodation in contact situations. From this perspective, it seems plausible that one consequence of the relative lateness and rapidity of the French social mobilisation process would have been the diminution of pronunciation differences and the consequent simplification of phonological systems in the developing *oïl* cities. Labov (1972b: 300) expresses the situation in the following terms: '[...] rapid language mixing seems to follow a kind of classic structural reductionism, and it would not be difficult to argue that it is a sub-type of the same process that produces contact languages [...] One of the universal constraints on change seems to be operating here — that in contact situations, [linguistic] mergers expand at the expense of distinctions.' The parallel with the pidginisation process is an obvious one, and one would expect this model, as suggested above, to predict regional urban varieties that are levelled with respect to the surrounding rural dialects, but that are nevertheless distinct from one another. But as we have emphasised at several points here, the distinctiveness of the French situation is the extent to which the spread of Parisian French has eliminated regional urban pronunciation differences. Rural pronunciation differences appear to persist, in part no doubt as a result of the still large rural French population relative to comparable countries. The study under discussion here certainly demonstrates that rural accents are perceived as persisting.

ii.   The second conclusion one can draw from the results presented above relates to the social function of accent differentiation across societies that are organised hierarchically in social-class terms. If the results shown in Figures 2 and 3 are representative of the situation for 'levelled' French generally, then it appears that French speakers can identify social-class provenance from accent. This raises the rather fundamental question whether social class is the most salient variable in marking social variation across speech communities; certainly much discussion in the sociolinguistic literature of concepts such as linguistic markers and indicators has been discussed in terms of the interaction between social class and style differentiation; cf. Chambers and Trudgill (1998: 70–3). This emphasis on social class reflects a perception shared by sociolinguists that this speaker variable is 'the most likely independent variable to correlate with linguistic innovation' (Chambers and Trudgill 1998: 153). Clearly however, this quotation reflects the preoccupations of scholars of linguistics rather than speakers' perceptions. If one considers the contrast between the French and English situation with regard to variable phonology in terms of socio-historical factors, it appears that the English language has developed such that its speakers have a resource, the regional component of the social-regional accent, that French speakers may lack. We do not of course wish to present a teleological argument here; the French language did not evolve 'so that' its speakers could retain the possibility of identifying one another's social-class origin; even though, as suggested above, this aspect of identity, signalling as it does a social actor's access to wealth and power, is perhaps the aspect that speakers who are unknown to one another may most urgently wish to determine at a first encounter. We merely note further here that French appears to represent a counterexample to the otherwise rather plausible generalisation put forward by Hudson (1996: 43), that 'we use pronunciation in order to identify our origins (or to *imply* that we originated from some group, whether we did or not)' (emphasis in original). If we interpret 'origins' here in the sense of regional origin, which clearly is an ascribed social characteristic that has the potential to be highly valued by its possessors, and which further is an attribute that broadly is not susceptible to modification (unlike social class), then it seems very remarkable that French speakers should lack the resource to identify this feature through pronunciation, as the results shown here seem to suggest they do. Any argumentation concerning this issue must however remain tentative, since we have here suggested at most a certain lack of success regarding the identification, rather than the expression, of regional identity through accent.

iii.   A further conclusion concerns the perceptual aspect of how variable pronunciation functions in French; if connected-speech processes (elision and neutralisation phenomena) constitute the principal variable pronunciation resource available to French speakers, how can we explain their value as sociolinguistic variables if we assume that salient phonological variables generally have a regional as well as social component? As suggested previously, the answer may be that these processes diverge in an easily perceptible way from the orthography of French, which continues to be inculcated in French schools in a highly normative way. For example, the elision of /r/ in word-final syllables, as in a word such as *quatre* 'four', results in the reduced form [kat], whereas the canonical realisation is [katʀ]. The example of this rather frequent word is perhaps not the most apt that could have been chosen, but a speaker who consistently elides /r/ word-finally, in infrequent as well as frequent lexical items, may well attract unfavourable social judgments. Thus, the divergence between the standard pronunciation, reflecting as it does the orthographic ⟨r⟩, and the non-standard where an orthographic element has been lost, is perhaps more sharply apparent in less frequent r-final words such as *lièvre* 'hare'. Deletion of /l/ also results in deviation from the standard pronunciation as represented in the orthography, as in *elle parle* 'she speaks' pronounced [ɛpaʁl] (standard [ɛlpaʁl]); or even more saliently, in full lexical words such as *escalier* 'staircase' realised as [ɛskaje], where the canonical form is [ɛskalje]. Variables of this kind recall those in English already mentioned: (h), (ng) and the glottal stop, discussed by Chambers and Trudgill (1998: 72). Chambers and Trudgill suggest that these may be subject to overt stigmatisation as a result of 'the divergence between pronunciation and orthography' mentioned above. Thus the deletion of schwa, /l/ and /r/ may be 'natural' in the sense discussed above, but in a country such as France which has a very strong normative tradition, these processes will certainly not be regarded as natural by speaker-listeners who have internalised this normative attitude to language variation and who focus on these variables as social-class markers. In the following chapter we examine the socio-stylistic value of these French variables using some behavioural results, in the light of this apparent tension between natural linguistic processes and normative pressures.

We touched above on English variables of the type which depend on ease-of-articulation processes and which, while resulting in divergence from the spelling, appear not to attract strong disapproval, suggesting that variables of this kind are subject to stringent linguistic constraints governed by ease of articulation, which when violated do indeed result in stigmatised forms. However, it may be added from impressionistic observation that before a pause, word-final three-consonant clusters may indeed reduce in formal MC speech to a single lengthened consonant, as in 'tests' reduced from [tɛsts] > [tɛsː], and 'coasts' [kəʊsts] > [kəʊsː]. Specifically, the present writer has quite often noticed consonant-cluster reduction of this type in speech events such as televised news broadcasts and weather forecasts. That professional speakers in rather highly formal speech situations should eschew spelling pronunciation in this way, might at first suggest a parallel between variables of the [tɛsts] > [tɛsː] type and French schwa, /l/ and /r/, given that ease of articulation is involved in both cases. No quantitative intraspeaker data appear to be available for English consonant-cluster reduction of this type, so that the social-stylistic value of such variables is unclear, as least as indicated by variationist methods.

We conclude this chapter by discussing briefly the distinctive nature of the French situation with regard to its regional-social pronunciation pattern, having first sketched some of the historical factors responsible.

2.8 Historical factors influencing the levelling of French

One question that emerges from the foregoing data and argumentation is whether one can talk of a normal or 'default' socio-regional state of affairs in a given language. One could argue that the British English situation is rather idiosyncratic in this respect; social and regional pronunciation differences are intimately linked in British English, such that regional accents, especially urban accents, have by and large until quite recently been perceived to be lower-class accents. The English accent that was formerly the most overtly prestigious, RP, is also the so-called 'regionless' accent. More recently, the continuing decrease in the acceptability of 'marked' or 'hyperlectal' RP in English has been accompanied by processes of levelling in the UK that see highly localised accents absorbed into wider regional areas (Foulkes and Docherty 1999a). At the same time, the UK tertiary sector and broadcast media seem increasingly to exploit the now largely positively perceived social information encoded in these less finely differentiated regional accents. Despite these relatively recent changes, what remains striking in the UK situation is the rather large number and national prominence of social-regional accents.

The situation sketched above seems not to obtain in France, where pronunciation has been standardised more successfully, apart from the very salient north–south split. Hawkins (1993:56) remarks that 'it is impossible to tell, simply from listening to a speaker of standard French, with a standard accent, where that speaker comes from'. This formulation clearly raises the further question of what criteria need to be framed to define a standard spoken language, and may be reformulated by reiterating the point we have developed above, namely that an *oïl* accent contains rather few regional features. It is also important to note in this connexion the difference between a 'standard' French or English accent, and RP. This latter accent is controlled by relatively few speakers, whereas at the pronunciation level, standard French appears to be the property of the majority of *oïl* speakers.

The historical reasons for the rather successful standardisation of French pronunciation are complex, and it is difficult to determine the role of the state in this process. Nevertheless, it is undeniable that, as Judge remarks (1993:7), 'France is famous for the degree of state interference in linguistic matters'. The French tradition of strong government from the centre, with concomitant, often ruthless suppression of parallel or regional power centres, dates back at least to the initiatives of Louis XIII's chief minister Richelieu in the early 17th century, and this centralising policy was reflected in a concern to codify the written standard language. However, there appears to have been little concern before the Revolution to impose the standard language on the mass of the rural populace via schooling; the state was 'at best indifferent to the language used by the mass of its subjects, at worst very ready to exploit the advantages it gained from the linguistic exclusion of the peasantry from economic and political power' (Lodge 1993:213).

By contrast, a prominent feature of the post-revolutionary period was the state's will to impose centralisation on all citizens. The linguistic aspect of this will was expressed in the motto: *La langue doit être une comme la République* '(Our) language, like the Republic, must be one and the same'. The French language came to be closely identified with national identity, and correspondingly, regional languages (Breton, Alsatian, Catalan etc.) were associated with disloyalty to the republic. However, the means necessary for the attempt to impose language planning throughout France, notably in the form of free universal primary education, were substantially lacking until the late 19th century, and as Lodge (1993:215) remarks, 'the intrusion of Parisian power into every corner of society [...] almost certainly had a more decisive impact on the diffusion of the standard language into the provinces than did the state's overt moves into the domain of language planning'. These efforts certainly contributed to the imposition of what has been called the 'ideology of the standard' (Milroy and Milroy 1991), the view that presents the standard language as the only correct variety, and all dialects as imperfect approximations to it. However, one must look to geographical, social and economic factors to account for the relative uniformity of pronunciation in northern France.

Firstly, it is evident that the central position in northern France of the Île-de-France region, from whose historical dialect ('Francien') the modern standard derives, facilitated, and no doubt still facilitates, its diffusion into the provinces. Apart from such factors as substrate influence (von Wartburg 1967), it is no doubt significant that the north-south linguistic division has been and continues to be perpetuated by the geographical distance of Paris from the south.

Lodge (1993:219–29) adduces further socio-economic factors which may explain the levelling of northern French pronunciation: universal conscription, dating from the Revolution and the subsequent wars of intervention; increasing geographical and social mobility as a result of the development of national markets; the relatively late urbanisation and industrialisation of France, which prevented the formation of distinctive urban vernaculars, such as are found in the old industrial centres of Britain. Lodge (p. 229) makes the further point that it is not only standard Parisian linguistic forms which have diffused into the provinces: 'if the diffusion of Parisian French into the provinces had been solely top-down and principally the result of official education policies, we would have expected speakers of French in the provinces to use few forms derived from the Parisian vernacular'. But non-standard linguistic forms patently have diffused from Paris to the provinces; the distinctiveness of the French situation lies in the fact that these forms appear to be largely lexical. Variation in the French lexicon will be discussed below, but it appears that the pronunciation norms that were diffused from Paris to the provinces were not working class. This reflects the absence of a distinctive Parisian working-class accent analogous to Cockney, for example; the reasons for this virtual absence are again complex, but the Parisian non-standard linguistic forms adopted by the provinces appear to be lexical and syntactic, rather than phonological.

The northern French standard naturally admits of regional variation, but we have seen that regional and social variation do not appear to be so closely tied in French as in English, so that regional French pronunciation is not automatically viewed as lower-class. Clearly, however, social class variation expressed in pronunciation is observable: as discussed above, French speakers do refer to the *accent de banlieue*, and this is of course a social-class judgment, but once again, as noted above, not a regional judgment.

2.9   The distinctive nature of the French situation

The foregoing sketch is designed to show that, although the phonology of a language may in principle be resistant to standardisation, it is possible for social and economic factors to combine to render pronunciation relatively homogeneous over a fairly wide area. Clearly, every nation has its own distinctive sociopolitical history, which will have contributed to its current linguistic situation. As suggested above, the historical reasons for the rather successful standardisation of French pronunciation are complex, and it is difficult to determine the relative roles of institutional and other factors (social, geographical and economic) in this process. The crucial point which emerges from the foregoing is that the history and present state of French goes against the rather intuitive notion that pronunciation will tend to be more resistant to standardisation than grammar. This seems plausible of one accepts that language standardisation largely proceeds through the promotion of literacy. According to this view, societies with a literate tradition appear to eliminate non-standard grammar from writing, while in contrast, the standard pronunciation will not be favoured unless orthography maps onto pronunciation in a transparent way.

This notion has found expression in the sociolinguistic literature. Hudson (1996: 43–5) suggests a distinction between variation on the different linguistic levels in the following terms (p. 45):

> [...] differences in syntax tend to be suppressed, whereas those in pronunciation and vocabulary tend to be favoured and used as markers of social differences. There do not appear to be any examples of communities in which this relationship is reversed, with less variation in vocabulary and pronunciation than in syntax.

Against this plausible suggestion, the example of French appears to show that societal factors can operate to level pronunciation to a high degree across a wide area (we examine the case of French vocabulary in a later chapter). Of course, the observation that French pronunciation has been standardised or levelled in large measure remains to be tested systematically through behavioural as well as evaluative studies, but agreement on its uniformity, if largely impressionistic, seems widespread. The evaluative evidence presented above gives preliminary, if indirect confirmation of these impressions. We proposed above some shortcomings of the study described above that should lead us to urge caution in the interpretation of results concerning the supposed regional uniformity of French pronunciation. As has already been stated, no doubt the principal limitation of the study is that the results emerging from it are based on perceptual, not behavioural data, and are correspondingly indirect. However, the advantage corresponding to this shortcoming is that a perceptual study has the possibility of eliciting native-speaker intuitions concerning socially sensitive pronunciation features of which a linguist (especially a non-native-speaker) may be unaware. We suggested above further that the rather limited range of pronunciation variables reported in the sociolinguistic literature on French may be an accurate reflection of what is available. The perceptual study reported here seems to confirm this.

To summarise, the data presented above suggest that in French, a language whose pronunciation has been levelled to a relatively high degree, certainly relative to English, the relationship between social and regional variation is quite distinctive compared to what obtains in other languages. In the following chapter we explore the implications of this for the audience design model of socio-stylistic variation proposed by Bell.

CHAPTER 3

Socio-stylistic variation
in French phonology

3.1 Introduction

In the previous chapter we suggested that French variable pronunciation may be distinctive in largely lacking a regional component. In this chapter we explore the implications of this issue for the relation between interspeaker and intraspeaker variation in French and the influence of linguistic and social factors upon this relation. Some evidence that we discuss below suggests that certain factors, which hitherto have apparently received relatively little attention in the literature, need to be considered as potential input to a theory of this relationship: notably the nature of the linguistic variables involved in stylistic variation; and the prominent role that standardisation has played in the evolution of French, and continues to play in the contemporary dynamic operating between the standard and vernacular varieties. Specifically, our concern in this chapter is to discuss the various factors influencing hyperstyle variation in two corpora of spoken French, with a view to assessing the possible implications of these results for the theories so far put forward of the relationship between inter- and intraspeaker variation. To reiterate, we will suggest that any explanation of this relation needs to take account of several related factors not previously fully considered: (i) the elicitation methods used in sociolinguistic enquiry; (ii) the linguistic factors influencing the variables involved; (iii) and the normative traditions prevalent in the community which may influence language production. Another way of expressing this latter issue is by reference to the relation between spelling and pronunciation inculcated in French speakers at school.

3.2 The French linguistic variables under discussion

The linguistic variables we examine here are schwa and the liquid consonants /l/ and /r/, which undergo variable deletion in French in certain linguistic contexts.

Results will first be presented for /r/-deletion in the contexts which are relevant to the present discussion. We shall see that the distinction between the influences of linguistic and extra-linguistic or social factors is rather blurred, but for ease of presentation we present them separately.

3.3   The corpora

We present below some behavioural language data, as opposed to the attitudinal data discussed previously, which bring the social-stylistic relationship characteristic of French pronunciation into sharper focus. These data are drawn from two corpora of spoken French, the first recorded in north-eastern France in 1990 (described fully in Armstrong 1993). This corpus of speech was recorded in Dieuze, a town of some 5,000 inhabitants in the Moselle *département* or administrative district in the Lorraine region of north-eastern France. The recordings were made in the town's *collège et lycée* or 11–18 secondary school, in which all the informants were pupils, and where the researcher had some years previously been English language assistant. We refer below to 'the Dieuze data/informants', etc. The second set of corpora were recorded in 1989 and 1992–3 in Paris (Hansen 2000). Again we refer later to 'the Paris corpus/informants/data', etc.

3.3.1   The Dieuze corpus

In Dieuze the informants were recorded in two speech styles, designated henceforward 'interview' and 'conversation'. In interview style, informants were recorded one-to-one with the researcher, the present author who is an advanced English non-native speaker of French. We consider below in the appropriate places the ways in which this factor may have contributed to the hyperstyle effects we are discussing. Conversation style was elicited by the use of 'peer conferences', i.e. the recording of two or three informants of the same age and sex, in the absence of the researcher. Interview style has been assumed to be the more formal of the two. The first ten minutes of each informal recording was excluded from study in all phonological and grammatical analyses of the corpus that are discussed here. Correspondingly, the first ten minutes of the interviews were not excluded, in view of the intention to study intraspeaker variation across two styles that should be as sharply differentiated as possible.

The direct influence of social class was not examined in the Dieuze corpus, but one might expect that the influence of this variable would be associated, at least indirectly, with the two demographic variables whose influence has been examined, sex or gender (gender henceforward) and age. The social variable of gender may be expected to influence linguistic behaviour, given that many previous sociolinguistic studies have reported a tendency on the part of females towards greater use of the non-localised linguistic forms that are also generally associated with the higher social classes. As discussed in the previous chapter, more recent analyses, such as that of L. Milroy (1992) and J. Milroy *et al.* (1994), have interpreted male–female differences in terms of the use by male speakers of linguistic forms that are more highly localised than those favoured by females, often irrespective of social class and of the 'standardness' of the linguistic variable. Watt and Milroy (1999) is the most recent summary of this issue. A further recent (and French) example of gender variation operating independent of social class is reported in Armstrong and Unsworth (1999). Gender can therefore be considered as a social variable that influences linguistic behaviour independently of other social variables, at least for some linguistic variables, in some communities, and depending on whether the variable in question is stable or innovating. We discuss this issue more fully below.

The social variable of age was expected to show up a pattern of the progressive acquisition of stylistic competence through the greater use, with increasing age, of linguistic forms to signal appropriate speech styles, these forms again drawn from various points on the social class dialect continuum.

The sub-sample of 20 or 16 informants is therefore differentiated by the social variables of age and gender. Two age groups were recorded: 11–12 and 16–19 years. There are four or five speakers per group in all tables presented below that refer to the Dieuze corpus. In view of the fact that not all speakers were very talkative, and that a good deal of background noise was present in some cases, sub-samples were chosen according to the copiousness and/or clarity of the speech the informants produced. Thus for example, clarity was important for the analysis of rather indistinct variables such as schwa and the liquid consonants /l/ and /r/, while copiousness of speech was of more importance for lexically conditioned variables such as *ne* or liaison. Social class was not included as a variable, since no consistent patterning of the data with this variable was observed. Most informants were in any event drawn from social classes intermediate in the continuum, and in view of their age the indirect relation between the informants' social class, determined by reference to that of their father or mother, and their linguistic behaviour is perhaps unsurprising, given the often close relation between occupation and social class.

3.3.2   The Paris corpora

The Paris results discussed below are based on those reported by Hansen (1994, 2000). The first corpus, described more fully in Hansen (1994: 30–1), derived from the speech of 24 informants recorded in Paris in 1989: 16 younger speakers (eight aged 15–19, eight aged 20–25) and eight older speakers aged 40–55. Again, three speech styles were elicited (in descending order of presumed formality): the reading of four texts; a questionnaire-based interview between an informant and the interviewer (Hansen; a Danish advanced non-native speaker of French); and a conversation between an informant, a friend and the interviewer. Again, we discuss below in the appropriate place the significance of the fieldworker's non-native status, but we note here that since rates of schwa deletion were very similar in interview and conversation, for clarity we give results below (Table 13) for interview as the only unscripted style. The 1989 informants can be defined as middle-class; Hansen (2000) refers to them as 'Parisiens cultivés'. They were thus sampled with regard to their level of education: the adults had all completed higher education (at least three years at a university or at an equivalent level). The young informants all had at least one parent that had completed higher education and were themselves either lycée students or students at a university or at an equivalent level, depending on their age.

The second speaker sample was recorded in Paris in 1992–3, and comprises Parisian informants who are working class or (Hansen's term) socialement défavorisés. The sample was composed as follows: five adults who had had a short technical or practical training, and had not obtained the more academically oriented baccalauréat, obtained at the age of eighteen. The five young informants were allocated to the WC sample in terms of their parents' educational level. The same speech styles were elicited as for the first corpus, and the same reading passages proposed. All of the Parisian informants had lived more than half their lives in Paris or its suburbs.

3.3.3   Analysis of the data

Certain of the findings discussed here which showed interesting patterns of social and/or stylistic variation, and where the researcher wished to make substantive claims concerning the patterns, were tested for statistical significance using the test known as Analysis of Variance (ANOVA). This test investigates the extent to which variation between two or more sets of observations is attributable to factors other than random fluctuation; the suitability of ANOVA to the present results stems from the fact that the test also takes into account variation within a set of observations. As is conventional in the social sciences, significance in the results reported here was tested at 'the five per cent level'; that is, a result was accepted as being statistically significant if it is shown that the probability (p) of its occurring by chance is equal to or less than one in twenty, or 5% (p≤.05). Chi-square tests were applied to the Paris results. Results of significance tests will be given in the appropriate places below.

3.4 The /r/ variable in the Dieuze corpus: Influence of sampling and elicitation methods

The linguistic variable we examine first is the consonant /r/, which undergoes weakening and variable deletion in French in certain linguistic contexts, principally syllable-finally in word-medial and -final positions. The consonant is indicated in citation forms (e.g. in dictionaries) as a uvular trill, but it is generally realised as a fricative, approximant or as zero. Results will first be presented for /r/-deletion in the contexts which are relevant to the present discussion. Table 1 below shows a relationship between social and stylistic variation that was found to be typical of almost all phonological variables studied in the Dieuze corpus.

Table 1. Total numbers (N) and percentage deletion rates % for /r/ before a consonant, e.g. in *l'autre jour*, and before a pause, e.g. in *j'en ai quatre*: both contexts aggregated

	Interview		Conversation	
	(N)	%	(N)	%
Males 16–19	143	58.7	155	78.1
Females 16–19	124	62.1	198	79.3
Males 11–12	83	57.8	225	84.0
Females 11–12	176	47.2	162	58.6

Table 1 shows variable deletion rates for French /r/ in the phonological context: obstruent + /r/ in a word-final syllable (*Or* henceforward), an environment where the consonant is very susceptible to elision. The two phonological contexts of pre-pause and pre-consonant have been aggregated because deletion rates are similar in these contexts, and because aggregating data in this way gives higher values for N and hence more reliable results. Deletion of /r/ in these contexts is a well-known feature of everyday spoken French Thus for example, *l'autre jour* 'the other day' (full form [lotʀɘʒuʁ]) will reduce very often in non-formal styles to [lotʒuʁ]; similarly, *j'en ai quatre* 'I've got four' will often reduce: [ʒãnekatʀ] > [ʒãnekat]

It is evident that for this variable, the effect of style is more important than other extra-linguistic factors, in this case gender and age. This style effect has been tested for statistical significance using ANOVA, which shows the effect to be highly significant for all groups aggregated ($p < .002$). It can be seen that style shift exceeds social variation quite considerably, most notably for the older males and females, who behave almost identically in terms of their deletion rates in both interview and conversation styles. If one leaves aside the younger females, who relative to the other three groups consistently showed little style shift for most variables, one interpretation of the results in Table 1 is that the older males and females and the younger males appear, irrespective of the demographic factors which differentiate them, to be in agreement in treating the *Or* context as a salient marker of speech style.

The social-style relationship is broadly the inverse of that typical of the marker variable commonly reported in English and other languages, where intraspeaker variation as elicited through the methods generally used does not normally exceed variation between social groups. The largest degree of inter-speaker variation in Table 1 is between the older males and younger females in conversation style (19.5%); the largest degree of intraspeaker variation is 26.2%, and is shown by the younger males. The compass of interspeaker variation is rather compressed in interview style relative to conversation, a result that echoes others, for instance Trudgill's discussed in the previous chapter. Thus in interview style the greatest interspeaker difference is 14.9%, between the older and younger females. Only the younger females show a degree of style shift that is lower than this figure. Overall, the results in Table 1 show no large degrees of differentiation along either of the interspeaker axes of age and gender; at the same time intraspeaker variation, although generally exceeding interspeaker, is no case dramatic.

We suggested above that the fairly large degrees of style shift shown in Table 1 may be due to an awareness on the Dieuze informants' part of the socio-stylistic value of the *Or* variable. As discussed in the previous chapter, this explanation has been applied to the marker variable, where speakers are both socially differentiated by their treatment of the variable in question, and where they (or at least the lower and intermediate groups) show considerable degrees of style shift; this pattern suggests that some speaker groups are highly aware of the sociolinguistic value of a marker. This awareness impels speakers both to differentiate their linguistic behaviour from that of other groups, and to distinguish carefully between speech styles. Chambers and Trudgill (1998: 72–5) suggest various reasons for this state of affairs: the variable may be the subject of unfavourable comment in the community, perhaps because of the way in which it is marked in the orthography; it may be involved in linguistic change, in which case speakers are aware of its value in differentiating certain social groups; or its absence, or the fact of variation between the standard and non-standard variants, may involve a phonological contrast.

However, these explanations leave intact the following problem: if the Dieuze speakers are aware of the fact that a connected-speech feature such as /r/-deletion in *Or* is the object of unfavourable comment, why does this feature not appear to function like a marker variable, sensitive to social as well as style variation? The answer may of course be simply that the Dieuze speaker sample is not differentiated enough socially to show large degrees of variation along the social dimensions in question.

Bell remarks (1984: 198–9) that 'studies which show style but not social variation are invariably based on a socially narrow sample'; 'socially narrow' appears to refer here to social-class differentiation. We saw in the previous chapter that English phonological variables commonly show considerable degrees of social differentiation according to social class: Chambers and Trudgill (1998) discuss well-known differentiation patterns according to gender (pp. 61–3) and age (pp. 151–3, 157–9). Differentiation along these dimensions was demonstrated indirectly in the case of French, through the results issuing from the Rennes–Nancy evaluative test. A regraphing of the results presented in Table 4 in the previous chapter, as shown in Table 2 below, reveals a fairly close correspondence between perceived and actual social class if the Nancy informants are grouped into WC and MC categories, as presented below. Table 2 shows a fairly highly polarised WC–MC pattern of differentiation; the exception of the OMCF speaker, discussed in the previous chapter, disrupts the otherwise rather impressively regular grouping that shows WC speakers (apart from the YWCF) rated by a large proportion of the Rennes informants as being of WC origin, while the MC speaker have correspondingly low scores. This indicates a close correspondence between WC and MC origin and accent, albeit in an indirect way. The pattern of gender differentiation in Table 2 is unclear, largely because of the effect produced by the aberrant OMCF speaker. Nevertheless the YWCF speaker's score, although it does not rate highly alongside her WC counterparts, does contrast sharply with that of her female MC equivalent, the YMCF.

Table 2. Rank order of Nancy speakers by perceived working-class accent, grouped into WC and MC categories

Nancy informant	% agreement on WC accent
YWCM	92.5
OWCM	87.5
OWCF	70.0
YWCF	35.0
OMCF	57.5
YMCM	27.5
YMCF	5.0
OMCM	2.5

On the direct behavioural level, the rather few results reported for variable *oïl* French pronunciation are rather inconclusive, showing patterns of social-class differentiation that are not very sharply polarised and not very different from gender differentiation. For instance, Ashby (1991:5) reported a 71% deletion rate of the consonant /l/ in clitic pronouns for the highest social class that he sampled (all groups aggregated), against 78% for the lowest. Compared to this, gender-related differentiation in Ashby's corpus was 70% for female speakers against 80% for male, for all groups aggregated. Pooley (1996:241, 244) reported a greater social-class than male–female differentiation pattern of /l/-deletion in the French of Roubaix. Social class was defined in terms of educational level, and Pooley reported 48% /l/-deletion for speakers under 30 with post-16 education, against 78% for those without. Speakers aged over 45 showed a similar pattern: 55% /l/-deletion for those with post-16 education, against 88% for those without. Curiously, the intermediate 31–44 group showed a reverse social-class effect: 72% /l/-deletion for those with post-16 education, against 50% for those without. The result reported by Pooley showing gender differentiation in the expected direction was slightly more modest: 58% /l/-deletion for females under 30, against 78% for males of the same age.

These results seem to suggest, albeit not very strongly, that social class can often be a more important differentiating variable than gender in French; this is certainly true in the case of Montreal French, as the results shown in Table 3 below reveal.

Table 3. Patterns of /l/-deletion in Montreal French by social class and gender (adapted from Chambers and Trudgill 1998:62)

	MC	WC	Male	Female
impersonal *il*	90	100	97	99
ils	75	100	90	94
personal *il*	72	100	84	94
elle	30	82	59	67
les (pronoun)	19	61	41	53
la (article)	11	44	25	34
la (pronoun)	13	37	23	31
les (article)	9	33	15	25

It can be seen from Table 3 that /l/-deletion in Montreal co-varies with social class to produce much sharper differentiation patterns than with gender. The implication for the Dieuze data presented here might be that style shift exceeds social differentiation for the variables presented above, partly because the social range of the speaker sample is relatively narrow, i.e. because gender tends to reveal less sharp patterns of differentiation than social class. This is clearly true of /l/ in Montreal; Table 3 shows some 8% difference for all linguistic environments aggregated across males and females, compared to almost 30% between MC and WC. As discussed in the previous chapter, social class has tended to be regarded as the most salient factor differentiating social groups, and discussion of linguistic markers and indicators has generally been discussed by Bell (1984) and by others (Chambers and Trudgill 1998:70–5) in terms of the association between social class and style differentiation. It is difficult to draw a direct comparison between the Dieuze results and those reported by Trudgill and discussed in the previous chapter. Nevertheless it is apparent from Table 4 below that if one compresses the social-class range of the speaker sample, as indicated by the boldfaced area, then hyperstyle variation results.

In Table 4 (identical to Table 1 in the previous chapter save for the addition of boldface) the maximum style shift is 82% between WLS and CS by UWC speakers, while the maximum degree of interspeaker variation is 73%, between LMC and MWC speakers in FS. This is hyperstyle variation, clearly, although the difference between 82% and 73% is not dramatic. Further compression of the social-class range would of course produce higher degrees of hyperstyle variation.

Table 4. Variation in Norwich (ng) by class and style, from Trudgill (1974:92)

	WLS	RPS	FS	CS
MMC	000	000	003	028
LMC	000	010	015	042
UWC	005	015	074	087
MWC	023	044	088	095
LWC	029	066	098	100

To reiterate, the point at issue is therefore whether the hyperstyle variation shown in Table 1 in the present chapter is to be expected in view of the rather modest but nevertheless clear degrees of gender differentiation that other scholars have reported in French. It is perhaps unsurprising that little age-related differentiation is apparent in the Dieuze sample, given the rather narrow difference between the two age groups; but larger degrees of gender-grading might perhaps have been expected. The relative youth of the Dieuze sample does not necessarily rule out the possible of gender differentiation, since findings from other languages show that large degrees of differentiation responding to this variable can emerge early. Perhaps the most striking result showing gender differentiation at an early age is that reported by Romaine (1979:144–57) for Scottish English, and cited in the form given below in Chambers and Trudgill (1998:63).

Table 5. Gender differentiation among Edinburgh children in the variable use of /r/

	% realisation of variant			
Age	Male		Female	
	[ɾ]	[ɹ]	[ɾ]	[ɹ]
10	57	15	45	54
8	48	37	40	54
6	59	16	33	50

Table 5 shows differentiation according to gender and age in the variable use of non-prevocalic /r/ in Edinburgh: percentage realisations of the localised variant, an alveolar tap, are shown in each left-hand column under 'Male' and 'Female', while the right-hand columns show the supra-local alveolar approximant. The columns do not total across to 100% because percentage realisations of the standard English zero variant, which is also available, have not been included. Thus in Edinburgh English, 'word' can be realised [wʌɾd], [wʌɹd] or [wʌd]. Table 5 shows a classic instance of the sociolinguistic gender pattern where males of all age groups have a preference for the localised variant, whereas the females show the opposite tendency. What is rather curious in this display is the fluctuation in degrees of differentiation between the gender groups as a function of age; while the six-year-olds are quite sharply differentiated in their use of /r/, the gender effect is much less pronounced for the eight-year-olds. Against this, the ten-year-olds again show a sharp difference in their use of the national variant, while converging in their use of the non-localised variant compared to the six-year-old usage. The example from Edinburgh suggests therefore that the near absence of a gender effect in the Dieuze speaker sample is not due to the relative youth of the informants.

Turning to the interaction between the effects of gender and social class, we may mention the two examples adduced by L. Milroy (1992: 163–179), (glottalised stops on Tyneside and despirantisation of interdental fricatives in New York City) that show considerable degrees of sex differentiation within social classes and largely independent of class variation. Milroy and Milroy (1978) report a further example of quite spectacular patterns of sex-differentiation within a homogeneous social class sample, from their findings in Belfast. Again therefore, it seems that the relative homogeneity of the Dieuze speaker sample in social-class terms does not in principle rule out the possibility of gender variation; indeed, the results on /l/-deletion reported in Ashby (1991) showed quite considerable gender differentiation within a social-class group, with males of the lowest social-class group having 90% /l/-deletion against the females' 75%.

Therefore the absence of a clear gender-grading pattern in the Dieuze sample, or more precisely its disappearance with the increasing age of the informants, remains puzzling. One may speculate that this relative absence reflects the rather lower degree of sociolinguistic salience of the variable pronunciation level in French, resulting in a later emergence of socio-stylistic competence in variable phonology. The distinctiveness of the pattern apparent in Table 1 may be that the younger females are in the process of adjusting their variable phonology so as to converge more closely, in a more non-standard direction, towards that of their male counterparts. We shall see in Chapter 6 that variable lexis differentiates the Dieuze speaker sample very sharply along the gender and intraspeaker axes, but with no dramatic age effect, suggesting that communicative competence emerges early on this level and continues to be salient.

The foregoing explanation assumes a macro-level, society-wide view of gender differentiation. At the micro-level of the community in question, one can argue that sharp patterns of gender differentiation are not inevitable in every speech community, and one can suggest that the community in question, a small rural town, differed considerably from those typically studied by urban dialectologists; specifically, the sharp patterns of social stratification typical of many cities were less salient in Dieuze, and indeed it seems intuitively plausible that a small, relatively isolated community should show more social cohesion than a large city, where fragmentation along several demographic dimensions seems inevitable. Against this however, as we have remarked immediately above, sharp patterns of gender differentiation have been observed in the Dieuze corpus on the lexical level, and it seems more likely, as is argued at length by Eckert (1989) that gender differentiation is a universal that is largely independent of local conditions and 'resistant to small-scale economic differences' (p. 255). What may be distinctive in the French situation is therefore differentiation in the linguistic levels at which gender grading becomes apparent.

Thus the relative absence of gender differentiation in variable phonology in the Dieuze speaker sample is one major effect that produces a hyperstyle pattern of the type alleged by Bell (1984: 153–4) to be untypical of the relationship between intraspeaker and interspeaker variation. As mentioned above, the pattern shown in Table 1 is representative of many of the results in the Dieuze data. To summarise, these results concern the variable deletion of weak phonological segments whose socio-stylistically diagnostic value has been demonstrated in the speech of French adults, although not often in the large degrees evident in other languages, but which appear to be in process of acquisition at the interspeaker level by the Dieuze speaker sample.

We suggested in the previous chapter that *oïl* French variable pronunciation may be distinctive in largely lacking a regional component. If true, it is clearly necessary to consider the implications of this for the intraspeaker dimension of variation, and the viewpoint of a contrast with English seems suitable given the comparison pursued so far. In the previous chapter we discussed the often linguistically arbitrary character of phonological variation in English. An example is variation between northern [o] and standard [əʊ] in a word such as 'hope'. Vocalic variation of this kind is linguistically arbitrary since ease-of-effort arguments are inapplicable, or if applicable, in this case suggest that the standard, diphthongal realisation [əʊ] involves less effort than the localised pure monophthong [o]. Obviously, non-standard variants such as northern [o] are dialectal remnants that so far have resisted the standardisation process. We need to distinguish in English between four overlapping types of variable or perhaps alternant, since type (iv) below can be thought of as not being composed in any great measure of sociolinguistic variables in the Labovian sense of their differentiating speaker groups to marked degrees:

i.   variables that involve alternation between arbitrary variants;
ii. variables whose sociolinguistic value is related to their representation in spelling;
iii. variables that perceivedly depend on ease-of-articulation processes;
iv. those that depend in reality on ease-of-articulation processes.

As was stated in the previous chapter, the widespread perception that the realisation of non-standard variants is motivated by ease-of-articulation factors has little foundation in fact (Chambers 1995: 232–7). The contrary case is that connected-speech processes such as elision and assimilation are found in rapid, casual speech styles and appear to be the property to varying degrees of all social groups. These connected-speech processes are of course not phonetically arbitrary, and the correlate to this appears to be their lesser sociolinguistic prominence. With reference to the typology in (i)–(iv) above, we can summarise the argument presented in the previous chapter by suggesting that variables such as (ng) are difficult to conceptualise straightforwardly as sociolinguistic variables because they share properties of all types (i)–(iv): there is alternation between /ŋ/ and /n/ that appears to be arbitrary, although alternation between [wɔːkɪŋ] and [wɔːkn̩] involves reduction in the loss of the vocalic segment /ɪ/ and syllabification of /n/. At the same time the non-standard form is perceived as deviating from the spelling. We suggested further (Chapter 2, Section 2.7 (iii)) that the French type of sociolinguistic variable is essentially similar, although the parallel with English was not drawn explicitly at that point. Again with reference to (i)–(iv) above, we reproduce for convenience in abbreviated form the list of French pronunciation variables given in the previous chapter:

1. Deletion of the liquid consonants /r/ and /l/, especially word-finally, as in *genre* 'type, kind'; *ronfle* 'snore. Non-standard realisation of genre [ʒãː]; standard realisation [ʒãːʁ]. Non-standard realisation of ronfle [ʁɔ̃f]; standard realisation [ʁɔ̃fl].

2. Deletion of schwa between two consonants, as in: *la semaine* 'the week'. Non-standard realisation [lasmɛn]; standard realisation [lasəmɛn].

3. Alternation between, or neutralisation of, oral mid-vowel contrasts. The French oral mid-vowels are [e] and [ɛ], as in *thé* 'tea' [te] and *taie* 'pillowcase' [tɛ]; [ø] and [œ], as in *peu* 'little' and *peur* 'fear'; and [o] and [ɔ], as in *paume* 'palm' and *pomme* 'apple'.

4. Neutralisation of nasal vowel contrasts. Front nasal vowels [ɛ̃] and [œ̃]: non-standard realisation of *quelqu'un* 'someone' [kɛlkɛ̃]; standard realisation [kɛlkœ̃]. Back nasal vowels [ã] and [ɔ̃]: non-standard realisation of *élément* 'element' [elemɔ̃]; standard realisation [elemã].

5. Insertion of schwa word-finally: so-called 'schwa-tagging'. This takes place both orthographically and intrusively. Non-standard realisation of *c'était Pierre* 'it was Peter' [setɛpjɛʁə]; standard realisation [setɛpjɛʁ] (orthographic example). Non-standard realisation of *bonjour* 'hello' [bɔ̃ʒuʁə]; standard realisation [bɔ̃ʒuʁ] (intrusive example).

6. Variation between front and back (a), as in *pas* 'not'. Non-standard realisation of *pas* [pa] or [pɔ]; standard realisation [pa].

7. Centralisation/fronting of [ɔ] in the direction of [œ] as in: *joli* 'pretty'. Non-standard realisation [ʒœli]; standard realisation [ʒɔli]

It may be that deletion of French schwa, /l/ and /r/ are variables which on the one hand derive their sociolinguistic value from their representation in spelling, and on the other depend on ease-of-articulation processes. Items 5–7 of the list above seem to fall into category (i), i.e. those variables that involve alternation between arbitrary variants. As noted previously, the possible mergers and chain shifts involving the nasal vowels (item 4) do not fit comfortably in the present categorisation, owing to the fragmentary and contradictory nature of the evidence concerning them. We discuss items 1 and 2 here, since intraspeaker results are available for them. These are weak phonological segments that are susceptible to elision in casual speech, which suggests that intraspeaker variation in French may be 'natural' in regard to these variables in a way that it is not in English. At the same time the representation of the prestige variant in spelling may increase their sociolinguistic salience, at least in some less frequent phonetic contexts; we discuss this issue more fully below.

If true, the consequence of this state of affairs for Bell's theory would be that the relationship between interspeaker and intraspeaker variation which seems to hold in English, is not valid in French for certain variables. For convenience we summarise the pertinent elements of Bell's theory again here: the inter-speaker and intraspeaker axes of variation are linked because most linguistic variables are sensitive along both axes. Speakers adjust their language along the intraspeaker axis in response to the perceived social (interspeaker) characteristics of their hearer. Bell's audience design principle seems to apply to a language such as English because speakers employ the mechanism of self-monitoring to select (among others) certain arbitrary phonological variables that they feel to be appropriate for the purposes of accommodation to their interlocutor's social status. Self-monitoring is involved because of the awareness on the part of speakers of the disapproval to which certain variables are subject. Speakers therefore avoid these variables in more formal styles: that is, when speaking to interlocutors whom they do not know well, and whose social-linguistic attitudes they therefore cannot gauge; or to speakers whose approval they wish to canvass, perhaps because an asymmetrical power relation obtains.

As remarked in the previous chapter, interspeaker variation exceeds intraspeaker, firstly because no one speaker or speaker group controls the entire range of socially-conditioned language confidently; a further, perhaps more important factor is that short-term linguistic accommodation is a complex process that often does not imply mere imitation on a speaker's part of an interlocutor's language production, but rather a degree of compromise, although close imitation can happen in service encounters where the distribution of power between interactants is highly asymmetrical, as illustrated by Coupland's (1980) well-known travel-agency study. Some evidence is available to show that speakers are capable in principle of controlling the full socio-stylistic range of certain variables: Lemieux and Cedergren (1985: 96) reported high rates of insertion of *ne* by Montreal adolescents in role-play situations, in sharp contrast to the very low rates found in the informal sociolinguistic interviews they conducted. As discussed in the previous chapter, other variables such as the English [ʌ] ~ [ʊ] lexical split may be difficult to acquire fully, because of the complexity of the linguistic constraints in play. We shall see in Chapter 5 that French liaison provides an analogous example. It is manifest that the variables under discussion here are omissible ones whose representation in spelling is for the most part straightforward, and which speakers might be expected to learn to control fairly early in their progressive mastery of communicative competence. If /l/, /r/ and schwa are indeed variables of this type, i.e. easily learnable at an early age and perhaps dependent on allegro-speech processes, what would be the implications for a possible explanation of the hyperstyle pattern seen above in Table 1?

The implications concern the question whether the hyperstyle pattern in Table 1, rather than being 'sociolinguistic' in the sense used here so far and discussed immediately above, is rather indicative of variation caused by a somewhat different type of audience design that prompted greater and less degrees of self-monitoring, these in turn perhaps reflecting slower and faster articulation rates in the interview and conversation styles respectively. This would imply that the French phonetic /l/, /r/ and schwa behave similarly to cluster simplification in the 'tests' and 'coasts' examples discussed in the previous chapter, since although these French variables appear to have intraspeaker value, a simulacrum of audience design may have been operating in the Dieuze corpus. In other words, the hyperstyle pattern in Table 1 may have resulted from 'audience design' in the sense that the informants assumed less shared knowledge, both linguistic and non-linguistic, on the part of the fieldworker, as a result of his non-native-speaker status. By shared linguistic knowledge is meant acquaintance with the sometimes radically reduced phonetic forms, as well as non-standard grammatical and lexical features, characteristic of colloquial spoken styles of French.

We do not wish to imply by the foregoing discussion that French speakers do not self-monitor; the hypothesis expressed immediately above would still assume Bell's analysis of self-monitoring as a mechanism whose function is to ensure the accuracy of audience design; but the Dieuze situation recalls a Bernsteinian duality in terms of 'restricted' and 'elaborated' language production, rather than the polarity implying formal–informal, power–solidarity, etc. which Bell postulates and which, as discussed above, refers essentially to the stimulation of language production in response to the degree of intimacy subsisting between speakers, and perhaps more importantly the power relations that obtain in any given interaction. We have already discussed in the previous chapter the relation between natural and elicited style shift, mentioning Milroy's (1987b: 173) formulation that 'the contrast between spontaneous speech and reading styles is a simulation, for experimental purposes, of differences in the amount of attention paid to speech which crop up in natural interaction'. Regarding the elicitation of unscripted styles, Giles (1973) has the interesting criticism that researchers interviewing informants in the context of a sociolinguistic interview may be responsible for inducing style shift by themselves unconsciously accommodating their speech in the direction of the production they expect to elicit. This is of course a reflex of the observer's paradox, expressed in somewhat subtler terms than is customary, and can plausibly be argued to be a natural tendency that one would expect to occur in non-experimental conditions; in any event it is difficult to see how it could be resisted in experimental conditions, given the unplanned nature of most unscripted speech production. If true however, one might presume that the tendency that Giles postulates would have the effect of compressing shift between unscripted styles to degrees smaller than might have been expected otherwise. This is because a tape-recorded interview between interviewer and informant might be expected to produce, following the concern of the field-worker to elicit an adequate volume of language data, more informal speech than is implied by the label 'formal style' used by Trudgill (1974: 46–7), following the model of Labov (1966). In contrast, casual style in the interview is defined as occurring in response to cues such as interactions with speakers other than the interviewer, and narratives that induce the informant to reduce self-monitoring, such as the celebrated danger-of-death stimulus.

Whether or not Giles's objection is generally valid (Trudgill (1986: 5–11) devotes considerable space to rebutting it with regard to his own Norwich results), the salient difference between the elicitation methods discussed above and those used in the Dieuze survey is clearly that in Dieuze the informal language data were collected in peer dyads or triads and in the researcher's absence, while the formal data were elicited through an approximation to the standard sociolinguistic interview, with informants interviewed one-to-one with the researcher. The significance of the fieldworker's non-native-speaker status for the purposes of the present discussion is that this status may well have brought about more formal interview conditions than are common, as a result of the fieldworker's limited capacity, relative to a native speaker's, to operate the type of 'downward' accommodation that would encourage informal speech production by informants. We discuss below some repairs made by informants in response to the fieldworker's incomprehension; these indicate a less ready receptive competence on the fieldworker's part of rapid colloquial speech. This reflects in turn the product of a pedagogical method relying for the development of listening competence on the exploitation of relatively formal speech such as broadcast news and interviews, speech produced by the highly educated. We do not wish to imply the production by the Dieuze informants for the fieldworker's benefit of 'foreigner talk'; there is no evidence in the corpus of the use of drastically simplified morphology or syntax, of disjunctive pronouns where the standard language has conjunctive, or other features reported in the pidgin and creole literature. Nor did any informant ever attempt to communicate in English. To reiterate, the point at issue here is therefore the consequence upon interview style of the fieldworker's relatively restricted capacity to produce rapid colloquial speech.

It may be therefore that the fieldworker's speech contributed somewhat, in the minds of a majority of the informants, to the creation of a rather highly formal speech situation, analogous perhaps to any highly 'tense' situation (in Bourdieu's phrase) with which adults will be acquainted. This hypothesis can of course be entertained alongside the Bernsteinian duality referred to above, as both are concerned with the influence of elicitation methods. One theoretical issue of interest here is the factitious, or at least uncontrolled, nature of the elements than can combine to produce a successful simulation of a formal speech style; the argumentation presented above is *post hoc*, and the field-worker's non-native-speaker status was not an element that provided a con-scious input at the fieldwork-design stage. Nevertheless this element may well have been the only one available to produce the simulation that resulted; it seems likely that children and adolescents do not possess the 'script' (the detailed awareness of a highly structured speech or other social event) for highly formal situations such as a job interview. In contrast, it seems that among adult speakers the possession of such a script can override other extra-linguistic factors: Milroy (1987a: 66–7) has the example of a young working-class Belfast man who helped in Milroy's fieldwork by interviewing his sister. As Milroy expresses the situation: 'The fact that this sample of interview style was structur-ally identical to the others [recorded by Milroy] suggests that discourse patterns are constrained by the speaker's definition of the speech event, as well as by the social relations of the participants to each other'.

To summarise, the hypothesis emerges from the foregoing that the fairly large degrees of style shift apparent in Table 1 may result, on the mechanical linguistic level, from substantial differences in articulation rates across the two styles, motivated by a perception on the informants' part either of a consider-able formality in the interview style, or indeed by their perception that the fieldworker was not a fully adequate interlocutor. We discuss therefore in the following section the implications raised by the issue of variation in articulation rates across speech styles.

3.5 Differences in articulation rate across speech styles in the Dieuze data

We devote here an extended discussion to various questions connected with the issue of the measurement of speech rate across different speech styles, because the issue appears not to have been discussed thoroughly in relation to French from a cross-stylistic, variationist point of view, and also because this issue sheds light on the elusive nature of a robust definition of speech style. This latter question is of course a central concern of the present study. The measurement of speech rate has been quite thoroughly discussed in the literature, and the connected issues are summarised at some length in Laver (1994:158; 539–46). Laver distinguishes (p.158) on the one hand speaking rate, which '[...] relates to the rate of speech of the whole speaking-turn. It therefore includes all speech material (linguistic or non-linguistic), together with any silent pauses, that are included within the overall speaking-turn.' On the other hand the measurement of articulation rate excludes silent pauses '[...] by virtue of the definition of an utterance, which begins and ends with a silence. But it includes all audible speech material within the utterance [...]' (ibid.). Thus a calculation of articulation rate will include filled pauses and lengthened syllables. Articulation rate is conventionally measured in syllables or segments per second, speaking rate in words per minute.

Perhaps the principal difficulty attending the calculation of speaking and articulation rates concerns the variability present within any given speech style. As Laver remarks (1994:543): 'comments about overall rate of articulation mask [an] underlying quasi-random variability from one occasion to another [...]'. We may take issue with the term 'quasi-random' here, as the factors responsible for this variability will be to some extent sociolinguistic; nevertheless, in the measure that individual variation within a given speech style depends on idiolectal factors, this kind of 'micro-style' variation will certainly be in principle unpredictable. However, if we take 'occasion' to mean 'series of utterances' as well as 'utterance', then Laver's comment may be applied to speaking rate as well as articulation rate; indeed its application to speaking rate is perhaps more pertinent, given that any conversation which is at all prolonged (as in the Dieuze corpus) will feature a greater or smaller number of pauses, each of which may be relatively long or short. Clearly the inclusion of pauses in a calculation of speaking rate across an entire conversation may affect the result considerably. If on the other hand we restrict Laver's comment to articulation rate, then the influence of fluency or continuity is important; speakers may differ individually, as well as in response to stylistic and other extra-linguistic factors that we discuss below, in the extent to which they maintain a more or less uninterrupted stream of speech, including filled pauses, at the utterance level.

A further issue is that the measurement in syllables per second of differences in articulation rates across speech styles can raise problems of comparability, since casual styles will tend to be characterised by a simpler syllable structure; that is, syllables may undergo processes such as consonant-cluster reduction.

Thus speakers have the possibility of articulating simplified syllables at a higher rate than more complex ones having consonant-heavy onsets and codas, irrespective of other factors governing their articulation rate. The same problem attends a calculation rate in segments per second, since a surface count will feed fewer segments into the calculation (consequent on elision), thus inflating the articulation rate further. The solution suggested by Roach (1998: 152–3) is to count the canonical segments in the utterances quantified irrespective of whether they are present in speech, i.e. 'to count not the sounds actually observable in the physical signal, but the "underlying phonemes" that [...] would have [been] produced in careful speech'. We shall present and evaluate below some results obtained by applying this method to utterances taken from the Dieuze data. At this point we may however remark that when applying this method to French, it seems defensible to count underlying tokens of deletable segments such as schwa and the liquid consonants, but not variable liaison consonants, as they appear to be subject to insertion rather than deletion rules. A further issue is that a calculation of underlying segments should not include tokens of the negative particle *ne*, as the variable treatment of the particle is constrained by syntactic factors that appear often to be unconnected with surface deletion phenomena. This issue is discussed in the following chapter.

As we have seen, phonological reduction takes place in French through the deletion of weak consonants such as /l/ and /r/, although deletion also affects other syllable-final and/or weak consonants such as /b/, /v/ and /k/ in the following common examples; *problème* 'problem' [pʀɔblɛm] > *pro'lème* [pʀɔlɛm]; *avec* 'with' [avɛk] > *a'ec* [aɛk]; *expliquer* 'explain' [ɛksplike] > *espliquer* [ɛsplike]. A second common fast-speech reduction phenomenon in French is of course the deletion of schwa; this results in reduction in the number of syllables articulated, as in the example *il me dit* 'he says to me' (full form [il. mə. di.]) reducing to *i'm'dit* [im.di.]. A full stop indicates a syllable boundary in these and following transcriptions. Deletion of schwa can thus increase the number of consonant groups of two or more: the rather spectacular example adduced by Malécot (1976: 98), of *parce que je crois* 'because I think' realised as [pskʃkʀwa], demonstrates that frequently-collocating groups (in this case -*ce que je*) will reduce radically in connected speech; and without producing stigmatised forms, judging by the nature of Malécot's speaker sample, upper-middle-class Parisians recorded surreptitiously in conversational style.

However, we need to qualify these statements regarding the role of schwa deletion in the accretion of consonants clusters. Schwa deletion in faster speech causes the reorganisation of syllables by bringing consonants together and by working against the strong tendency in French to *enchaînement* (linking), or the opening of syllables through forward resyllabification, that is the attachment of (citation form) word-final consonants to following word-initial vowels. We discuss this tendency in more detail in Chapter 5 on liaison. The deletion of schwa often closes syllables through the reverse process of backward resyllabification, as in the example of: *c'est le cas* 'it is the case'. This sequence is realised standardly as: [sɛ.lə.ka]. Deletion of schwa is followed by attachment of /l/ to the preceding syllable: [sɛl.ka]. Thus while consonants come to be juxtaposed consequent on schwa deletion, the result is the closure of syllables which are canonically open, rather than heavier consonant clusters within syllables. Similarly, although the example given previously, of *parce que je crois* realised as [pskʃkʀwa], appears to result (if we include the semi-consonant /w/) in the seven-consonant cluster /pskʃkʀw/, in fact this sequence syllabifies as follows, as the fricatives /s/ and /ʃ/ lengthen and become syllabic: [ps:.kʃ:.kʀwa].

Malécot (1976: 93–4) suggests that if it continues to increase, the closure of syllables following schwa deletion may have important implications for the phonological structure of French, perhaps resulting in a preponderance of closed syllables in a language whose open syllable structure has been much remarked. However this may be, connected-speech reduction phenomena in French have opposing effects: we have seen that word- and syllable-final consonant clusters are often reduced in conversation style in the Dieuze data through deletion of /l/ and /r/. Against this, schwa deletion increases the number of consonantal syllable codas through backward resyllabification. However, the overall effect is indeed a reduction in the number of segments articulated in faster speech.

Examples illustrating the converse, i.e. the insertion of linguistic material in more careful styles, come easily to hand. The phonemic status of French schwa does not rest upon broad foundations, as its varying with zero or other vowels gives rise to rather few minimal pairs. Miscomprehension in context between native speakers due to the absence of schwa seems unlikely, as between *dehors* [dəɔʀ] 'outside' and *dors* [dɔʀ] 'sleep' (2nd-person verb form). At the same time, schwa occurs more frequently in formal speech styles, partly perhaps as an aid to comprehension among locutors who are non-intimates, and who therefore may well have less shared knowledge. This was strikingly illustrated in one of the Dieuze interviews, when a younger female speaker was describing to the author (older, male, non-French-native speaker) the composition of couscous, and provoked the following interchange. A = informant and B = field-worker in the following examples:

(1) A: c'est de la s'moule [sɛdlasmul] 'it's semolina'
     B: comment? 'pardon?'
     A: la semoule [lasəmul] 'semolina'

A corresponding example in grammar is given by Coveney (1996: 56), concerning an informant who inserted a token of the negative particle *ne*, which in most utterances is functionally redundant but which in Coveney's example was inserted to repair a miscomprehension. A precisely parallel case was observed in the Dieuze corpus, as follows (a gloss is given below):

(2) A: je m foule pas
     B: comment?
     A: je n me foule pas.

The negative particle was inserted here again as an aid to comprehension. The phrase *se fouler* has the sense, in colloquial French, of 'to work hard'. In each of these examples, respectively from pronunciation and grammar, the addition of a syllable is the strategy used for repair.

Thus it seems plausible that greater redundancy, or at least more linguistic substance, will be found in comparable utterances in formal speech compared to casual, and that correspondingly, reduction will characterise less formal speech styles. This is certainly true of certain differences across speech and writing; for example, French marks considerably more gender and number agreements in writing than in speech. The phonological reduction phenomena discussed above appear also to operate largely irrespective of lexical input, as shown in the following section.

3.5.1   Lexical input, connected speech processes and articulation rate

A brief consideration of the relationship between lexical input and connected-speech processes (CSPs) seems appropriate here, since the question raises issues of theory and method that concern the comparison of articulation rates in different speech styles.

Wright (1989: 359) defines CSPs as 'those processes which occur at word boundaries in the stream of speech' and not 'at the word boundaries of isolated or citation forms'. It seems legitimate to widen this definition to include the processes that occur at syllable boundaries in casual or rapid speech, since the CSPs of interest here also operate word-internally. Wright further asserts that 'in connected speech [...] collocations are not fixed, and so the occurrences of these processes [CSPs] depends far more on phonetic conditioning than on phonological environment'. The CSP relevant in the present case is elision. The variables discussed below are again schwa, /r/ and /l/. These three variables have been shown to be susceptible to elision across languages; this is because they are articulated relatively weakly and do not bear stress. Thus 'phonetic conditioning' appears to be a major factor influencing the elision of these variables in connected speech. However, to turn to the question of lexical input into CSPs, Wright's implication that fixed collocations, and by extension the question of lexical frequency, can be excluded from a study of CSPs, throws an interesting light on the measurement of articulation rates. Plainly, this question is relevant to the study of any segment which is variably deleted, and which is distributed more or less equally across both frequent and infrequent lexical items, as most such phonetic segments are likely to be; Wright appears to be asserting that phonetic processes such as assimilation and deletion will operate on segments in fast connected speech irrespective of the frequency of occurrence of the words or phrases in which the segments occur.

The statement that CSPs will operate independently of lexical input is manifestly false in respect of 'idiom chunks' such as, in French, elision of schwa from *de toute façon* 'in any case', *je veux dire* 'I mean', *tout le monde* 'everyone'; these phrases are susceptible to reduction, through schwa elision and subsequent deletion or lenition of consonants, in all but the most careful speech styles. The decision may therefore be made, if it is found that such chunks are sufficiently frequent, to exclude them from a quantification of articulation rates across two or more relatively informal conversational styles, since their inclusion might depress differences in articulation rates and thus skew results. The opposite case concerns words or phrases which, by reason of their infrequent occurrence, may be thought to be less susceptible to CSPs. Certain examples from French cited by Dell (1980:97) are relevant to the present study: Dell describes syllable-final /r/-deletion as being 'blocked' in the idiolect of most speakers in bookish words such as *astre* 'star' (in a literary register; the more common word is *étoile*) and *piètre* 'paltry'. This consideration is perhaps less pertinent to a study of stylistic variation between relatively casual styles, since infrequent words seem almost by definition unlikely to appear in more informal styles, unless used for some special stylistic effect, e.g. facetiously or in mock-solemnity. Nevertheless, the issue of lexical frequency is by no means wholly irrelevant in this connexion, as we shall see below.

To illustrate various issues relating to lexical input in the calculation of articulation rates across speech styles, one may take the example of /r/-deletion and note first that reduction is very common in both speech styles in the

Dieuze corpus in words having largely a functional component, such as *pour* 'for', *sur* 'on' *avoir* 'have', which occur frequently and are arguably less semantically salient than full lexical words. One might thus postulate a two-tier deletion process whereby on the first tier it is for the most part frequently-occurring function words that undergo reduction; on the second tier, characterised perhaps by a faster speech rate, almost any word may be subject to reduction. This second process may be illustrated by the example of /r/-deletion in an utterance from the Dieuze data, produced by an older female in conversation style:

(3)   J'en ai ma*r*re, j tombe toujou*r*s sur un o*r*dinateu*r* qui ma*r*che pas, moi
        'I'm fed up, I always get a computer that doesn't work'

This stretch illustrates various aspects of the issue under consideration. All possible pre-consonantal occurrences of /r/ (italicised) were elided. One word, *toujours*, while it can hardly be categorised as a function word (unless the decision is made to distinguish a set of frequent adverbs as a functional class, which seems controversial), is nevertheless of frequent occurrence, and may be expected to undergo reduction accordingly. The phrase *j'en ai marre* can reasonably be described as a frequent idiomatic phrase, with a corresponding susceptibility to /r/-deletion. The other words, *ordinateur* and *marche*, seem at first sight to belong in the 'full' lexical category. However, the informant was studying secretarial skills, so one might expect *ordinateur*, and other words in the same lexical field, to occur frequently in her idiolect, with a consequently increased likelihood of reduction. Deletion of /r/ in the remaining word, *marche*, may be adduced as illustrating the vulnerability of any lexical item to reduction in allegro speech; again, however, *marcher* may be argued to be something of a frequent 'broad spectrum' verb, used in casual speech rather than a verb of higher socio-stylistic value such as *fonctionner* 'to work', 'to function'. We discuss in Chapter 6 the question of variation between lexical pairs such as these. The utterance given above seems therefore to illustrate the more or less self-evident fact that infrequent lexical items are rather unlikely to be found in casual speech. Less self-evidently, if such items are rare in informal speech, it seems plausible that they will be correspondingly less likely to undergo reduction as a result of faster articulation rates. Against this, several lexical items observed in the Dieuze corpus do seem to confirm Wright's assertion that CSPs (deletion of /l/ and /r/ in this case) will operate on less frequent items: for example, *lièvre* 'hare'; *ongle* '(finger)nail'; and *maigre* 'thin'. These items have been observed in conversation style, reduced respectively to [ljɛv] (full form [ljɛvʁ(ə)]); [ɔ̃g] (full form [ɔ̃gl(ə)]); and [mɛg] (full form [mɛgʁ(ə)]. These examples endorse Wright's notion that CSPs will override lexical input in allegro speech. What is not clear is whether casual speech is necessarily allegro speech; we now discuss this question.

3.5.2   Articulation rate and speech style

So far in this discussion, we have assumed implicitly that faster articulation rates will be associated with more informal or casual speech styles. It seems demonstrable that informal styles will be characterised by reduced linguistic forms; what is less clear is whether these forms will tend strongly to be articulated at faster rates. Laver (1994: 544) suggests that 'speaking rate and formality of speech style seem to have no direct correlation, at least in English.' We may suggest further that the formal–informal distinction is a gross one, and that within any given speech style, micro-style variation will occur in response to many factors. Therefore Laver's suggestion that there is no direct relation between formality and articulation rate seems justified. We shall have occasion to discuss micro-style variation more fully in a later chapter on grammatical variation, but in relation to articulation rate we may again note that intra-speaker variation, in 'audience design' terms, responds to factors such as the degree of intimacy and the nature of the power relations subsisting between interlocutors, (these are perhaps the principal factors), as well as topic, tone, mood of the speakers, and nature of the interchange: narrative, interview, quarrel, etc. Laver (1994: 545), quoting Gimson (1989: 286) notes that mood may increase or decrease the articulation rate: 'a rapid rate of delivery, for instance, may express irritation or urgency, whereas a slower rate my show hesitancy, doubt or boredom [...]'.

Laver (p. 545) cites the taxonomy of Siptár (1991: 27–9) that takes into account speech style as well as articulation rate, and that has categories, drawing on examples from Hungarian, ranging from 'guarded speech' to 'fast-casual speech'. What is relevant here is that in Siptár's taxonomy, casual speech and fast speech are not co-referential; a 'guarded' style such as news broadcasting may be associated with a fast articulation rate. This observation is undoubtedly accurate, as news broadcasters are demonstrably capable of producing speech whose pronunciation is rapid as well as canonical; a stretch of television news-broadcast speech analysed by the present author was found to have an articulation rate of some 13 segments per second. Nevertheless one may question the representativeness of this kind of mismatch, found in the speech of trained professional speakers. This example provides a further illustration of the fact that the formal–informal speech-style continuum is not uniplex; while a (serious) news broadcast is highly formal in terms of topic, from the point of view of the relationship between locutor and addressee the news broadcast raises problems of comparability with face-to-face speech styles. This is reflected in Bell's (1984) elaborate 'audience design' model, which is non-linear in terms of the formal–informal opposition and which classifies audience design in radio speech as 'initiative referee design'. The term's complexity reflects the number of factors that can influence style variation. This problem of the closeness of comparability of speech styles is illustrated by some results reported by Fónagy and Magdics (1960: 179–92) concerning different articulation rates across speech styles: 9.4 segments per second in a poetry-reading style against 13.83 per second in a sports commentary. This difference lines up with one's intuitive expectation, but it is again apparent that the two speech styles are incommensurable along the dimensions at least of scripted vs. unscripted and face-to-face vs. broadcast speech. Regarding the issue of an average articulation rate, Calvert (1986: 178) remarks: '[…] it is interesting to note that speakers average a rate of 10 sounds/second in conversation. At faster rates it is difficult to co-ordinate articulation and errors begin to occur. At the rate of 15 sounds/second, errors are frequent and speech is distorted.' We shall see below that considerably faster rates are characteristic of much of the speech in the Dieuze corpus.

We may mention finally, and perhaps most importantly for the purposes of the present analysis, that articulation rates, considered as a permanent individual characteristic, can vary considerably across individuals broadly irrespective of stylistic variation that responds to the factors discussed above. A fast articulation rate appears to be positively regarded in many societies, as indicating competence in general and perhaps a high level of intelligence in particular (Giles 1992: 133). It is no doubt significant that rustic speech is stereotypically portrayed as occurring at a slow articulation rate. Nevertheless, individual rates probably need to be considered as idiolectal and, even if they are the object of evaluative judgments of this kind, are unlikely to be affected by these judgments. We consider the significance of idiolectal differences in the following section.

3.5.3   Factors influencing articulation rates in the Dieuze corpus

We examine now the various factors influencing articulation rates in the Dieuze corpus. We shall have occasion in Chapter 4 to discuss at the grammatical and (briefly) the discourse-analytic levels the difference between the two speech styles recorded, but this discussion may be foreshadowed here briefly. While both interview and conversation styles were broadly devoted to discussion and narratives, conversation style was often characterised by an emphasis on the affective aspect of the topic under discussion, with interviews tending to be more narrowly focused on the informational dimension of variation. In interview style, informants typically talked about school, school subjects, their family, their home town or village etc., in response to the interviewer's questions. The speech thus elicited can therefore be defined as being broadly 'message-oriented', using Brown's (1982:77) definition, where the aim of the interchanges tends to be the 'communication of a propositional or cognitive (information-bearing) message to the listener'. Brown distinguishes between this type of speech and 'listener-oriented' speech, where, as seemed often to be the case in the Dieuze conversations, the goal is often to maintain friendly relations, and where 'it is often the case that speakers [...] don't seem to be talking about anything very much'. The distinction between interview and conversation styles in the Dieuze corpus is probably less sharp than that expressed by Brown, and there will of course be a continuum between these two poles. In any event is difficult to imagine an extended interchange that is wholly non-informational. The distinction between the two styles in the Dieuze data might be more aptly expressed in terms of the pragmatic use the speakers make of the subjects being discussed. Thus the speech elicited in interview style may be broadly described as message-oriented; by contrast, speakers in conversation style, although they discuss specific subjects, often appear to do so in order to express or produce an emotional effect. A more suitable broad distinction between interview and conversation styles might therefore be expressed respectively in terms of an 'ideational or 'propositional' orientation on the one hand, and on the other an 'affective' approach.

Bearing these differences in mind, we can compare and analyse the articulation rate of some utterances in the Dieuze data from the viewpoints of interspeaker and especially intraspeaker variation. Below is an utterance produced by an older female in conversation style, when she was describing a driving lesson. The five non-standard phonological reductions in the passage are given in ordinary spelling thus (in the order in which they appear below): *il*>i; *me*>m; *vous*>v; *tu*>t; *je*>j; the prefix *re-*>r'. This practice is followed in subsequent examples. The pronoun *il* refers to the driving instructor:

(4)   et i m dit vous v garez de gauche à droite en côte t sais trois fois j l'ai
      loupé trois fois i m'a fait r'commencer j'ai chialé dans la voiture
      'and he said to me, "park from left to right up the hill" / three times I
      couldn't do it and he made me start again / I cried in the car'

This utterance contains 34 syllables (including the orthographic schwa at the
and of *voiture*, discussed below) and lasts six seconds, giving an articulation rate
of 5.66 sylls/sec. This ranks towards the lower end of the range of 4.7–6.8
sylls/sec for French cited by Laver (1994:542) (from Gósy 1991:66). If we add
the five canonical syllables that have been elided, this gives a rate of 39/6 or 6.5
sylls/sec. Comparing canonical (89) with realised segments (81) gives 14.83
against 13.50 segments/sec. Even this latter, 'unadjusted' rate seems quite rapid,
being fairly close to the 13.83 segments/sec in a sports commentary, mentioned
above. One may note in this connexion that this stretch contains three syllables,
droite and *trois* (uttered twice) that contain five and four segments respectively.
The significance of this is that heavy syllables such as these are uncommon in
the other stretches of speech sampled for measuring articulation rates, so that
this stretch is not an example of the fastest rate the speaker produced.

The utterance is however noteworthy on the discourse-analytic level for its
continuity; perhaps the most substantial sense-break in the utterance is between
recommencer and *j'ai chialé*. However, no pause is perceptible at this juncture.
The boundaries between the various sections or 'chunks' of this utterance
(Boomer (1978:246–9) suggests the term 'phonemic clause' to designate
'successive packages of sound, syntax and sense') are marked, not by pauses but
by intonation features such as variations in pitch and loudness. This high degree
of continuity reflects perhaps the 'involved' style of talk that characterised many
of the Dieuze conversations; in the stretch of conversation under discussion
here, a group of older females were exchanging stories about their often
stressful experiences undergone while learning to drive. Each informant had a
story that she was eager to tell, and so there was a good deal of competition for
the floor. Clearly, a locutor has available various devices for ceding the floor,
both linguistic and paralinguistic: perhaps the most obvious linguistic cues are
pauses and lengthening of segments, or series of segments, that a speaker wishes
to signal as utterance-final. Paralinguistic cues include the use of eye contact.
One linguistic resource that French speakers have available to cede the floor is
the use of 'schwa-tagging' mentioned previously, i.e. the insertion of a word-
final schwa after one phonetic consonant and before a pause, either orthographically or intrusively. The utterance-final word *voiture* was in fact pronounced
[vwatyʁə] in the stretch of speech given above, with perhaps the intention, and

in any event the result, of yielding the floor.

We mentioned above the broad contrast between speakers' orientations in the two styles: affective or involved in the conversations, ideational or informational in the interviews. The two stretches of language from the Dieuze corpus given below in (5) have variation on all linguistic levels and are comparable in that while the topic and text-type (narrative in this case) are held constant, the addressee varies. In text A below, a 12-year-old girl describes for the benefit of the interviewer the plot of a film she had seen recently, *Chéri, j'ai rétréci les gosses* 'Honey, I Shrunk the Kids'. The description is given in response to a request by the interviewer. In Text B the same informant describes the same film in response to a question from a peer of the same speaker group framed in rather vaguer terms: *'c'est comment?'* ('what's it [the film] like?').

Obliques indicate silent pauses, and colons after words, lengthened vowels filling pauses. Phonetic transcriptions are given in square brackets to indicate deviations from standard pronunciation. Suspension marks in square brackets [...] indicate a chaotic passage where the colocutor intervened substantially, making comprehension, and hence transcription, difficult. As in the example given above, non-standard reductions are given in ordinary spelling: *puis*> pis; *il*> i; *ils*> i or iz; *se*> s; *de*> d; *tu*> t; *il y a*> y a.

(5)   Text A (interview)

Fieldworker: c'est quoi l'intrigue du film? c'est un drôle de titre.

SM: oui / c'est un: un chercheur / i cherchait pour rétrécir les objets parce qu'il avait [py:] / plus d place dans sa maison sa femme [l]e disputait tous les: tous les jours / et: ça marchait pas / et il a laissé i a laissé une formule et les enfants sont allés dans son laboratoire / et: iz ont rétréci / et puis i leur arrive plein de d'aventures quand i sont tout petits une abeille qu[i] les empor[te] dans un nid: ah / i tombent dans les fleurs / i s met à pleuvoir y a l'orage iz arrivent dans les poubelles / et tout ça pis à la fin ça ben: s finit bien i i redeviennent adultes[1]

---

1. Fieldworker: what's the plot of the film? it's a funny title.
   SM: yes / it's a a researcher / he was doing research to shrink objects because there was no / no more space in his house his wife was arguing with him every day / and: it didn't work / and he left he left a formula [lying around] and the children went into his laboratory / and: they shrunk / and then loads of adventures happen to them when they're little a bee takes them into its nest er: / they fall into flowers / it starts to rain there's a storm they go into dustbins / and everything then at the end: well it ends well they grow up again

Text B (conversation)

SP: c'est comment?

SM: ben: c'est: c'est un [mm] un chercheur un peu / i: cherche à rétrécir les objets / pis euh ça marchait pas / pis y a les enfants qui sont allés jouer dans son laboratoire et: ça marchait / alors iz ont rétréci [l]es enfants bien évidemment / et pis alors euh i rétrécissent / et pis: y a euh c'est euh i / i leur arrive plein d'aventures t sais plein de misères aussi des parfois i sont heureux parfois i sont tristes euh et tout ça parfois i s disputent [...] et pis à la fin ben: i r'grandissent[2]

Text A is composed of 395 surface segments and lasts 33 seconds, which gives an unadjusted rate of 11.96 segments/sec. Adjusting from actual (395) to canonical realisation (415) gives 12.57 segments/sec. As noted above, the segments elided are overwhelmingly schwa, /l/ and /r/. In addition, the sequence *empor[te] dans un nid* features the assimilation of the word-final /t/ of *emporte* (standard realisation [ãpɔʀt]) under the influence of the following word-initial /d/ of *dans*.

Like the driving-lesson stretch discussed above, text A is in the average-to-fast range. There are however no errors of articulation, although it is noticeable that repetition of segments is fairly frequent; this may reflect the speaker's concern with organising the turn without pausing. Although expressed in segments per second, the above are speaking rates in Laver's definition cited previously, since they are contained with a relatively extended speaking turn that comprises several short pauses. It is worth remarking however that text A is interrupted by no substantial pauses; no pause indicated by an oblique is longer than a second, and most pauses coincided with continuers contributed by the fieldworker. These features are typical of the relatively uninvolved, ideational character of most interviews. Text A illustrates that the distinction between speaking rate and articulation rate is, in this case at least, a factitious o ne; there is little difference between articulation rates of the various stretches making up the speaking turn, although the initial utterances are slightly slower than the final ones. Indeed, in view of the cohesive and coherent character of text A, and of the often messy nature of actual utterances (stretches of speech cleanly

---

2. SP: what's it like?

SM: well: it's it's a [mm] a researcher sort of / he's doing research to shrink objects / then er it didn't work / then the children go and play in his laboratory and: it worked / so they shrunk the kids did naturally / and then er they shrink / and then er it's er it / loads of adventures happen to them y' know they're unhappy lots some sometimes they're happy sometimes they're sad er sometimes they have arguments [...] and then at the end well they get big again

separated by silence are certainly rare in the Dieuze data) it seems defensible to regard text A as an extended utterance characterised by a speaking rate or articulation rate capable of being averaged over the entire speaking turn, in view of the small degrees of variation apparent between the constituent utterances.

Turning to text B, a quantification of the articulation rate of the stretch from: *ben: c'est: c'est un* [*mm*] *chercheur* to: *et pis alors euh i rétrécissent bien évidemment*, which again can be regarded as an extended utterance in view of its relatively uninterrupted structure, lasts 13 seconds and contains 154 surface segments, thus showing an unadjusted articulation rate of 11.84 segments/sec. Adjustment from actual (154) to canonical realisation (163) gives 12.54 segments/sec. These rates are very nearly identical to those observed in text A, and we can suggest that the communicative intent, which in both cases is partly the concern to provide a coherent narrative, has overridden other audience design considerations. Indeed we may go so far as to say that the communicative intent is to a large extent co-referential with the audience design here, although from a discourse-analytical point of view one might wish to point out the ideational bias of text A compared to the stress laid on the affective aspects of the film's plot in text B (see Armstrong 1998 for a fuller discussion of the two texts).

Clearly, two passages such as texts A and B cannot be regarded as representative of differences in articulation rates across the speaker sample; we present a quantification below that depends on different principles. Nevertheless, bearing in mind this caveat regarding representativeness, it is worth pointing out that the difference between canonical and actual realisation in text A, expressed as the difference between the canonical and actual figures divided by the canonical figure, is 20/415 or 4.8%, against 9/163 in text B, a figure of 5.5%. This is not a large difference, and of course these passages are too short to give an accurate picture of the probabilistic nature of phonological variation. The only striking feature on this level in text B, in the sense of non-standardness, is the elided /l/ in *iz ont rétréci* [*l*]*es enfants*. This is however paralleled in text A by the elision of /l/ in le in the sequence: *sa femme* [*l*]*e disputait tous les: tous les jours*.

3.5.4 Relation between articulation rates and variable deletion of weak segments

We alluded previously to the idiolectal character of speaking rates. We present below in Table 6 a comparison of degrees of variation across the individual rates of two speakers, i.e. along the interspeaker dimension, with those across the intraspeaker axis for the same speakers.

Table 6. Variation in articulation rates of two younger females in the Dieuze speaker sample; in segments per second, both unadjusted (−) and adjusted (+)

Articulation rate	Interview				Conversation			
	slowest		fastest		slowest		fastest	
Gender / Age	−	+	−	+	−	+	−	+
F 11–12								
SP	9.0	9.1	11.6	12.6	5.7	5.7	14.7	15.2
SM	10.2	11.2	13.8	14.6	8.0	8.0	14.2	19.8

In Table 6 it can be seen that the articulation rates of a sub-sample of only two informants have been measured. Given that articulation rates were found to vary widely and in an unpatterned way among individuals in the speaker sample, representativeness could not be aimed at. We can therefore assume that while articulation rate is to a large extent idiolectal, variable deletion of the segments of interest here is socially conditioned. These two informants were therefore sampled with a view to illustrating in a clear and economical way the largest interspeaker differences in articulation rates present in the sample as a whole, by selecting the fastest and slowest speakers available from all gender/age groups. The hypothesis that motivated this experiment was as follows: if large idiolectal differences in articulation rate between speakers were observable, this would disconfirm the view of articulation rate as an important intervening factor in the types of audience design operating across the two styles. This is because large degrees of variation in articulation rates would stand in contrast to the quite high degrees of conformity, as indicated by the low p-values resulting from most ANOVA tests, shown by speakers in their treatment of the weak phonological segments that are susceptible to elision in fast speech styles. We develop this point further below.

Fastest and slowest articulation rates were sampled by scanning a fifteen-minute segment at the beginning and end of each recording (after a lapse of ten minutes in conversation style), on the assumption that speakers would be more relaxed at the end of a session than the beginning. As mentioned previously, the first ten minutes of each informal recording were excluded from study in all phonological and grammatical analyses of the corpus that are discussed here, and the first ten minutes of the interviews were not excluded. A suitable utterance of at least five seconds duration was then sampled from each fifteen-minute segment, since no evidence from the corpus suggested that the length of an utterance was a factor influencing its articulation rate. Given our concern here with micro-style variation, utterances sampled were not excluded on the grounds that they were characterised by irritation, boredom, impatience, excitement or other communicative elements cited above as being capable of producing a faster or slower articulation rate. This fifteen-minute scanning procedure is clearly somewhat arbitrary, in view of the variability in articulation rates present within any given speech style and the fact that this variability responds to factors other than those normally thought of as sociolinguistic. The consequence is that a notably slow or fast passage is in principle capable of occurring at almost any point in a recording. Nevertheless the procedure presents the advantages of methodological ease and of a reasonable degree of representativeness with regard to each recording; indeed, in the case of the 35-minute interviews with SM and SP, the segments scanned represented almost the entirety of the recording.

Turning to the figures in Table 6, it is worth remarking firstly that slower articulation rates generally show a smaller difference between unadjusted and adjusted rates, for the obvious reason that speakers generally elide fewer phonetic segments when speaking at slower rates; correspondingly, faster rates are of course generally associated with higher rates of elision. This is not always so, however. For instance, slower articulation rates are often used when speakers are reciting lists, as in the following example from SP who was enumerating her school subjects:

(6) y a le sport y a mathématiques y a dessin / y a aussi euh sciences naturelles
     'there's sport, there's maths, there's art, there's er biology as well'

This stretch has an unadjusted articulation rate of 6.14 segments/sec, but an adjusted rate of 7.28. This difference is due to the systematic reduction by the speaker of *il y a* to *y a*. The significance of this example is that elision of /l/ in impersonal *il* was found to be near-categorical in the Dieuze corpus, and this stretch of speech shows very clearly that the articulation rate is quite orthogonal to the case of /l/-deletion in a phonetic context that has very little sociolinguistic value indeed for the Dieuze speaker sample.

However, what is most strikingly apparent in Table 6, as was pointed out above, is the unpatterned nature of the degrees of variation along the dimensions of interest. Although the fastest articulation rates increase for both speakers in conversation style, for both speakers the slowest rates show a reverse effect, i.e. they are slower in conversation than in interview. The crucial point

here however is that the fastest rates in the conversation styles do not correspond in any systematic way with higher elision rates; correspondingly, the
slowest rates in interview style show no direct correspondence with lower
elision rates. We noted above the categorical deletion of /i/ and /l/ from *il y a*
irrespective of articulation rate. A more striking example concerns /r/-deletion
in a context that proved to have socio-stylistic value for the Dieuze speaker
sample, *Or* before a consonant or a pause: e.g. in *l'autre jour, j'en ai quatre.*
Variation in this context for the speaker sample as a whole has already been
discussed in connexion with Table 1 above. Below is an extended utterance that
illustrates a typically rather slow articulation rate from SP accompanied by two
instances of deletion of /r/ in *Or*+ consonant. Here SP is describing part of the
daily work routine of her father and mother, who ran their own bakery and shop:

(7)   i part euh i part dans les aut(res) [ot] villages / vend(re) [vã] du pain et pi
       ma maman eh ben elle vend au magasin
       'He goes off er he goes off to the other villages to sell bread and Mum
       sells in the shop'

Here both words having the *Or* structure, *autre* and *vendre*, undergo /r/-dele-
tion. We discuss below in Section 3.7 the influence of phono-lexical factors
upon deletion rates in the *Or* set, but briefly, frequent *Or* words such as *autre*
show higher rates of /r/-deletion than less frequent words such as *vendre*.
Nevertheless the likelihood of variable deletion in both lexical sets is inherently
probabilistic, and the above sequence provides a glimpse of this type of variation in operation. The sequence illustrates also the independence of variable
deletion in relation to articulation rate; SP's speech was in general rather slow,
and this stretch was articulated at an average (unadjusted) rate of 9.8 seg-
ments/sec, 11.6 segments/sec adjusted. This example shows therefore in
miniature what the figures in Table 6 indicate as a whole: an indirect relation
between articulation rates and socio-stylistic variation in phonology of the kind
we have been discussing in the present study. Table 7 below shows observed
frequencies as well as percentages of /r/-deletion in *Or*+ consonant or pause for
SP and SM.

Table 7 shows that while both informants show awareness of the socio-stylistic
value of this variable by style-shifting in the expected direction, SP is actually
deleting /r/ at a considerably higher rate in conversation than interview style,
despite her notably lower articulation rates in both styles. These figures suggest
strongly therefore that the Dieuze informants are indeed operating audience
design, perhaps in the modified, Bernsteinian sense discussed previously, in

Table 7. Observed frequencies (N) and percentage deletion rates % for /r/ before a consonant and a pause (aggregated): e.g. in *l'autre jour, j'en ai quatre.* Two younger female speakers, SP and SM

Gender/age	Interview		Conversation	
Females 11–12	(N)	%	(N)	%
SP	13/37	35.1	30/46	65.2
SM	10/44	22.7	23/65	35.4

their treatment of the phonological variables discussed here, the liquid consonants and schwa. It seems likely that the informants' concern to operate audience design results from their awareness of the socio-stylistic value of these variables. The alternative explanation would that the variables resemble certain connected-speech phenomena, such as the reduction of certain final consonant groups in English discussed in the previous chapter, in having no sociolinguistic value for the informants; and that greater deletion rates across the two styles are therefore the result of faster speech rates in the informal style. However, this is not borne out by the lack of correspondence between the figures in Tables 6 and 7. Thus it appears very likely that variable deletion of these segments is indeed subject to self-monitoring.

We may point out finally in connexion with the rather difficult question of the precise mechanisms that govern self-monitoring the assertion of the neurologist Sacks (1985: 48; referring to Martin 1967) concerning the role of auditory feedback in the monitoring of speech production:

> Normally this [auditory feedback] is subsidiary, and rather unimportant in speaking — our speech remains normal if we are deaf from a head cold, and some of the congenitally deaf may be able to acquire virtually perfect speech. For the modulation of speech is normally proprioceptive, governed by inflowing impulses from all our vocal organs.

Proprioception is defined by Sacks (p. 42) as the part of the human sensory system composed of 'that continuous but unconscious sensory flow from the movable parts of our body [...] by which their position and tone and motion is continually monitored and adjusted [...]'; literally, proprio(re)ception is the self-receiving or -perceiving mechanism. If correct, these observations go some way to explaining the rather inconclusive results reported by the psychologist Mahl (1972), who interfered with the auditory feedback of an experimental subject in order to study its effect upon the subject's speech production. He did this by filling the ears of a speaker with white noise, and found that the influence of the visible presence of a colocutor was as important as that of auditory feedback in influencing speech production; although results differed across the socially sensitive variables studied. The influence of what Bell (1984: 148) refers to as 'visual monitoring' was controlled by causing the informant to sit facing or turned away from the colocutor. It may be that the rather contradictory results reported by Mahl reflect the fact that the proprioceptive mechanism is as important as auditory feedback, if not more so, in providing information on speech production.

The previous sections have been concerned principally with the effect of elicitation methods upon degrees of style shift in the Dieuze corpus. We turn now to the influence of linguistic and discoursal factors.

3.6   Influence of phonological factors upon style shift

In the three following sections we examine the effect of linguistic and discoursal constraints upon degrees of style shift in the Dieuze corpus. This issue appears not to have received much treatment in the literature; or rather, there has been a tendency to study linguistic factors in isolation from the psychosocial factors responsible for style shift. This is strikingly illustrated by Bell's (1984: 145) introductory comments in his paper formulating audience design:

> Sociolinguists have commonly distinguished two initial categories of factors which correlate with linguistic variation [...] First are the linguistic factors — phonological, morphological, and syntactic constraints which promote or inhibit the application of a variable rule. Thus, following consonant promotes consonant cluster reduction — *wes' side* — and following vowel inhibits it — *west end*. Then there are the extralinguistic factors, also divided into two categories [i.e. interspeaker and intraspeaker].

We will argue here that where intraspeaker variation is in question, linguistic and extralinguistic factors need to be considered conjointly for certain linguistic variables. In this connexion we again consider the case of variable /r/-deletion in the Dieuze corpus. Table 8 below shows a pattern of hyperstyle variation that is considerably more striking than that discussed above in relation to Table 1. Table 8 shows degrees of interspeaker and intraspeaker variation for /r/-deletion in the sequence *Or* followed by a vowel. The figures in Table 8 show very clearly that the effect of following linguistic context is to produce much higher degrees

Table 8. Total numbers (N), percentage deletion rates % and style shift for /r/ in the sequence Or+V: e.g. in *de quatre à cinq* 'from four to five'

	Interview		Conversation	
	(N)	%	(N)	%
Males 16–19	25	24.0	55	78.2
Females 16–19	32	31.2	42	69.0
Males 11–12	30	23.3	37	70.3
Females 11–12	40	12.5	30	43.3
All groups	127	22.1	164	67.7

of style shift with respect to *Or*+V than for *Or* followed a consonant or pause, the contexts discussed in relation to Table 1 above. Small numbers of tokens per speaker group unfortunately preclude statistical testing of these results, but the results are intuitively very striking; interspeaker variation is dwarfed by the style effect. Analogous results have been reported by other researchers on the social dimensions of social class, age and gender. For example, Macaulay (1977) describes sharper stratifications along these dimensions in Glasgow Scots for /t/ realised non-standardly as a glottal stop in medial and pre-pausal positions. It thus appears that the linguistic environment in which a socially diagnostic variable appears exerts a strong influence on its interaction between the interspeaker and intraspeaker axes of variation. This observation not wholly new; Labov's well-known study (1966) of non-prevocalic /r/ in New York City took account of this context, finding that pre-pausal /r/ was more sensitive both socially and stylistically than pre-consonantal /r/. The result shown in Table 8 recalls Labov's result, but at a higher level of style shift and in a more naturalistic way; it will be recalled that Labov distinguished between an initial, non-emphatic speech style, and a more careful style which was characterised, in Labov's terms, by a higher degree of self-monitoring; the latter style was elicited by Labov's simulated failure to understand the initial, non-emphatic utterance 'fourth floor'. The general conclusion seems to be that phonological variables that are more cognitively salient have higher social-stylistic value than others (see Yaeger-Dror (1994: 203–4) for a summary of findings concerning cognitive salience). A further factor relates to phono-lexis; we discuss this in the following section.

The linguistic context: *Or*+V generally disfavours /r/-deletion, as the overall deletion rate indicates: at 44.9%, this is a lower figure than for *Or*+consonant or pause (52.9%). The linguistic factor which appears to inhibit /r/-

deletion before a vowel concerns the resyllabification that takes place in this context; thus, the full form of *l'autre année* syllabifies to the form [lo.tʀa.ne.], where *enchaînement* or forward linking causes consonants to attach to following vowels, opening syllables and producing the CV.CV. tendency characteristic of spoken French. The consonant /r/ in this context is therefore less susceptible to deletion, since *enchaînement* places the consonant in syllable-initial position, where segments tend to be more stable, and also more salient. This factor appears indeed to have inhibited /r/-deletion in the more formal speech style, characterised, as we have suggested above, by higher degrees of self-monitoring. One aspect of self-monitoring may therefore be the awareness on the part of speakers of the 'unnatural' character of the deletion which takes place in contexts such as *Or*+V. A comparison of Tables 1 and 8 shows that what distinguishes *Or*+V as a stylistically sensitive variable is the fact that deletion rates in interview style for *Or*+V are low for all speaker groups: 22.1% for *Or*+V compared to 55.6% for *Or*+consonant or pause. This appears to endorse the notion that the informants were conscious of the non-standard or even stigmatised nature of /r/-deletion in this context in the relatively formal interview style. By contrast, lower self-monitoring, as well as the solidarity-based nature of the relations between locutors, may have overridden these considerations in conversation style.

3.7   Lexical input into /r/-deletion in *Or*: A phono-lexical analysis

Although almost all words in the *Or* set are susceptible to /r/-deletion in *Or*+consonant or pause, if only in informal style, deletion in *Or*+V is blocked for most words in this class, as a result of the syllabic structure which characterises *Or*+V. Deletion of /r/ in *Or*+V is largely confined to a small set of frequently-occurring words. This set has been noted in the Dieuze data as consisting principally of *autre* 'other', *être* 'to be', *peut-être* 'maybe', *mettre* 'to put', *mètre* 'metre' and compound words suffixed by -*mètre* (*kilomètre, centimètre* etc.). Deletion rates in both phonological contexts are much higher in this subset than in the rest of the *Or* lexical set. It must be acknowledged, however, that the distinction between the set of words exemplified by *autre* (hereafter referred to as AUTRE) and the rest of the *Or* lexical set was drawn at a somewhat arbitrary point. As will be seen below, deletion rates for /r/ are some 25% higher in AUTRE than in the rest of the lexical set for all following phonological contexts aggregated, and almost 50% higher in pre-vocalic position. Clearly, however, there exists a gradual relationship between lexical frequency and /r/-deletion rates in the entire *Or* lexical set. As Milroy (1987b:131) points out, it is not possible to draw a distinction on principled grounds within a phono-lexical set.

Nevertheless, the decision was made to divide the lexical set into AUTRE and the residue at this point in order to improve ease of analysis of *Or*, in terms of the interplay between lexical and phonological factors. It needs to be borne in mind, therefore, that the results set out below represent a rather schematised account of a phono-lexical situation which is not in fact binary, but continual. However, the findings of Laks (1977) endorse in large measure this distinction between AUTRE and the rest of the lexical set. Laks included an element of lexical analysis in his observations on deletion of schwa and /r/ in Or by Parisian working-class adolescent males. In a series of linguistic profiles of his eight informants, he reported that some speakers deleted /r/ from *quatre*, *être* and *autre* 100% of the time, irrespective of following phonological context. He attributed the high deletion rates in these lexical items to their frequency.

Deletion of /r/ in the frequent word *quatre* was found to be heavily constrained linguistically in the Dieuze data, and this item has therefore been excluded from AUTRE. The criterion for the inclusion of a lexical item in AUTRE is essentially that the item's frequency overrides the tendency for /r/-deletion to be blocked in Or + V. Deletion of /r/ in *quatre* in pre-vocalic position does occur in the data, but is lexically constrained; thus, /r/ elides in the frequent collocations de *quat' à cinq/six* etc., but in unfixed collocations /r/ in *quatre* is retained in conformity with the syllabic schema described above.

Before presenting figures for AUTRE + vowel, we may comment on the patterns of interspeaker variation in Table 8. These show that the two older groups' behaviour is rather homogeneous in both lexical contexts. Because of rather small numbers of tokens, the deletion rates for the younger males in interview style, and hence the degree of style shift, probably need to be regarded with caution. However, it is apparent that the younger males display conformity with the two older groups rather than with the other members of their age group, the younger females. This discrepancy is quite largely attributable to discoursal factors. A common finding across all the variables studied in the Dieuze corpus is that the younger males talked the least in interview style, while they were a good deal more relaxed and loquacious in conversation style; although Table 8 does not show this tendency, it can be seen clearly in Table 1 above. It seems plausible that a less guarded speech style will be characterised by a greater use of reduced, non-standard phonological forms, and this is of course a major premise of the present study, but a point which is more pertinent to the present discussion is that the discoursal functions found in interview and conversation styles are rather different.

We have already touched on this issue above in relation to articulation rate, and we develop it further in subsequent chapters, but in connexion with the present area of variation, the younger males engaged in a good deal of narrative in conversation style, relating incidents seen in films or television programmes (this is also true of the older groups, but less so of the younger females, oddly, as is implicit in the figures in Table 8). This type of narrative seems to require the frequent use of *l'autre* and *les autres*, as the activities of one character, then 'the other(s)' are recounted. One group of younger males also engaged in a prolonged discussion of aeroplanes, which entailed the frequent use of *mètre* and its derivatives. The frequent use of *autre* in a narrative style also gives rise to high deletion rates in AUTRE in pre-vocalic position, and large degrees of style shift as a consequence. Tables 9 and 10 show this difference quite clearly:

Table 9. deletion of /r/ and style shift in AUTRE + V

	Interview		Conversation	
	(N)	%	(N)	%
All groups	42	38.1	98	85.7

Table 10. deletion of /r/ and style shift in *Or* + V other than AUTRE

	Interview		Conversation	
	(N)	%	(N)	%
All groups	85	14.1	66	40.9

Tables 9 and 10 show the influence of lexical input into /r/-deletion in *Or* + V. As noted above, the principal difference in stylistic value between the two lexical contexts (i.e. between AUTRE and the residue) stems from the high pre-vocalic deletion rates in conversation style in AUTRE. Deletion in AUTRE in interview style is relatively high at 38.1%, but deletion for AUTRE in conversation is very much higher at some 85%. As mentioned above, this deletion rate can be partially explained by discoursal factors; the relation of narratives in conversation style entails a frequent use of *autre*, which deletes at a very high rate in all phonological contexts. It appears therefore that the high degree of style shift found in AUTRE here is a result of discoursal patterns which are perhaps peculiar to the speech events elicited, rather than of the intrinsic value of AUTRE as a style marker. In pre-vocalic position, *autre* is often found in the Dieuze data in dislocated constructions such as the following:

> et pis l'aut i fait... [epilotifε]
> lit. 'and then the other one [he] says'

where *fait* is being used colloquially for *dit*. This type of doubled construction, where a pronoun redundantly expresses person and number already conveyed in a NP leftwards in the string, is of course very common in everyday French, and has been adduced as evidence of an ongoing cliticisation of the French personal pronouns, a process brought about by the non-contrastive character of the French verb paradigms in the present tense (cf. Harris 1988: 231–2). We discuss this issue further in the following chapter, in relation to *ne* deletion in the Dieuze corpus. However one may wish to divide the above utterance syntactically (and if one regards the pronoun as cliticised it is plausible to consider this string as composed of subject + verb form, i.e. analysable as S[*l'aut'*] V[*i' fait*]), it certainly seems legitimate to regard *autre* as occurring in pre-vocalic position on the phonetic level where no pause is discernible after *autre(s)* in this type of construction, as often occurs in the Dieuze data.

Where a pause occurs unambiguously across a syntactic link, as in:

(8)   et pis l'aut' euh i' fait... [epilotøifε]
       'and then the other one er he says'

it is always filled, as above, perhaps to assure continuity and to retain the floor. Contexts such as that given above have also been counted as pre-vocalic. The fact that /r/ in AUTRE deletes at such a high rate in pre-vocalic position suggests that the underlying form for *autre* for example may now be /ot/, with a rule for /r/-insertion in careful styles. Indeed, Laks's (1977: 114) evidence suggests that such a rule may be valid for the entire lexical set of *Or* for some speakers, at least in pre-consonantal position. He cites one of his (male L/MWC Parisian adolescent) informant's replies, in response to Laks's enquiry about the occupation of one of the other informants. The exchange is worth quoting in full:

(9)   Laks: Qu'est-ce qu'il fait déjà Gérard?
               'What does Gérard do again?'
       J.P.:   Il liv(re) (...) 'He delivers...'
               [i livə] (...) [emphasis in original]

The standard pronunciation here would be *il livre* [i(l)livʁ(ə)].

J.P.'s reply appears to be self-contained syntactically, perhaps better translated as: 'he's a delivery driver...', rather than: 'he delivers, er...', if only because the 'er' of hesitation is generally realised in French as [øː]. Thus, the final vowel [ə] which Laks transcribes here may be interpreted as a token of the schwa which is held by generativists to be underlyingly present after a single word-final consonant (cf. for example Dell 1980: 164–8), although a schwa in this position may be variably realised phonetically as schwa, as one of the front rounded mid-vowels or as a vowel close to [a], all with or without a degree of nasalisation. The realisation of a schwa in this position implies the possibility for this speaker of an underlying form /liv/ and a rule for insertion of /r/ in more careful styles. Nevertheless, a speaker who had the phonological form /liv/ may be presumed to be capable of producing the utterance: *il liv' euh ...*, equivalent to 'he delivers, er...' with a filled pause inserted. It is thus immaterial whether J.P.'s utterance, quoted above, is self-contained or not.

However this may be, Laks merely remarks that this speaker has no categorical rule responsible for the maintenance or deletion of /r/ in this environment. In the same conversation, Laks cites J.P. as maintaining and deleting /r/ within the same utterance, although in different phonological environments; /r/ is retained or inserted in *livre* (with the same meaning as that given above) in prevocalic position, and deleted in *livre* before a consonant. The fact that /r/ is maintained before a vowel argues against the interpretation given above, i.e. of /liv/ as an underlying form.

Laks's cautious interpretation of these data is doubtless the more prudent one. The interest of this example from the point of view of the Dieuze data is that even for speakers of a very non-standard variety such as Laks's informants, a full lexical item such as *livre* should remain resistant to /r/-deletion in prevocalic position, i.e. in the least favourable environment for deletion. It can be seen from Table 10 above that /r/ in *Or* in lexical items other than AUTRE does undergo deletion before a vowel in the Dieuze data, that this phono-lexical context is rather infrequent (151 tokens for 20 speakers in both styles aggregated), and that the overall deletion rate is not high: 25.8%, or 39 out of 151 tokens. Of these 39 instances of /r/-deletion, 24 or 61.5% take place after a nasalised vowel, as in *comprendre* 'to understand', *attendre* 'to wait'. This phonological context is thus clearly favourable to /r/-deletion; the phonetic reasons for this are connected with the considerable amount of articulatory energy required to produce lengthening of the nasal vowel in this phonetic context, and this is compensated for by weakening of the following consonant.

Further, the production of a lengthened nasalised vowel in this position requires the resolution of tension between the need to lower the velum so as to produce nasalisation, and the energy that tends to maintain the velum against the pharyngeal wall. Wioland (1991:69) states that this tension is resolved by the expenditure of a considerable amount of articulatory energy, compensated for by lenition of the following consonant(s).

In summary, the large degree of style shift observed in AUTRE + V is in large part due to the frequent use of *autre* in the narratives which are often found in conversation style. The category AUTRE is composed of only five frequent lexical items (and their derivatives), and this frequency must be accounted a factor influencing the tendency to high /r/-deletion rates in this category (71.4% overall). By contrast, the remainder of *Or* in pre-vocalic position is composed of many more individual lexical items, some rather infrequent. Correspondingly, this infrequency accounts in some measure for the low overall deletion rate of 25.8%. Deletion of /r/ in this phono-lexical context is also rather heavily constrained phonologically; a preceding nasalised vowel, as in *comprendre*, favours deletion.

The higher overall deletion rate for AUTRE can no doubt be attributed, in part at least, to the high frequency of the words in this set; Laks's (1977) findings on this phono-lexical context are comparable to those observed in the Dieuze data. Milroy (1987b:133), in her discussion of the influence of lexical input on phonological variation, reports, among others, Fasold's (1978) and Neu's (1980) analyses of final stop deletion in American English, where lexical frequency was found to be a heavily constraining factor. This well-known problem refers to the skewing effect that the inclusion of frequent items such as 'and' would produce on a quantification of deletion rates of /d/ in English. Clearly, the difference between this issue and the effect of AUTRE + V is that the latter phono-lexical set is embedded in certain types of discourse structure, and hence influences degrees of style shift, in a way that very frequent items such as 'and' almost certainly do not. This three-cornered relation between discourse structure, phono-lexis and hyperstyle variation appears not to have received attention in the sociolinguistic literature so far. A more fine-grained analysis within social groups between narrative and non-narrative discourse contexts would highlight micro-style differences reflected in /r/-deletion rather than the social-group/style differences shown in the tables above.

3.8   Further lexical factors:
Variable deletion in the context word-final obstruent + /l/

Deletion of /l/ was also quantified in the Dieuze corpus in the context obstruent + /l/ in a word-final syllable. This set is exemplified by *possible, exemple,
ronfle*, where /l/ elides variably following schwa-deletion, especially before a
consonant or a pause. Thus, *table de nuit* 'bedside table' or *sur la table* 'on the
table' will reduce very frequently to *tab' de nuit* and *sur la tab'* in everyday
speech styles.

Table 11. /l/-deletion in the context obstruent + /l/: all linguistic contexts, i.e. pre-vowel,
-consonant and -pause

	Interview		Conversation		Both styles	
	(N)	%	(N)	%	(N)	%
Males 16–19	84	25.0	58	50.0	142	35.2
Females 16–19	28	17.9	79	67.1	107	54.2
Males 11–12	32	34.3	16	50.0	48	39.6
Females 11–12	43	16.3	36	16.6	79	16.5
All groups	187	23.5	189	50.8	376	37.2
–par exemple	151	16.5	150	47.3	301	31.9

This set of words is not homogeneous in respect of frequency. The phrase *par
exemple* 'for example' is notably frequent in the lexical set, and is correspondingly more likely to undergo high /l/-deletion rates in both styles than less
frequent items. Table 11 above shows deletion rates and degrees of style shift
both for the whole lexical set including *par exemple* 'for example' in the 'All
groups' row, and with *par exemple* excluded, in the '*–par exemple*' row. Table 11
again shows the intraspeaker dimension to be more salient in this context than
the interspeaker. Small values for N in several cells make necessary a cautious
interpretation of the figures, and the degree of style shift for all groups aggregated is probably the most reliable result; here, the shift across styles is quite
considerable, and indicates the stylistic sensitivity of this linguistic context for
all speaker groups except the younger females, a characteristic result. For all
speaker groups aggregated the effect of speech style is highly significant:
p = .001. The frequent phrase *par exemple* undergoes high rates of /l/-deletion in
both styles (overall deletion rate 58.6%, against 31.9% for the lexical set with

par exemple excluded). The phrase also shows a low degree of style shift. The exclusion of *par exemple* highlights the stylistic salience of the rest of the lexical set, raising appreciably the degree of style shift for all groups aggregated.

In respect of speaker group scores, small numbers of tokens may well be skewing results; the very large degree of style shift displayed by the older females may be unreliable given only 28 tokens for five speakers in interview style. This observation also applies to the results for the younger males and females. However, the older males show a figure of 100% style shift, calculating shift as a percentage of the interview score, on the basis of reasonably large numbers of tokens.

The linguistic factor which may have influenced the high degrees of style shift shown in the context word-final obstruent + /l/, and which are increased when tokens of the frequent phrase *par exemple* are excluded, is perhaps the greater semantic weight of full lexical items. Diller (1983) reported a comparable tendency in relation to deletion of the French negative particle *ne*, such that the particle was deleted at higher rates before pronouns with an ambiguous or empty semantic reference. Similarly, it has been observed in the Dieuze data, and reported in other studies, for example Sankoff and Cedergren (1976) and Ashby (1984), that *il* with a personal referent shows lower deletion rates on the one hand, and on the other (in the Dieuze data) greater stylistic sensitivity than impersonal *il*. As discussed previously, it appears plausible that a less frequent (and presumably more meaningful) lexical item, bearing as it does more information, should call for more linguistic substance in its articulation. As Coveney remarks (1996:73), it is not clear how the semantic weight of subject pronoun could account directly for higher deletion rates; a clearer line of reasoning is that impersonal pronouns generally form part of pre-formed sequences, which are often subject to phonetic reduction.

In summary, we have seen that phonetic, lexical and discoursal factors are important in influencing degrees of style shift in the data discussed above. As stated above, these are aspects of intraspeaker variation which seem to have received rather little attention in the literature, although interspeaker correlates to the intraspeaker effects discussed above are implicit in several graphs and tables which show the influence of linguistic factors upon social class or sex differentiation. For convenience we again reproduce below the results of /l/-deletion in Montreal French reported by Sankoff and Cedergren (1976), summarised in the following form in Chambers and Trudgill (1998:62).

We have already discussed above these figures in connexion with the relative importance of gender and social-class differentiation. The aspect of this

Table 12. Patterns of /l/-deletion in Montreal French by social class and gender (adapted from Chambers and Trudgill 1998:62)

	MC	WC	Male	Female
impersonal *il*	90	100	97	99
ils	75	100	90	94
personal *il*	72	100	84	94
elle	30	82	59	67
les (pronoun)	19	61	41	53
la (article)	11	44	25	34
la (pronoun)	13	37	23	31
les (article)	9	33	15	25

display that is relevant here is the widely differing social value that /l/-deletion has as a function of the linguistic context in which it takes place. The Dieuze data on style shift presented on previous pages demonstrate that the large degrees of interspeaker differentiation which are apparent in Table 12, and which are largely conditioned by linguistic factors (principally semantic weight and lexical frequency) are echoed on the intraspeaker level. That is to say, /l/-deletion in contexts which show large degrees of interspeaker variation also show much style shift. This endorses Bell's view of the social–stylistic relationship, but we may add that linguistic factors can intervene in the relationship.

The foregoing statement that large degrees of interspeaker differentiation are conditioned principally by linguistic factors is of course in need of qualification; attitudinal factors undoubtedly also play an important role in the conditioning of variables that have high stylistic value. Speakers' awareness of the stigmatised character of certain variants (the stigmatisation connected in its turn perhaps with linguistic factors) will therefore be responsible for determining certain variables as salient markers of style. These two factors, the linguistic and the attitudinal, appear to be very intimately linked. An example which provides a close parallel to the Dieuze data can be found in Labov's (1972a:284) discussion of a well-known feature of African-American English Vernacular (AAEV) in New York City, non-standard subject-verb concord in the 3rd-person verb form. Labov reported that while adult AAEV speakers showed 70–100% realisation of standard forms, 'core' adolescents speakers, the gang members who were the custodians of the vernacular had 0–40% realisation rates. This general pattern is unsurprising, but a more detailed analysis showed that while adults had an invariable phonological rule blocking deletion of the standard 3rd-person marker -*s* before a following vowel (thus *'she go in'), the core speakers realised the inflection less often in this phonological context than in the others. The parallel with the Dieuze data presented here is striking; an elision phenomenon which tends to be resisted in process phonology, i.e. deletion of a syllable-initial segment, is associated, in the case of AAEV with those speakers whose usage is most non-standard, and in the case of the Dieuze data with variable /l,r/-deletion in certain linguistic environments which show very sharp degrees of style shift, reflecting speakers' perception of the stigmatised, or highly non-standard, nature of /l,r/-deletion in these contexts in formal styles.

3.9   Social factors influencing hyperstyle variation: The Paris corpora

In this section we examine schwa deletion from the point of view of the normative traditions prevalent in France that appear to influence language production. In this connexion a citation of Coveney (1996: 89–90) is pertinent: 'formal styles, which reflect the conservative written language, seem to involve, in certain respects at least, a quite different type of linguistic behaviour than informal styles [...]'. This is a formulation of a common-sense view underlying much of the sociolinguistic technique that relies on reading to elicit less vernacular speech styles. Coveney's formulation was expressed with reference to the variable realisation of French *ne*, and it is manifest, firstly that the conservative written language has invariable *ne*; and secondly, that formal styles reflect the conservative written language in the sense that these styles may be associated in the minds of many speakers with formal language instruction. As discussed above, this relation between speech and writing in French may also hold for certain phonological variables. Highly normative and formal teaching methods continue to be employed in French schools to teach the language, in contrast to the British English situation, and it may be the effects of these methods that are discernible in examples of socio-stylistic variation that differentiate scripted and unscripted speech styles in French. These examples are rare,[3] but one result in *oïl* French that shows both interspeaker and intra-

---

3. Lucci's partly quantitative study of situational variation in French (1983) covered a range of variables he termed 'phonostylistic'. He studied variation in schwa, liaison and mid-vowels, as well as intonation and intensive stress, in five male speakers from Grenoble, aged 35–55, three middle-class and two working, in five styles: lecture, two reading styles (lecture

speaker variation is shown in Table 13 below.

Table 13. schwa deletion in monosyllabic words in (V)C_C as in: *c'est dans lE bureau* (Hansen 2000)

Class / Age	Interview		Reading passage	
	(N)	%	(N)	%
MC Young	1204	72.3	787	21.1
MC Adult	606	58.9	403	26.1
All MC 1989	1810	67.8	1190	22.7
WC Young	281	71.9	242	12.4
WC Adult	347	68.6	243	12.8
All WC 1992	628	70.1	485	12.5

These results concern variable deletion of schwa in monosyllabic words preceded by a single consonant, a context that is favourable to schwa deletion. Thus *c'est dans lE bureau* 'it's in the office' (the schwa indicated by the orthography is capitalized) can be realised: [sɛdāləbyʁo] or, much more commonly, [sɛdālbyʁo]. A chi-square test showed a p-value of .01 for intraspeaker variation in this phonetic context, for all groups aggregated. The results in Table 13 are comparable to those presented in Table 1 above in showing hyperstyle variation, but much steeper hyperstyle ratios can be seen in Table 13. The largest degrees of interspeaker differentiation are 13.4%, between young MC speakers and MC adults, in interview, and 13.7%, between MC adults and WC adults, in the reading passages. At the same time degrees of intraspeaker variation are quite dramatic: the smallest shift is 32.8%, by MC adults across interview and reading styles, while the largest is 59.5% for young WC speakers.

The social-class differences in Table 13 do not show the classic pattern of close convergence in scripted speech relative to unscripted, and this is most clearly apparent if we compare the 'All WC' and 'All MC' results. While there is

styles (lecture and newspaper), interview and conversation (clearly, the working-class males were not lecturers, and lecture style was not elicited from them). Some stylistic variation was reported in the direction that one might expect, i.e. higher deletion rates in less formal styles. Curiously, however, no attempt was made to compare the linguistic behaviour of the speakers from the two social classes in the styles where it would have been feasible to do so, i.e. in reading style, interview and conversation. A socio-stylistic analysis of Lucci's results from the optic of interest here is therefore not possible.

rather little age and social-class differentiation in interview (MC adults providing the most notable exception) there is a systematic class difference in the reading styles, where deletion rates for the MC groups are higher than for WC. These results recall those reported by Armstrong and Unsworth (1999) in regard to schwa in southern French, and the explanation offered there (p. 149) may be applicable to the results in Table 13 also: 'this pattern fits Chambers and Trudgill's (1998:60) self-monitoring hypothesis if one assumes that WC speakers approach the task of reading aloud with lesser familiarity and hence greater attention to their performance'. We may mention in passing that the southern French results also showed hyperstyle variation in contexts that were structurally similar to those where variable deletion takes place in *oïl* French. Space precludes a discussion of these southern French results, but they provide further evidence that hyperstyle variation may be the norm rather than the exception in French.

To what extent can we formulate the criticism that the hyperstyle effects in Table 13 are unsurprising in view of the fact that the social-class range is compressed relative to what other studies have examined? If we consider again Trudgill's well known results on (ng) (1974:91–5) as reproduced in Table 14 below, and compress the social-class compass and style compass (indicated by the boldfaced areas) so that the results are comparable to those in Table 3, we see a hyperstyle effecting the Norwich results also. Maximum style shift is 82% by UWC speakers, against 45% social-class differentiation between LMC and UWC speakers in casual style.

Table 14. variation in Norwich (ng) by class and style
(adapted from Trudgill 1974:92)

	WLS	RPS	FS	CS
MMC	000	000	003	028
LMC	000	010	015	042
UWC	005	015	074	087
MWC	023	044	088	095
LWC	029	066	098	100

The salient difference between the hyperstyle variation in Tables 13 and 14 is that the French informants show a rather high degree of homogeneity in displaying high (and similar) levels of schwa deletion in interview style, and low levels in reading. By contrast, Trudgill's results show the familiar pattern of greater responsiveness of LMC speakers to normative pressures in both scripted and unscripted speech styles, differentiating themselves thereby from the class immediately below, UWC. It appear therefore that the Paris speakers perceive schwa to be a marker of style but not of class, while the Norwich sample perceive (ng) as a marker along both dimensions.

We can express this quite clearly in terms of a ratio between averaged intraspeaker and interspeaker variation (i.e. both social-class group scores averaged) of 3.9/1 for the Paris results. The averaged ratio for the Norwich results in the boldfaced area is also high — 3.6/1 — but whereas the French MC and WC ratios between (2.9/1 and 5.6/1) cluster fairly symmetrically round the average, the Norwich ratios for LMC and UWC are very different: 1.5/1 against 4.9/1. We discuss in the following section the question of the specifically French social characteristics that make possible the quantitative socio-stylistic relations shown in the tables here relating to variation in the French language. To reiterate and summarise, these relations appear to result from a uniform response to formal or reading styles that overrides the influence of social class or gender. This effect is quite clearly seen in Table 13, where the classic LMC/UWC effect might have been expected. The effect actually shown in Table 13 suggests that normative pressures are successfully applied in French across social classes to a greater extent than elsewhere. We now discuss this more fully; but note in passing that the influence of the interviewer's non-native speaker status appears to have been negligible, in view, as noted previously, of the very small differences in schwa-deletion rates across conversation and interview styles. What is at issue in Hansen's Paris results is the influence of spelling.

3.10 Discussion

We appear not to be in a position to answer definitively the question whether the quantitative socio-stylistic relation shown in the tables relating to variation in French is representative of the French situation generally, although three independent surveys carried out have shown similar findings: the Dieuze and Paris surveys discussed above, and that carried out in southern France (Armstrong and Unsworth 1999). The relative lack of findings on French precludes a definitive answer based on very large quantities of empirical data, but in view of the theoretical interest inherent in the question we discuss below the conditions that would be necessary to bring about such a state of affairs.

The impressionistic observation that hyperstyle variation is now the normal situation in *oïl* French can be found in the writings of several distinguished scholars of French sociolinguistics; for instance, Gadet (1998:67) expresses her view in the following terms:

> Je ferai l'hypothèse que le français, après avoir connu une période où l'axe décisif est diatopique (XIXe siècle), puis une phase de saillance diastratique correspondant à l'urbanisation (époque de fortes distorsions entre 'langues de classes', qui correspond aussi à la francisation radicale), serait actuellement dans un primat du diaphasique.

> 'I will suggest that French, having seen a period where the important social dimension is geographical (diatopique) (19th century), then a phase of social-group (diastratique) importance corresponding to urbanisation (a time of considerable differentiation between social-class dialects, which also corresponds to the intense promotion of French [at the expense of regional languages]), may currently be in a period where intraspeaker/style variation (diaphasique) is paramount.'

Sanders (1993b: 27) expresses a similar view:

> A major difference between English and French is the way in which spoken French has come to diverge from written French. Related to this — though not identical with it — is the distinction between 'informal' and 'formal' usage, which is much greater in French than it is in British English.

A view similar to these has been expressed orally to the present author by another distinguished French scholar of linguistics in relation to *ne* deletion (Yaguello, personal communication), which in this scholar's opinion has intraspeaker value but little interspeaker. Views such as these, expressed by distinguished linguists, some of whom are also French native-speakers, seem worthy of serious consideration. As stated above, insufficient data are available to endorse these views with any degree of certainty, so that we must confine our discussion to a consideration of the conditions necessary for a *'primat du diaphasique'*. There appear to be three principal issues involved. The first relates to the supposedly large degree of divergence between spoken and written French, in the present context most notably in comparison with English. If this situation does obtain, it is relatively straightforward to hypothesise why speakers in experimental conditions would show the high degrees of convergence that are necessary to produce hyperstyle variation. The second issue relates to the social conditions necessary to bring about a high degree of linguistic conformity both in scripted and unscripted formal speech styles on the part of a large proportion of the population. The third issue, spontaneous hyperstyle shift, is rather more difficult to explain, but we make the attempt below. Firstly however, the two factors inducing speakers to show high degrees of convergence in the scripted styles elicited by sociolinguists are as follows:

i.   It would be necessary, as discussed in Section 3.4 above, that many if not most French variables should derive their socio-stylistic value from their transparent representation in spelling. This would entail a ready recoverability of the standard variants in reading passages and word lists that would induce speakers to realise them in these styles. This appears to be true of the French phonological variables examined here, and applies also to items of morpho-syntax such as *ne*. The opposite case is the English vocalic variable exemplified by Norwich (a:); in these cases the relation of the variants to the spelling is more opaque.

ii.   The condition formulated in (i) is necessary but not sufficient to bring about hyperstyle variation. The high degree of convergence by all speaker groups in formal styles necessary for the hyperstyle effect implies that the influence of conservative written forms should have been successfully imposed upon many speakers, such that high degrees of convergence are produced in formal styles. We referred above to the highly formal and normative methods that are still used to teach the French language in France; to this factor we may add the training that French school pupils receive in the recitation of verse. Chambers and Trudgill (1998:60) explain the rationale for eliciting formal speech through word-list styles from the perspective of self-monitoring: 'reading out one word at a time is a much simpler task than coping with a passage of connected prose, and informants are therefore correspondingly more able to direct even more attention to their speech, rather than to what they are reading.' A further explanatory factor that relates directly to the Paris results is that in French different norms apply across different styles of reading. Therefore the response of French informants to a word-list style may well be influenced by the rules of versification, which for example broadly require the pronunciation when reciting poetry of all orthographic schwas in all contexts except the pre-vocalic; French school-pupils are of course taught to recite poetry according to these rules. Thus we can postulate that French speakers have available at least two reading-style norms: (non-elevated) connected prose, and verse. Evidence that school pupils do internalise these norms is provided by a stretch of speech from an 11-year-old female Dieuze informant, who produced in conversation style a fable of her own composition in the style of La Fontaine. The informant's recitation is notable in the present context for the tokens of schwa that were realised according to the French rules of metrication. These schwas are italicised below; they would of course not be pronounced in unscripted or connected-prose styles in *oïl* French:

(10)   Un moustique des plus piqueurs / S'en allait avec un*e* troup*e* de pro-meneurs [...]⁴

This stretch of speech provides evidence that French schoolchildren are subject to pressures designed to induce them to internalise the pronunciation associated with the conservative written norm. Evidence that all pupils are affected by these linguistic pressures is of course recalcitrant to rigorous quantification, but it is no doubt significant that authors such as Dannequin (1977, 1988) and Duneton (1984) have expended a good deal of polemic in criticising the highly normative methods used in French schools to teach the French language. The authors assert that these methods put a premium on rote learning and imitation of the linguistic model that the teacher provides, and of course a discount on the child's capacity for individual expression. The title of Dannequin's book (1977) and article (1988), *Les enfants bâillonnés* 'The children gagged' provides eloquent testimony of her view of the strongly repressive tendency of these methods. Dannequin's opinion is of course debatable, but certain of the facts she alleges are indisputable; for example, she mentions the very early age at which French children begin to come into contact with institutional linguistic normativism: from two or three years of age at the *école maternelle*. In addition to this factor, it may be mentioned that normative linguistic pressures are exerted, at least in principle, upon all French school pupils, in contrast to the UK situation where traditional methods of teaching English grammar are largely confined to the small fee-paying school sector, which represents less than 10% of pupils. Further, the post-16 staying-on rate in France is higher than in the UK, and all pupils who take either the academically oriented *baccalauréat* or more vocational qualifications such as the *brevet d'études professionnelles* take French as a compulsory component of their course of study. It seems likely that all of these factors contribute in some measure to condition (ii) stated above.

iii.   The further issue that we need to consider here is the language associated with the conservative written norm and its production in spontaneous, i.e. non-scripted formal styles. Essentially the same remarks as were formulated above apply in this connexion; what seems necessary for the hyperstyle effect to be widespread in formal spontaneous styles is that all, or a preponderant majority

---

4. An attempt to reproduce the jocular flavour of the original might give something like: 'A mosquito of the biting-most sort / Went out with a troop of strollers ...'

of French speakers, should be subject to the association between spoken and written French as it affects their ability to style-shift in formal situations. What is less clear is the precise way in which this association may be activated in psychosocial terms. As mentioned previously, it appears that many French phonological variables are of the type that can be internalised by reference to written norms, rather than by prolonged immersion in a highly exclusive socio-cultural environment. In addition to the Norwich (a:) variable already discussed, we may note again the UK English example of the type of variable exemplified by the vowels distributed in lexical splits found in pairs such as 'putt' and 'put', which are differentiated in southern/standard English by two distinct back vowels, respectively [ʌ] and [ʊ], and whose distribution is not reliably marked in the orthography. Words such as these are notorious shibboleths in English, but French examples depending on arbitrary variation between vocalic or consonantal pairs (as opposed to more complex areas such as variable liaison, where morphology and syntax are also involved) come less easily to hand. The inference is that the standard phonology is more widely and readily available to a substantial majority of French speakers compared to what obtains in the UK; and further that this greater availability depends partly on the more transparent relation between French phonological variables and their representation in spelling, and partly on the intensive promotion of the conservative written variety in the French school system. In psychosocial terms, we may note the probable association between the classroom, and formal situations encountered in adult life.

We may reiterate again briefly that a further factor contributing to this hyperstyle situation, if indeed it is widespread, appears to be the relatively modest degrees of interspeaker variation apparent in French phonology. Clearly, low rates of interspeaker variation will provide an input to the high hyperstyle ratios discussed above. One distinctive feature of the French hyperstyle situation, if indeed it is prevalent, may then be relatively modest degrees of interspeaker variation relative to intraspeaker, giving the effect of high ratios between the two dimensions of variation, and ratios which are moreover uniform across speaker groups.

3.11 Summary and conclusion

We have discussed here some examples of variable French language data that show an idiosyncratic pattern when compared to the social-stylistic relationship which is generally found in the literature, and upon which Bell's influential view of this relationship is based. The results presented here have shown that several factors are capable of influencing the social-stylistic relation, and further that some of these factors may be specific to an investigation of French language data. These factors as follows: the relationship of the researcher to the speech community being studied; the nature of the linguistic variables which are involved in social/stylistic variation; and the success of institutional pressures in inculcating in speakers' minds the 'ideology of the standard' (Milroy and Milroy 1991). This second factor especially seems to have received insufficient attention in the literature.

Bell's (1984) analysis concerns a society-level analysis of the relation between speakers' situationally-conditioned use of language and their social-group membership. By contrast, caution must be employed in relating the micro-level study which has been the principal focus of interest here relating to the Dieuze corpus, to the sharply stratified urban communities which are broadly typical of Western industrialised societies.

We discussed above the virtual absence of a clear gender-grading pattern in the Dieuze sample, or more precisely its disappearance with the increasing age of the informants. We speculated that this relative absence reflects the rather low degree of sociolinguistic salience of the variable pronunciation level in French, resulting in a later emergence of socio-stylistic competence in variable phonology. We have seen however that a certain number of findings (Ashby 1984, 1991; Pooley 1996) do indicate the presence of interspeaker variation in French phonology in adult speaker samples, and it seems likely that the contrast between the rather modest degrees of variation in phonology in the Dieuze speaker sample reflect the fact of the Dieuze informants' not having yet entered fully the 'linguistic market'. Against this may be set the sharp degrees of variation in lexis in the Dieuze sample (Chapter 6), a fact that suggests, as noted previously, that communicative competence emerges early on this level and continues to be important. This is due no doubt to the greater sociolinguistic salience of lexis as a result of its involvement in propositional meaning, a fact that is reflected in the perception on the part of non-linguists of the lexical level as being most susceptible to comment without specialist knowledge.

What is perhaps of greater theoretical interest in the Dieuze results is the consistent hyperstyle effect, perhaps produced, as we argued above, by the relatively unusual elicitation methods that arguably succeeded in capturing larger degrees of shift between unscripted styles than is common, as a result of the absence of the fieldworker in the informal style as well as of the influence of his non-native speaker status in the formal. The theoretical interest here refers to the influence of elicitation methods upon results, a point we develop below.

In addition, the French data presented here, and the accompanying analysis, may go some way towards explaining further why some phonological reductions are particularly stigmatised and avoided in careful speech styles. The existence of these striking patterns in the Dieuze data, as well as of Labov's AAEV data, suggests that such idiosyncratic variables may be more widespread than their relatively modest representation in the literature implies.

It should be pointed out that the unusual character of the Dieuze corpus undermines any claim to a universalistic theory of the quantitative relationship between interspeaker and intraspeaker variation; or even a theory seeking to generalise across societies that in many ways are rather similar, as are France and the UK. Nevertheless, it is by no means inconceivable that the results from the Dieuze corpus and (especially) the Paris corpora are reasonably representative of the social-stylistic situation in *oïl* French generally; very few regional features have been observed in the Dieuze corpus, and the observation that French pronunciation has been levelled to a high degree seems defensible in view of the results presented in the previous chapter. What the Paris results presented above show, for the purposes of our argument, is the strong influence that spelling exerts on many speakers.

We do not however wish to argue here that these factors, the regional levelling of French pronunciation and the strong influence of writing, have radically disrupted in French the social – stylistic relation that obtains in English, and that major factors other than audience design are responsible for style shift. The results regarding articulation rate discussed above go against such a hypothesis. As Bell argues (1984: 159), when speaking, 'persons respond mainly to other persons, [...] speakers take most account of hearers in designing their talk'. This is an admirably clear formulation of what audience design means in psychosocial terms, and it would be extraordinary indeed if this major motivation, which is rooted in a basic human need for approval and cooperation, differed across societies in any radical way.

In contrast to Bell's account, Finegan and Biber (1994: 315–47) propose an explanation of the social-stylistic relation that stresses the primacy of the stylistic dimension, with social class variation deriving from it. The results discussed here do not appear strongly to support this conclusion, except perhaps to endorse the emphasis which Finegan and Biber lay upon the need to account in any theory of the social-stylistic relation for the linguistic input to this relation, i.e. the fact that reduced phonological forms tend to be associated with casual styles, and full forms with formal. Finegan and Biber explain this tendency by reference to the tighter social networks generally associated with working-class groups; the high degree of shared information that speakers who contract tight social networks possess will thus result in their greater use of elliptical forms. This seems plausible on the phonological level, although linguistically arbitrary regional variants and non-standard pleonastic grammatical forms such as multiple negation are more difficult to explain using this approach.

Finally, in regard to the primacy of interspeaker variation over intraspeaker and the reflection of this relation in numerical terms, we have noted previously that this relation appears likely obtain generally at the performance level, in view of the circumscribed range of social contacts which most speakers contract, a fact that finds expression in the limited compass of socially conditioned language varieties controlled by a speaker or speaker group. Nevertheless, as we have seen above this generalisation needs to be nuanced to take account of the addressee and the linguistic variable in question; binary variables whose variants can be internalised with relative ease, perhaps principally on account of their clear representation in writing, may have a socio-stylistic distribution so far as linguistic competence is concerned that differs from that of more complex variables. For instance, Ashby (1991:11), citing Lemieux and Cedergren (1985:96) pointed out that 'when asked to play the roles of upper-class speakers in contrived skits, working-class adolescents from Montreal used the negative type with *ne*, even though the same speakers hardly ever used it in conversation.' As suggested previously, the *ne* variable is of the binary, relative transparent type referred to above, as are the liquid consonants and schwa, and we can suggest that the attempt to measure 'performance as the statistical reflection of competence' in regard to variables of this type is necessarily circumscribed by the experimental conditions that obtain.

CHAPTER 4

Grammatical variation

4.1 Introduction

In the paradigm of variationist sociolinguistics, the phonological level of analysis has presented and continues to present fruitful areas of enquiry, while in contrast, variation in morpho-syntax has proved more recalcitrant to Labovian-type analysis. Specifically, the analysis of variation on the morpho-syntactic levels raises not only serious methodological difficulties, but also very fundamental issues of sociolinguistic definition. These latter issues are in addition to those concerning the equivalence between grammatical variants on the semantic, pragmatic and discourse levels which have been much discussed in the literature (Sankoff 1973; Lavandera 1978; Labov 1978; Romaine 1981).

Grammatical variation is of course not monolithic, as implied by a conventional acceptation of the term 'grammar' that comprises morphology and syntax; thus variation in French grammar ranges from relatively low-level morpho-syntactic variables such as deletion of *ne*, and some variable liaison that has a morphological input, to more complex, meaning-bearing areas of variation such as subject- and object-NP doubling, interrogative sequences, the synthetic and periphrastic future tense forms, variation between auxiliary verbs (*avoir* and *être*) and pronouns with definite and indefinite reference (*nous, on, tu* and *vous*). Broadly, variationist methods have been most successful, in the sense of producing statistically robust results, when applied to the former type of variable.

In this chapter we compare the sociolinguistic distribution of some variable grammatical structures in French and English. The purpose of this comparison is to examine the proposition advanced by Hudson (1996:45) that languages tend inherently to suppress variation in grammar and to promote variation in phonology. At the same time we consider some difficulties of method and theory surrounding the analysis of grammatical variation.

4.2   Grammatical variation in French: The example of negation

As Milroy points out (1987b: 143–4), the salient difference between phonological and grammatical systems from the viewpoint of data collection and analysis is that any phonemic inventory, even though it will inevitably be subject to some 'leak' as a result of variation and change working within it, is a more or less closed system. Consequently one can expect speakers to employ phonological variables of interest relatively frequently, even if, as Milroy remarks, the full range of variants of a non-binary variable may be difficult to obtain within the limits of a standard sociolinguistic interview. In contrast, one result of the open-ended nature of grammatical systems relative to what obtains in phonology, is that in many cases speakers can exercise far greater choice in their use of grammatical structures to express the meaning they wish to convey. As stated above however, exceptions to this generalisation are provided by low-level morpho-syntactic variables such as French *ne*, an 'omissible item' in Coveney's (1996: 30) typology of grammatical variables. As Coveney remarks (1996: 55), the presence or absence of *ne* is 'possibly the best known sociolinguistic variable in contemporary French', and indeed we assume that a detailed description of the phenomenon is not required here. Deletion of *ne* in *oïl* French has been studied by several scholars, most recently by Ashby (1991, 2001) and Coveney (1996, 1999). We may briefly state that standard French can express negation through the 'embracing' structure that most commonly comprises pre-verbal *ne* and several post-verbal items: *pas, jamais, plus, rien*, and *personne* are the most frequent. In addition to these negative items, the restrictive adverb *que* is also frequent; this lexical item is not found phrase-finally, but can receive stress in sequences such as (stress is indicated by underlining): *ceux qui (ne) font que français* 'the ones that just do French' (taken from the Dieuze data). The issue here is of course that everyday spoken French overwhelmingly has no *ne*, relying instead on the negative and restrictive items listed above, which are more salient by virtue of the fact that they can receive phrase-final stress.

Table 1 below shows examples of a classification of the contexts in which deletion of *ne* can take place, taken from Smith's (2000) adaptation of Coveney's categorisation (1996) according to subject, as follows: (i) clitic pronoun, (ii) non-clitic and relative pronoun; (iii) subjectless expressions; (iv) negative item (*pas, jamais, rien* etc.); and (v) non-subject proclitic (i.e. object pronouns). These five criteria are exemplified in Table 1 below, with the element used as a criterion of classification underlined.

Ashby (1981) and Coveney (1996) have discussed in considerable detail the

Table 1. Linguistic elements used to classify loci of *ne* retention

Example	Gloss
i. Clitic subject	
on ne va pas vous accabler de chiffres	'we won't overwhelm you with figures'
nous ne nageons pas en pleine utopie	'we aren't living in cloud-cuckoo land'
ii. Non-clitic subject	
ça ne frappe pas que les pays les plus pauvres	'that doesn't affect only the poorest countries'
qui ne fait que creuser l'inégalité entre les hommes et les femmes	'which only accentuates the inequality between men and women'
iii. Subjectless expression	
ne soyez pas trop durs (imperative)	'don't be too hard'
ils avaient l'air de ne rien dire (infinitive)	'they seemed to be saying nothing'
comme n'étant pas du tout le retour en arrière (present participle)	'as not being in the least a retrogressive step'
iv. Negative item	
elles ne partent jamais du bas	'they never start from the bottom'
sinon, ça n'a rien changé	'otherwise, it changed nothing'
v. Non-subject clitic	
on n'en peut mais	'we can't go on'
ça ne me paraît pas une bonne chose	'that doesn't seem to me to be a good thing'

linguistic constraints bearing upon the deletion of *ne*; these are relatively complex, but no more so than the arrays constraining some phonological variables. Those weighing upon the variable omission of *ne* are connected with phonology as well as syntax: in oversimplified terms, *ne* in everyday spoken French is overwhelmingly deleted after clitic pronouns, with some variation due to phonological factors, but tends to be retained after full noun phrases and other complex syntactic constructions. We discuss more fully in a subsequent section some linguistic constraints responsible for the variable deletion of *ne*, principally in relation to its value as a marker of style. At first sight one might wish to argue that this similarity between *ne* and certain phonological variables is reflected in the sociolinguistic distribution that *ne* shows, a typical example of which is illustrated in Table 2 below.

Table 2 shows figures for retention of *ne* in a corpus of spoken French recorded in the 1980s in children's summer camps, chiefly in Picardy. The

Table 2. Variable ne-retention: Coveney's results (adapted from Coveney 1996: 86)

Speaker group	Retention of *ne* (%)
Age	
17–22 years	8.4
24–37	23.9
50–60 years	28.8
Sex	
Female	14.8
Male	16.1
Social class	
Working class	9.2
Intermediate	16.4
Upper class	19.3
All groups	17.0

informants were for the most part *animateurs* or monitors in the camps, and speech was recorded in an informal interview style. One or two classic patterns are observable: less retention of *ne* by younger and working-class speakers; against this, the degree of sex differentiation present is negligible. However, the principal feature of these results for the purposes of the present discussion is the way in which the rather low level of *ne* retention is distributed across all social groups; all speakers, whether differentiated by age, sex or social class, are involved in this area of sociolinguistic variation. Deletion of *ne* therefore fulfils one of the criteria proposed by Coveney (1996: 52–4), as being applicable in the identification of grammatical sociolinguistic variables. We need not list all of the criteria here; the requirement that is relevant to the present discussion (p. 53) is that the area of variation in question should be widely distributed across the community: 'the variants should be socially differentiated within the speech community'; and further 'the variants must occur in the vernacular style of at least some speakers in the speech community'. We can suggest that these criteria stem from the concern of the Labovian programme with the diffusion of variation and change through linguistic systems, which by and large are assumed to be the property of all of their speakers; items diffusing through the system generally originate in vernacular speech varieties. Exceptions to this pattern of community-wide distribution are provided by 'dialect divergent' situations, reported for example by Newbrook (1982) and Johnston (1983). In these situations, considerable structural differences between the standard and vernacular varieties produce patterns of social-stylistic variation running contrary to the situation described above. Further exceptions are 'embryonic' and 'vestigial' variables (Trudgill 1999a), i.e. those in the process of entering or leaving a speech community; these also show a distribution that is restricted to certain speaker groups or even individual speakers. We shall see below that some French grammatical variables appear to behave in this way.

We now consider an example of grammatical variation in English, with a view to discussing the sociolinguistic distribution that appears typically to obtain in that language.

4.3 Grammatical variation in English

Chambers (1995:51–2; 241–2) suggests that patterns of grammatical variation tend to be sharp or 'qualitative', while variation in phonology is generally quantitative or probabilistic. Chambers appears to use the term 'qualitative' merely in opposition to 'quantitative', so that while all speakers in a given speech community usually participate in the use of phonological variables, and in terms of degrees of more or less that are amenable to quantification, grammatical variables may be distributed less evenly, with some speaker groups showing a qualitative or near-total avoidance of certain variants. Thus a qualitative pattern by no means implies a lesser degree of evaluative judgment by speaker-listeners of the linguistic 'quality' of a variable involved in quantitative variation. Another way of expressing this is that the typical grammatical pattern has a quasi-complementary distribution, such that some speaker groups show near-total avoidance of the standard variant, while others almost categorically avoid the standard. In contrast, virtually all members of a community who share a language variety (e.g. all speakers of Tyneside English) will have in common variable pronunciation features, albeit to differing degrees. As noted above, we need to qualify any sharp overall distinction between variable patterns in grammar and phonology by reference to dialect divergence, and to embryonic and vestigial phonological variants. Nevertheless, the tendency to sharp patterns of differentiation in grammar is very clearly illustrated by a comparison of rates of non-standard subject-verb concord in Norwich (UK) and Detroit (US), shown in Table 3 below. The results shown are taken from Trudgill's Norwich survey (1974:55–63) and Wolfram's report on Detroit speech (1969:135–41). This table shows a sharp or near-qualitative pattern in the use of non-standard verb concord, as in 'she go'. There is a dramatic contrast between lower middle-class and upper working-class use of the variable feature; and this is true of two widely-separated speech communities although the UK pattern is more sharply polarised. Other English grammatical variables showing the same pattern as that in Table 3 are multiple negation and copula deletion (Chambers 1995: 117–18).

Table 3. Percentage of 3rd-person verbs without -s in Norwich and Detroit (Trudgill 1995: 32)

Social class	Norwich	Social class	Detroit
MMC	0	UMC	1
LMC	2	LMC	10
UWC	70	UWC	57
MWC	87	–	–
LWC	97	LWC	71

Several inferences can be drawn from this pattern: one refers to the effects of standardisation in literate societies; another, related inference has to do with speakers' evaluative reactions to grammatical variation, such that grammatical variation is perhaps perceived as being in some way less arbitrary than phonological variation. Table 4 below exemplifies this latter point.

Table 4. Percentage use of post-vocalic /r/ in New York City (US) and Reading (UK) (Trudgill 1975: 35)

Social class	New York City	Reading
UMC	32	0
LMC	20	28
UWC	12	44
LWC	0	49

We have already discussed the pattern in Table 4 in connexion with the relatively levelled character of *oïl* French variable phonology. As stated previously, the pattern in this table shows very clearly that the social value of linguistically arbitrary phonological items can vary orthogonally between two locations. The variable phonological pattern is not difficult to explain: no propositional meaning is involved at the lower level of 'double articulation', so that while rhoticity in Reading may convey elements of social meaning such as rusticity and lack of education, considerable knowledge of the British English dialectal pattern is necessary to decode this. The same is true mutatis mutandis of rhoticity in New York City. Patterns of use and evaluation in variable phonology can therefore be localised to an extent that is less common in grammar. By contrast, Table 3 shows speaker groups in Norwich and Detroit appearing to share much the same pattern of evaluation regarding non-standard subject-verb concord. We must assume therefore that the absence of a dramatic contrast between MC and WC use of /r/ in both speech communities also indicates a qualitative difference between patterns of evaluation of non-standard phonology and grammar.

One way of explaining these different patterns is by reference to the effects of standardisation: pronunciation is more resistant to this process than grammar, because if it is granted that language standardisation largely proceeds through the promotion of literacy, in most languages that have a written system the orthography does not strongly favour any particular variety; this is certainly true of English and French (cf. Milroy. and Milroy 1991:66–7). One qualification that needs to be added is that the vocalic system is indicated less transparently in spelling than the consonantal; examples discussed in previous chapters were English long (a) and the 'put'/'putt' lexical split. A more numerically important example is the vocalic variable (a): the standard variant of (a:) is a long low-back unrounded vowel, as in southern/standard British English 'bath' pronounced [bɑːθ], while the northern/non-standard variant is short and low-front: [baθ]. As mentioned previously, the lexical split between English front and back (a) is complex and not reflected very accurately in the spelling, with certain exceptions.

Broadly therefore, standardisation can be argued to exert normative pressures more effectively on the grammatical level. The written language, leaving aside marginal phenomena such as vernacular literature and the reproduction of non-standard language in mainstream literature, overwhelmingly uses the standard grammatical forms. Thus Table 3 can be interpreted as showing the effect of 'top–down' standardising pressures as it were squeezing non-standard grammar out of the linguistic system of middle-class speakers. Standard grammatical forms are perceived therefore as being readily available to those who wish to learn them, while phonological forms are not, or less so; an important exception is of course the spoken media, where talk is conducted for the most part using standard accents, or has been until quite recently. Thus we seem to be concerned here with different evaluative axes of language variation where phonology and grammar are in question: while variable phonological features encode aspects of a speaker's social/regional origins, variable grammar may be evaluated as being more 'cognitive', in the sense of referring to a speaker's level of education, literacy, and therefore perhaps intelligence. We return to this question below, after discussing this 'cognitive' dimension of the evaluation of variable grammar.

We mentioned above the further inference that can be drawn from the patterns of variation shown in Tables 3 and 4, and in particular the gradient of differentiation characteristic of each variable: in Romaine's terms (1984:85–6), a steep gradient for verb-marking, implying a very high level of consciousness on the part of middle-class speakers of the stigma attaching to use of the non-standard morphology. In contrast, the gradient in Table 4 is non-sharp for rhoticity, correspondingly implying perhaps a degree of consciousness that variable use of /r/ prompts a more tolerant or less normative judgment by speakers of the variable use of phonological items.

It was suggested above that grammatical variation is evaluated by speakers as being in some way less arbitrary than phonological; we have not yet considered why this should be so. Firstly however, we need to define what is meant by applying the term 'arbitrary' in this connexion. We noted above that a phonological variable can be used in a linguistically quite arbitrary way in different speech communities to signal sharply contrasting social characteristics or values. Thus for example, there is no *a priori* reason why in Britain a back (a) should be overtly prestigious in certain lexical sets, while a front (a) should not; that is nevertheless the situation. The same proposition can be applied to certain French variables, perhaps the closest parallel in the contemporary variable phonological system is the fronting, already discussed in some detail above, of the mid-vowel [ɔ] to [œ] in words like *joli*.

One can argue that many grammatical items share this arbitrary or unmotivated quality: English present-tense verbs in the standard variety require -*s* in the 3rd-person singular in an otherwise undifferentiated paradigm, but other, non-standard varieties have verb-marking systems possessing just as much internal consistency as the standard system. Similarly, a linguistic system using non-standard multiple negation, as in 'I don't want none', consistently (if variably) selects 'none' rather than standard 'any'. From a different perspective, a further example of non-standard grammar, levelling of past-participle and preterite verb forms ('She hasn't went') shows the paradoxical result of non-standard varieties ironing out variation by bringing irregular verb forms into line with the regular majority, while of course still attracting stigmatisation. We can suggest therefore that on purely linguistic grounds, variable morpho-syntax and phonology share the characteristic that the standard language selects and promotes a variant that is unmotivated in relation to its exponent function. Tables 3 and 4 above show nevertheless that the kind of low-level morpho-syntactic variation exemplified by non-standard NP-verb concord is highly stigmatised in English in a way that many variable pronunciation features are not. This is true even though all non-standard grammatical variants are as functional or efficient as the standard counterpart; as we have seen in the case of the levelling of past-tense verb forms, some may be more so.

The motivations that appear to underlie the stigmatisation of grammatical variation are expressed most vividly by folk-linguistic arguments, stating for instance that multiple negation is illogical on the analogy of mathematical formulae, where two negatives express a positive. This type of argument, although of course inapplicable to natural languages, nevertheless provides a clue to the difference between the two evaluative patterns implicit in Tables 3 and 4.

It is pertinent to mention here Hudson's suggestion (1996:43–5) that speakers express different aspects of their social identity on different linguistic levels, and that while morpho-syntactic variation tends to be suppressed, phonological variation is cultivated in order that speakers can express various 'acts of identity'. As Hudson expresses it (p. 43): 'it could be that we use pronunciation in order to identify our origins', while 'we may use morphology, syntax [and vocabulary] in order to identify our current status in society, such as the amount of education we have had.' This argument is summarised and further developed 'very tentatively' as follows (p. 45):

> syntax is the marker of cohesion in society, with individuals trying to eliminate alternatives in syntax from their language. [...] Pronunciation reflects the permanent social group with which the speaker identifies. This results in a tendency for individuals to suppress alternatives, but in contrast to the tendency with syntax, different groups suppress different alternatives in order to distinguish themselves from each other [...].

Hudson's phrase 'in contrast to the tendency with syntax' is in line with his suggestion that syntactic variation tends not to be socially diagnostic, with the result that the suppression of all grammatical variants is aimed at; in contrast with pronunciation and vocabulary, where non-standard alternants are kept alive. As he expresses it (p. 45):

[...] differences in syntax tend to be suppressed [across languages], whereas those in vocabulary and pronunciation tend to be favoured and used as markers of social differences. There do not appear to be any communities in which this relationship is reversed, with less variation in vocabulary and pronunciation than in syntax.

The evidence that Hudson adduces in support of the argument that grammatical variation has an inherent tendency to be suppressed is taken both from standardised and unstandardised languages. As he points out, the relative paucity of reported variation in grammar compared to pronunciation in languages with a writing system could, as well as a product of the difficulties attending the study of grammatical variation, be an artefact of the standardisation process, for the reason to do with literacy discussed above. But several well-known examples show that syntactic structures can spread across typologically different languages in contact that are not highly standardised; the two examples of syntactic levelling cited by Hudson are of the adoption of copular 'be' from Marathi and Urdu, both Indo-European languages, into Kannada, which is non-Indo-European; and second, the diffusion across Albanian, Bulgarian and Romanian of post-posed definite articles. The latter is a less straightforward example, as one would not wish to call these languages unstandardised; nevertheless the point at issue here is that one can plausibly assume that these syntactic changes came to be accepted by speakers in a non-coercive way through peer contact, and not through the institutional pressures characteristic of language standardisation. Indeed, the adoption of a grammatical feature from one language into another subverts the standardisation process by increasing variability, if only temporarily.

Thus it may be that the factors responsible for the suppression of grammatical variation are essentially similar across standardised and unstandardised languages. In any event, the distinction that can be drawn in principle, between on the one hand levelling across or within languages, and standardisation on the other, is largely factitious at the level of the individual speaker. We have defined levelling as the diminution of linguistic differences resulting from acts of accommodation taking place relatively 'horizontally' or non-hierarchically, at the level of peer groups; and standardisation as the process of the suppression of linguistic variation in response to institutional, 'top-down' initiatives, perhaps most notably through pressures exerted in the educational system. As already stated, these processes are inseparable in practice, since a speaker who is participating in a relatively non-coercive levelling process will also be responsive to institutional pressures. Correspondingly, the diminution of differences between sets of varieties that have an asymmetrical power relation implies a degree of upward convergence belied by the term 'levelling'.

If, as Hudson suggests, it is generally true that speakers actively wish to suppress alternatives in syntax, what are the factors or motivations alluded to in the previous paragraph which prompt them to do this, while at the same time continuing to cultivate variation in phonology and lexis? One issue is the extent to which the suppression of grammatical variation contributes to the social cohesion that communicative efficiency can be argued to promote. Broadly speaking, one can suggest that the higher the level of the syntactic structure in question, the greater the extent to which meaning, and hence possible miscomprehension, are involved. J. Milroy (1992:33) has the following example of a serious misunderstanding on the part of speakers of standard UK English:

(1)   A: How long are yous here?
       B: Oh, we're staying till next week.

       (silence of about two seconds)

       C: We've been here since Tuesday.
       A: Ah well, yous are here a while then.

Speaker A, a Hiberno-English speaker, has a non-standard temporal system which uses the present tense where standard English has the present perfect: 'How long have you been here?'. Speaker B misinterprets A's first utterance as meaning: 'How long are you/will you be here (for)?', and confusion prevails until C repairs the situation. Milroy (p. 34) states that 'there is no doubt that [communicative] breakdowns arising from the different [grammatical] structures of divergent dialect are quite common'. Examples such as (1) certainly provide clear evidence of the relation between syntactic differentiation and social (in)cohesion, such that syntax has the possibility to function as the marker of cohesion in society in a way that much variable pronunciation does not. What is less clear is why low-level grammatical variants, which present no risk of miscomprehension, should be the object of such unfavourable evaluation. We now discuss some possible explanations.

We have already mentioned the perceived association in folk-linguistics between non-standard grammar and cognitive deficit, whereby the use of multiple negation is held to indicate illogicality. Certain examples like multiple negation are clearly susceptible to criticism using arguments drawn from logic and mathematics, but the use of all non-standard grammatical constructions is popularly associated (in Anglophone countries at least) with lack of education at best; from this, it is only a short step to perceived deficient cognition. It may be that what is popularly perceived as the ready 'corrigibility' of low-level grammatical constructions in English (Matthews 1981:6–7) increases the stigmatisation to which non-standard alternants are subject. By corrigibility Matthews means the possibility of the application of a clearly definable rule of syntax or morphology that 'corrects' an unacceptable sentence; as opposed to the essentially arbitrary tendencies of lexical co-variance which govern collocational restrictions ('To toast the bread', not *'To grill the bread'), and which are properly the domain of the lexicon. In discussing this distinction Matthews uses the example of subject-verb agreement, as follows (p. 6):

> For a constructional or syntactic relation we will […] require [when defining the scope of syntax] that it should be subject to a *rule*, or that a rule should be associated with it. An obvious instance is the agreement in, for example, 'It sounds good' and 'They sound good' […]. Combinations like 'They sounds good' or 'It sound good' are errors which could in principle be corrected, or put into more acceptable English, by any speaker who said or encountered them. To learn English is, in part, to learn to conform to the rule by which this is so. (emphasis in original)

Later (p. 7), discussing examples of ungrammatical word order, Matthews asserts that 'in ordinary [i.e. non-poetic] speech such forms are as wrong, and as corrigible, as those which *gratuitously* break the rule of agreement [discussed previously]' (emphasis added).

The implication in this discussion, which clearly shows a normative bias, is that such rules as subject-verb agreement are simple, low-level, and easily learnable 'in principle' by all members of a speech community. Thus the perception may be that while the ready control of certain relatively complex grammatical constructions, such as (in English) correlative constructions or the use of the subjunctive, are inaccessible without prolonged education, the basic morpho-syntax of the language is open to all; those who fail to internalise it show a perverse resistance to education, self-improvement and social mobility. We may contrast this with the situation in variable phonology, where, as suggested above, certain (especially vocalic) standard variants are not easily learnable; vowels are furthermore not so clearly definable targets as grammatical items; and phonological variables, lying below the semantic level of double articulation, are not involved in conveying meaning and are perhaps therefore not perceived in the same way from the point of view of the cognitive load they represent.

A further contrast may be suggested between the attitude of French and English speakers towards their respective language: impressionistically, French speakers often consider their language to be difficult to speak well, and have a corresponding tolerance of foreign learners' mistakes in grammar. It is of course unclear whether this attitude is widespread, but in any event, as noted in the previous chapter, it may in part be a product of the still highly normative and formal teaching methods employed in French schools to teach the language; these methods of course promote the standard morpho-syntax of French. As a result these methods may inculcate in French pupils' minds the notion that their own language, in its standard written form, is hard to master fully; if only by setting up an association with grammar and the boredom and/or distress caused by its highly formal teaching. When questioned by the author, the Dieuze informants consistently nominated French as their least favourite school subject. This normative tradition is in sharp contrast to the British English situation, where the formal teaching of English grammar was largely discontinued in the 1960s except in fee-paying schools, and has only recently begun to see a revival.

The foregoing lines of argument are implicitly presented from the viewpoint of middle-class speakers who are presumed to wish to eradicate non-standard grammatical variants from their speech, and indeed this is the viewpoint adopted by Hudson in the quotation presented above: 'syntax is the marker of cohesion in society, with individuals *trying to eliminate* alternatives in syntax from their language' (emphasis added). However, the pattern shown in Table 3 above suggests that while this is true of middle-class speakers, we must assume that working-class speakers are either extremely unsuccessful if they are trying to eliminate alternatives in morphology and syntax; or that they choose to maintain these non-standard alternatives. The pattern of social differentiation in Table 3 suggests that grammatical variation in Detroit and Norwich may function as a marker of interspeaker divisions in a quite different way from what obtains in variable phonology. On either side of the broad MC – WC division, where very sharp differentiation takes place, the MC speaker groups show a high degree of convergence with one another, as do the WC groups. This is especially true of the Norwich sample, where both MC groups show near-total avoidance of non-standard forms, while the MWC and LWC groups are relatively little differentiated by their very high use of non-standard forms (87% and 97% respectively). Further to this observation, it has been suggested more recently by Cheshire (1997) that English non-standard grammatical variants are maintained especially in perceptually prominent sentence types such as questions, which involve speaker and hearer more closely than other structures (because a question generally expects an answer). Grammatical variation in English may thus be more tightly constrained than variable pronunciation in how it is distributed, and it may serve to signal aspects of a speaker's social identity in a more salient way than pronunciation. We discuss this view in more detail in Section 4.8 below, when we come to examine intraspeaker variation in grammar.

We may suggest tentatively therefore that grammatical variation in English may typically have a different social distribution to what obtains in French. We now examine a further area of variable French syntax in order to examine this proposition in more depth.

4.4   Variable interrogation in French

We considered in Section 1 above a French morpho-syntactic variable that, like English non-standard subject-verb agreement, is relatively straightforward in terms of the linguistic constraints in play. We noted also that *ne* shares certain properties with some phonological variables: it varies with zero; further, since *ne* is functionally redundant in the majority of cases, few problems of semantic equivalence arise. We saw further that variable *ne* deletion appears to be distributed socially in a way that bears resemblances to what obtains in variable phonology. In the previous section we contrasted the French situation with regard to variable grammar to the English pattern, suggesting that even low-level grammatical variation in English is subject to evaluative norms of a quite different order to those applied to phonology. Could it be that French speakers share norms regarding relatively 'meaningless' variable grammatical items such as *ne* that are less stringent than those current among English speakers, while reserving their strictures for higher-level variants?

To address this question, it is worth extending the present discussion to the variationist study of *wh-* questions in French, an area of French syntax that is undoubtedly socially and stylistically diagnostic, and which raises issues of method and theory that are more fundamental and more complex than those associated with low-level grammatical items such as *ne*; or indeed than the study of *yes/no* interrogatives. As Gadet (1997b: 7–8) points out, French speakers potentially have available a considerable array of *wh-* interrogative variant structures, although as we shall see, not all speakers use all of the variants available. Some of these are listed below under (2)–(8), in descending order of socio-stylistic value. All are translatable by 'when are you coming?' although, as noted below, some are focused to greater extent than others. The surface syntactic structure of each interrogative sequence is indicated schematically after the example, using Coveney's (1990: 117) notation where: Q = *wh-*

word or phrase; V = verb; S = subject; NP = subject noun phrase; CL = clitic pronoun; E = the interrogative sequences *est-ce que/qui*; k = *que*; sek = *c'est que*.

(2)	quand venez-vous?	[QV-CL]
(3)	quand est-ce que vous venez?	[QESV]
(4)	vous venez quand?	[SVQ]
(5)	quand vous venez?	[QSV]
(6)	quand que vous venez?	[QkSV]
(7)	quand c'est que vous venez?	[QsekSV]
(8)	quand que c'est que vous venez?	[QksekSV]

Gadet lists 14 variants in total; as we shall see below, (3)–(5) are among the most frequent in everyday French, while (2), (3) and (5) are probably unmarked pragmatically. Thus leaving aside their socio-stylistic value, it is of course plain that not all of the constructions listed above are equivalent to each other in all discourse contexts, in respect of the strong criteria for setting up grammatical variants formulated by Labov (1972b: 271): 'social and stylistic variation presupposes the option of saying "the same thing" in several different ways: that is, the variants are identical in reference or truth value, but opposed in their social and/or stylistic significance'. Reference and truth value are clearly irrelevant to the study of variation in interrogatives; what is at issue here is pragmatic equivalence. Thus for instance, (4) and (7) are probably the constructions most frequently used as echo-questions; but accompanied by a level intonation pattern, they can also function as unmarked interrogatives with full equivalence to (2), (3), (5) and (6). At a formal level of analysis, intonation can be seen therefore to be an additional constraint operating on the decision to include a variant as possessing full equivalence to the others in the set; although of course within a discourse-analytic optic, the acceptability of a variant in a given context will ultimately depend on the linguist's judgment, perhaps endorsed by those of native speakers. As Coveney points out (1996: 121): 'there is a certain irony in the fact that a variationist analysis should require the use of intuitive judgements of this kind, since sociolinguists have in the past attacked the uncontrolled use of intuitions as practised by linguists of other persuasions'.

We now discuss the results shown in Table 5 below, which are presented by Valdman (1982: 225). Valdman's figures are in turn adapted from a quantification of variable *wh*- interrogatives carried out by Behnstedt (1973). In addition to the constructions (2)–(8) listed above, Behnstedt quantified the two listed below as (9) and (10).

(9)   quand viennent les enfants?
    'when are the children coming?'   [QV NP]

(10)   quand Jeanne vient-elle?
     'when is Jeanne coming?'   [QSV-CL]

Clearly, these differ from (2)–(8) in having a full NP subject as opposed to
((9)), or as well as ((10)), a clitic pronoun. Thus whereas all members of the
(2)–(8) set are in principle interchangeable with one another in certain contexts, (9) and (10) constitute an additional set having partial overlap with
(2)–(8). It will be seen that the total of the figures in each of the three remaining
columns in Table 5 below is 100; we must assume therefore that Behnstedt
simply expressed the number of occurrences of each variant as a percentage of
the total number of *wh-* questions used by each speaker sample. The shortcoming of this method is that since the nine constructions in the left-hand column
of Table 5 are not interchangeable in all combinations, these constructions are
sociolinguistic variants in a weak sense. Thus for instance, where a token of QV
NP occurs, variation is manifestly not possible between it and QV-CL unless the
referent is identical in both cases. The method used to arrive at the results
shown in Table 5 is therefore rather rough-and-ready. Furthermore, these
results need to be treated with caution, since although total token numbers are
considerable, especially for *français soutenu* or 'formal French' the distribution
of token numbers is not transparent. Thus 21 speakers are represented in the
français familier 'colloquial French' data, giving in principle some 21 tokens per
speaker per variant, but in practice it is unknown how numbers of tokens are
distributed across the variants, as the original figures are not recoverable.

Behnstedt's choice of terms to designate the three varieties of speech studied
is rather unhappy, as they evoke speech styles as well as varieties: *'français populaire'* refers here to working-class speech which was collected when the researcher was working as co-driver of a lorry; *'français familier'* refers to colloquial
middle-class speech; and *'français soutenu'* was recorded from radio interviews
and discussions: it is therefore both formal and middle-class (Behnstedt's term
is the German *Rundfunksprache* or 'radio speech'). The social status of the
participants in these radio discussions was presumably not known with certainty, although it seems defensible to assume that they would be highly educated
MC speakers in view of the exclusive character of formal radio discussions. We
need to bear these limitations in mind as we consider the patterning observable
in Table 5.

Table 5. Variable *wh*- interrogation: Behnstedt's results
(adapted from Valdman 1982:225)

Social class/style	'français populaire' (WC)	'français familier' (MC)	'français soutenu' (MC)
wh- construction	% use	% use	% use
QSV-CL	0	0	3
QV-CL	0	3	47
QV NP	9	2	12
QESV	8	12	3
SVQ	12	33	25
QSV	36	46	10
QkSV	26	0	0
QsekSV	3	4	0
QksekSV	6	0	0
Total tokens	587	446	4367

The *wh*- variants in Table 5 are listed in approximate descending order of socio-stylistic value: QSV-CL and QV NP, the variants that raise problems of comparability, are ranked in accordance with their socio-stylistic distribution across these speaker samples. QV NP, QESV, SVQ and QSV are the most frequent variants, accounting between them for 69% of all occurrences. The relative infrequency of QESV seems surprising, even though all speaker groups show variable use of the construction. However, what is striking in this display is the overall distribution across speaker groups and styles of the array of variant constructions. The distribution recalls that adapted from Coveney's study and shown in Table 2 above, in that it is 'quantitative' or probabilistic for the use of the variants in the boldfaced area of the table. That is to say, all speaker groups are participating in what one might call the 'core' of this area of variable syntax: QN VP, QESV, SVQ and QSV. At the same time the 'periphery' of high-value variants (QSV-CL and QV-CL) and low-value variants (QkSV, QsekSV and QksekSV) are not distributed in this way: the high-value variants are used exclusively by MC speakers, overwhelmingly in the most formal style, while low-value variants are almost solely the property of WC speakers. Another way of expressing this difference is in terms of the distinction between 'indicators', which show social but little style differentiation, and 'markers', which show both; QV-CL can be thought of as a marker in these terms. Table 6 below, showing Coveney's results (1996) for *wh*- interrogation, partially confirms these results.

Table 6. Variable *wh-* interrogation: Coveney's results
(adapted from Coveney 1996:234)

| *Wh-* form | QV-CL | QESV | SVQ | QSV |
Speaker group	% use	% use	% use	% use
Age				
17–22 years	0	46.4	26.3	56.3
24–37 years	6.2	49.2	27.9	51.4
50–60 years	16.7	50	1/4	2/7
Sex				
Female	4.4	69.6	35.3	1/10
Male	4.4	41.4	24.4	63.4
Class				
Working class	0/7	4/7	3/7	0/5
Intermediate	6.8	56.8	15.4	13/19
Upper class	2.7	42.1	34.6	47.8
All speakers	5.8	48.6	27.7	50

Table 6 shows the results of Coveney's analysis of *wh-* interrogatives, taken again from his Picardy corpus. As Coveney himself points out, these results need to be treated with caution: the mean number of interrogatives per speaker is 2.7, and where results are unreliable because of small numbers of tokens per speaker group, observed rather than relative frequencies are shown (i.e. fractions, not percentages). The variants are again ranked in descending order of socio-stylistic value from left to right, and it is clear that all speaker groups share use of the 'core' of variable interrogatives (in this case QESV, SVQ and QSV: QV NP was excluded from the analysis, for reasons discussed below) while QV-CL, although little used, also shows a variable distribution, being used by almost all speaker groups.

It is worth devoting a brief discussion to Coveney's analytic methodology, as it is more sophisticated but perhaps less intuitive than Behnstedt's. We noted in connexion with Table 5 the relative crudity of the figures that results from analysing variants that are not all mutually commutable. The difference between Behnstedt's and Coveney's methods of calculation is most clearly illustrated by the fact that in Coveney's results, the percentage realisation rates across each row do not total 100%. This is because tokens of interrogatives where variation was judged to be impossible, because no equivalents were available, were excluded from the analysis of each variant construction. The totals behind the percentages given in each row are therefore different, but have partial overlap and form differing proportions of the total value for N for the variable (represented by the total of occurrences of all the variants) treated by each speaker group. Thus the figure in each cell in Table 6 represents in percentage terms the number of times a variant construction was realised where variation was possible. Observed frequencies have been for the most part omitted from Table 6 for clarity, but Coveney's method is illustrated more clearly in Table 7 below, which show Coveney's analysis of variable *yes/no* interrogatives. Examples of ESV and SV constructions are as follows below, all translatable as 'do you often go to Paris?' No occurrences of the V-CL variant were noted.

(11) Allez-vous souvent à Paris?   [V-CL]

(12) Est-ce que vous allez souvent à Paris?   [ESV]

(13) Vous allez souvent à Paris?   [SV]

Table 7. Variation in *yes/no* interrogatives: all speaker groups aggregated (Coveney 1996: 233)

Interrogative form	SV	ESV	Total N
Observed frequency	77/95	32/106	109
% realisation rate	81.1	30.2	

Again, the totals in each column are not the same and the percentages in the '% realisation rate' row do not total 100%. This is again because interrogatives without full equivalents were excluded from the analysis of each variant. Coveney (1996: 121) gives the following example of a *yes/no* interrogative that has no variants of equivalent structure:

(14) tu coupes un petit peu? 'will you switch [the tape-recorder] off for a bit?'

Here the pragmatic function (request) cannot be expressed using the ESV or V-CL constructions, unless a modal verb is used, as in:

(15) Est-ce tu peux couper un petit peu?

An example taken from the *wh-* set is the following:

(16)   qu'est-ce qu'il y a?

which cannot be realised using all other *wh-* variants without its idiomatic force ('what's the matter?'/'what's wrong'?) being lost. Thus (17) is available to express this idiomatic meaning, but not (18):

(17)   qu'y a-t-il?

(18)   il y a quoi?

As Coveney points out (1996: 201–2), such examples are rather trivial: another is *'comment dirais-je?'*, which is a tag whose variants are limited in a similar way to those of (16). But others are far from being trivial: rhetorical questions in French such as the following appear to have no other variants:

(19)   qu'est-ce que tu veux? 'what can you do?'

(20)   où est l'inconvénient? 'what's the problem?'

Coveney (p. 202) points out that tokens such as (19) and (20) were numerous in his data in relative terms, and in contrast to the tags and idioms discussed above, questions of this kind are clearly productive. The obvious result of the exclusion of many 'quasi-variants' such as these is small numbers of tokens, and thus potentially low reliability of results. The results shown in Tables 6 and 7 were drawn from a corpus of some 250,000 words; from one point of view, it is of course unsurprising that rather few direct interrogatives were elicited from a sample of interviewees in view of the linguistic structure of most interviews, where rights governing turn-taking, topic control and the asking of questions tend to be controlled by the interviewer. Against this, Coveney points out firstly, that he felt that his interviews were rather informal, such that they might be more suitably described as 'elicited conversations' (1996: 17); secondly, he points out (p. 91) that indirect interrogatives framed by interviewees are frequent in his corpus; no doubt as a consequence of this relative informality. Thus the example of Coveney's 'narrow' variationist quantification of interrogatives highlights very vividly the relation between the frequency and equivalence problems associated with the analysis of variable syntax.

Against these rather negative comments (which are prompted by the high degree of accountability that Coveney applied to the data he analysed), it should be said that the results in Tables 6 and 7 broadly confirm several features of those reported by Behnstedt; for instance, the fact that no speaker in Coveney's sample, including the most 'conservative' older female speakers, used the *yes/no* V-CL structure, and that very few occurrences of the *wh-* QV-CL variant were noted, suggests that this structure is now appropriate only in the more formal varieties of spoken French, as indeed Behnstedt's 'français soutenu' results show positively. Correspondingly, Coveney's figures complement Behnstedt's in showing that the variants in the low-value periphery such as QkSV are found only in low-status groups and/or in very informal speech styles, which Coveney's sampling and elicitation methods did not capture. As mentioned above, Coveney's results for *wh-* questions also endorse Behnstedt's in showing the *wh-* 'core' (QESV, SVQ and QSV in Coveney's data) being used variably by all speaker groups.

4.5   Intermediate conclusions

The results shown in Tables 5–7 suggest that variable French *wh-* interrogation, considered as a whole, has as it were a core and a periphery: the core of frequent variants is used variably (in the sense discussed in Section 4.2 above) by all speakers and is thus comparable in its social distribution to what obtains in English and French variable phonology and variable use of *ne*. Outside the core, there is a high-value and a low-value periphery showing a complementary distribution similar to what obtains for English non-standard verb concord, shown in Table 3: WC speakers show zero use of QSV-CL and QV-CL, the high-value peripheral variants, and correspondingly, the MC speakers in both styles have zero use of QkSV, QsekSV and QksekSV, the low-value peripheral variants.

If it is legitimate to draw a comparison between different types of variable morpho-syntax across English and French (a question we discuss in the following sub-sections), it is clear that the suggestions in Section 4.3 above designed to explain the high degree of stigmatisation applied to grammatical variation in English, are not wholly valid for French. Tables 2 and 5–7 appear to show French speakers sharing behavioural and evaluative norms regarding variable grammar that are quite different from the English pattern. It is also clear that French speakers tolerate and indeed maintain variation in the core of the area of 'high-level' syntactic variation that interrogatives represent; at the same time, the high- and low-value peripheral variants have strong affinities, at least so far as their socio-stylistic distribution is concerned, with the English grammatical variants discussed in Section 4.3. From a cross-linguistic perspective, the important distinction between these French and English variants appears to be that a French variant such as QV-CL is in process of becoming archaic, such that its socio-stylistic distribution is characteristic of the 'vestigial' variants discussed above, and hence typical of more formal and conservative speech varieties; we discus this type of distribution below when we come to examine intraspeaker variation in grammar. By contrast, multiple negation and non-standard subject-verb concord in English are vernacular variants that bear comparison with French interrogative structures such as QkSV in their community-wide, non-vestigial distribution.

If the results shown in Tables 2 and 5–7 are representative, one interesting conclusion that emerges from the difference between variable grammar in English and French is that non-standard grammar is not inevitably associated across languages with lack of education and therefore perceived low intelligence, as we have argued that it is in the minds of many English speakers. Thus there appears to be no direct or necessary connection between the more centrally 'structural' character of morphology and syntax, reflected in its ready 'corrigibility' in Matthews's terms (1981:7), and its susceptibility to standardisation. On the contrary, the French examples discussed here show that speakers can actively cultivate variability in grammar if it is one of the chief linguistic resources they have at their disposal to express their social identity, to complement perhaps in fairly substantial measure the rather diminished sociolinguistic resource that pronunciation may represent. Within this category of variable grammar, we can note the further striking fact that low-level, omissible morphological items such as *ne* are comparable sociolinguistically to areas such as some variable interrogation; this latter area involves alternating word order and hence, it may be presumed, operations at a higher level of cognition.

The foregoing claims are most clearly substantiated by the complementary data shown in Tables 2, 3 and 5–7 above, which imply that some French variable grammatical items resemble pronunciation in their social-stylistic distribution, and by inference in how they are evaluated. At the same time, the corresponding English situation with regard to variable grammar (represented in Table 3) shows evaluative norms more vividly: it seems legitimate to assume that English speakers will be quite highly aware of the grammatical variables which pattern in the polarised 'marker' way shown in Table 3. Trudgill (1995:35) has the further example of multiple negation in US English that shows the same polarised patterns as that of non-standard verb concord shown in Table 3. These grammatical variables, like some phonological sociolinguistic markers, will therefore be 'the subject of unfavourable comment in the community' (Chambers and Trudgill 1998:72). The English phonological markers discussed in this connexion by Chambers and Trudgill are the glottal stop, (h) and (ng). What these variables have in common for the purposes of the present discussion is that they are unambiguously marked in the orthography, and hence that their use is perhaps more closely connected to a perceived high degree of literacy, or perhaps a normatively-oriented 'social trajectory', than other standard phonological variants whose representation in spelling is less transparent.

Correspondingly, the more gradual patterns shown by the French grammatical variables in Tables 2 and 5–7 may be presumed to reflect less unfavourable evaluative community norms. Clearly however, more substantial evidence is required to reinforce this claim, and we present in Chapter 6 below on lexis some fairly direct evidence, in the form of self- and other-repair, showing that some French speakers have highly salient and overtly normative attitudes towards their own and others' use of non-standard lexical items, while variable phonology and grammar are not to the same degree 'the subject of unfavourable comment'. We shall see further that these attitudes are in turn reflected in very sharp patterns of social-stylistic lexical variation.

4.6 Issues of comparability: Variation and change in grammar

The hypothesis sketched above must of course remain tentative in view of the small number of findings available, of the fact that these findings are based on small numbers of tokens, and that the findings concern a small number of areas of variation. In the absence of adequate results on areas of variation in *oïl* French other than negation and interrogation, we can at most state the rather arid and obvious fact that these are the types of grammatical variable in this variety of French that have been most frequently analysed by researchers. This fact can perhaps least controversially be taken only as throwing light on issues of methodology, in other words that scholars have not considered insuperable the problems of identification, quantification, etc. associated with these variables. It would certainly be imprudent to suggest, as we did in a previous chapter in relation to phonological variation in French, that the grammatical variation in French reported by most researchers reflects reasonably accurately their intuitions that these are in fact the principal resource available in French variable grammar. Thus there are several grammatical variables in French that may well differentiate speaker groups in the polarised way seen in English. Table 8 below shows the variables that are commonly mentioned in the literature; as can be seen, several of these have been the object of variationist analysis in Quebec French.

Apart from Ashby (1992) and Coveney (2000a), no variationist analyses of

Table 8. Some French grammatical variables

Variable	Standard variant	Non-standard variant(s)	Researchers; Research site
auxiliary *avoir/être*	*je suis venu*	*j'ai venu*	Sankoff and Thibault (1980); Montreal
future	*j'irai*	*je vais aller*	Emirkanian and Sankoff (1985); Montreal
pronouns	*nous allons* (definite reference)	*on va* (definite reference)	Coveney (2000a); Picardy
	on va (indefinite reference)	*vous allez/ tu vas* (indefinite reference)	Laberge (1983); Montreal Ashby (1992); Tours
subject-doubling	*mon père il a une voiture de service*	*mon père a une voiture de service*	Nadsadi (1995); Ontario
complementiser *que*	*je pensais que c'était bien*	*je pensais c'était bien*	Cedergren and Sankoff (1974); Montreal

the grammatical variables tabulated above appear to have been undertaken on *oïl* French; the rather few studies available have concerned the Canadian varieties. The issues of relevance to the present discussion are on the hand, the relation between patterns of variation in grammar in Canadian and *oïl* French; and on the other, the relation between patterns of grammatical variability and incipient or ongoing change. We now discuss these in turn.

4.6.1 Grammatical variation in Canadian French

Studies of variable grammar in Canadian French have yielded diverse results. Given the focus of the present study, our intention here is not to present an exhaustive account of grammatical variation in Quebec French, but rather to consider two contrasting results in the light of the present discussion. Thus in the first instance, Sankoff and Thibault's (1980) study of variation between *être* and *avoir* in Montreal showed quite sharply polarised patterns of variation between groups of speakers who had high and low rates of use of the non-standard auxiliary. Their results also showed an interesting implicational pattern whereby one speaker group, ranked low in terms of social class or 'Linguistic Market Index' had some use of auxiliary *avoir* with common main verbs such as *aller*, where the standard past form is unambiguously *je suis allé* 'I went' (non-standard *j'ai allé*). Relative to other groups, this speaker group had high use of auxiliary *avoir* with all other relevant verbs, including very high use of *avoir* with those where in Montreal French there is optionality regarding the use of auxiliary *être* or *avoir*, such as *rester* 'to stay'. Conversely, speakers who had high use of optional *être* with verbs in the *rester* sub-set showed near-zero use of auxiliary *avoir* overall. Sankoff and Thibault (1980: 343) suggested that this pattern showed a 'tendency toward the regularization of the auxiliary system in French', arguing that the aspectual reference conveyed by the set of verbs that prescriptively have auxiliary *être* is not sufficiently uniform to resist the tendency.

Other variables that have been studied in Canadian French have shown less sharply differentiated results. Thus Emirkanian and Sankoff (1985) presented results that suggest a very advanced state of recession in Montreal French of the synthetic future tense: young speakers had 5.3% use, an intermediate age-group 9.9% and older speakers 13.5%. This result, as well as that discussed above concerning variation between *être* and *avoir*, suggest of course a relation between variation and change endorsed by the sociolinguistic literature: while sharp differentiation patterns may be indicative of a more or less rapid change in progress, more gradient patterns suggest near-complete change or stability.

Clearly, the question whether patterns of grammatical variation in Canadian French indicate change in progress or relative stability, bears an indirect relation to the central theme of the present study. This is because many quite advanced processes of variation and change appear in these French varieties to be incipient or even absent in the *oïl* variety. This seems to be true of complementiser deletion: although Gadet (1998: 21) reports the phenomenon in the speech of marginalised immigrant groups, it is not clear whether it is present in the variety of French of interest here. The relevance of the Canadian French findings on the sociolinguistic salience of grammatical variables other than those discussed in the preceding sections is therefore limited, as suggested above, to the information it provides on the relation between patterns of present variation in grammar and possible or likely change in progress. We now discuss this issue as it concerns *oïl* French.

4.6.2   Relation between variation and change: The example of *ne*

To what extent do patterns of variation indicate change in progress? The essential problem was aptly expressed by Weinreich, Labov and Herzog

(1968:188) in the following terms: 'Not all variability and heterogeneity in language structure involves change; but all change involves variability and heterogeneity'. To this formulation we may add that not all sharp patterns of variability in phonology and grammar may indicate change; instead, they may indicate the co-existence of sharply normative speaker judgments alongside relative linguistic stability. The question is central to our present enterprise, clearly, and is perhaps most easily approached retrospectively and using the recent example of a relatively simplex grammatical variable, French *ne*. In the following broad discussion, which concerns the relation between patterns of socio-stylistic variation on the one hand, and on the other with the twin issues of linguistic change and evaluative judgments of the variables in question, we take no account of the rather complex array of linguistic, pragmatic and discourse-analytic constraints which bear upon the realisation of these variables, and which of course may promote change in certain linguistic contexts while disfavouring it in others. The variable discussed below is of the type that can, for the purposes of the present (linguistically) broad discussion, be presented as being unitary. This is in contrast to other variables, such as English (be), that cannot be so described on account of the complex way in which variation operates across the different paradigms of the verb (cf. Tagliamonte 1998:153). In a subsequent section we consider constraints of the types listed above in connexion with stylistic variation in French *ne*.

To the extent that evidence is available of change in French in the areas of grammatical variation discussed in this chapter, recent diachronic evidence (Smith 2000) shows a rather gradual recession over some 35 years in the use of *ne* in two corpora of formal *oïl* French radio speech. Smith reported an overall ne-retention rate of 92.6% in a corpus recorded in 1960–1 (Ågren 1973), against 72.5% in a corpus recorded by Smith in 1995–6. We discuss in some detail below, in connexion with liaison (Chapter 5), the question of the extent of comparability between public and everyday speech, i.e. whether the decline of a linguistic feature found in the highly formal speech of highly educated speakers reflects a parallel decline in the wider speech community. Briefly however, it seems likely that radio speech tracks wider linguistic change rather than leading it, and that Smith's results represent, albeit at higher levels of realisation of the standard variant, a change in progress in the declining use of *ne*. Regarding the relation between this rate of change and the patterns of variation reported by Coveney and discussed above, we may point out that this relatively gradual decline in the retention of *ne* took place over a 35-year interval that has seen a period of considerable social upheaval in France; in this context the 'events' of May 1968 represented of course a sharp demarcation point, at least symbolically. The consequence has been, on the one hand a marked relaxation of social relations between the various social groups: young/old, MC/WC, male/female; and on the other the progressive ascendancy of youth culture, as against the perceived 'gerontocracy' who had directed France hitherto. Again, we develop this point more fully in relation to liaison below, but against this social background the decline in retention of *ne* reported by Smith seems gradual rather than abrupt, and we may suggest that the non-polarised patterns of *ne* deletion discussed in Section 1 above reflect, albeit of course indirectly, the relative stability of *ne*.

More direct results on the decline of *ne* have been reported by Ashby (2001), who compared deletion rates in his Tours corpus (recorded in 1976; first reported in Ashby 1981b) with rates analysed in a second corpus that he recorded in 1995.

Table 9. Variable *ne* retention: Ashby's 1976 and 1995 results (adapted from Ashby 2001)

Speaker group	Retention of *ne* (%)	
	1976	1995
14–22 years	19	14
51–64 years	52	25
Female	30	17
Male	42	20
Working class	15	9
Intermediate	47	17
Upper class	45	26
All groups	37	18

What the results in Table 9 seem to show is a fairly sharp convergence of the hitherto 'conservative' speaker groups (older, intermediate- and upper-class, female) towards more vernacular usage, while the guardians of the vernacular (young and working-class) show rather little change over this twenty-year period; this is especially true of the 14–22-year-old group. If one compares these retention rates with those reported by Coveney (1996) (record-ed in 1980) and shown above in Table 2, it is apparent that Ashby's 1976 data is rather formal compared to Coveney's, as it seems very unlikely that any regional variation is in question. The overall decline between the two Tours corpora, from 37% retention to 18%, is fairly large if expressed as a percentage of the 1976 figure, i.e. $(37-18) \div 37 = 51\%$. On the other hand the decline is from a rather low base, so that this method of calculating the shift can be argued to result in an inflated figure.

As organised above, the 1976 patterns of variation give no clear indication that a decline is imminent in the retention of *ne* among the speaker groups who show high retention rates. The 'raw' decline of 19% is incidentally very close to that reported by Smith (2000) for radio speech of 20% between 1960–1 and 1995–6; and Ashby's 1995 overall deletion rate of 18% is very close to that reported by Coveney (17%). In contrast to the gradual patterns of *ne* deletion shown in Table 9, an alternative presentation of some of the 1976 results gives a series of patterns that are quite dramatically different, as Table 10 shows.

Table 10. Variable *ne* retention in Tours: some of Ashby's 1967–8 results (adapted from Ashby 1981: 683–5)

Speaker group		Retention of *ne* (%)	
Social class	Sex	14–22 years	51–64 years
Working	M	9.7	39.6
	F	5.9	10.3
Intermediate	M	23.4	63.2
	F	14.7	67.8
Upper	M	38.4	70.3
	F	12.9	74.3

The results in Table 10 show very sharp patterns of age-related differentiation for all female speaker groups except the working-class; in contrast, all male groups show less sharp degrees of age polarisation. On the basis of these findings, Ashby (1981b, 1991) argued that a generational change was in progress in the retention of *ne*, an argument disputed by Coveney (1991). Ashby's subsequent real-time comparison, shown in Table 9, appears to have endorsed his earlier judgment; however, what is at issue here is rather the fact that the polarised results shown in Table 10 should have prompted a discussion of their significance in terms of the relation between present variation and possible change on the one hand, and age-graded stability on the other. The discussion was raised by the very sharp polarisation between use of *ne* between the younger and older age groups in all three social-classes sampled, with the exception of WC females. The steepest ratios in these patterns of polarisation are in the region of 6:1, while none are much lower than 2:1. It seems reasonable to characterise these degrees of differentiation as sharp or polarised, although a measure of consensus between researchers' intuitions seems ultimately the only guarantor of a judgment of this kind. Sankoff (1988:148–50), characterising the variationist paradigm as a 'descriptive-interpretive' one, describes one of the central procedures associated with the variationist study of grammatical variation as follows: 'the identification of function [of syntactic variables] has an unmistakably hermeneutic, or interpretive, component which is antithetical to positivist criteria'. This remark may also be made of any procedure in variationist sociolinguistics, whether applied to phonology or grammar, beyond the quantification of variants and the statistical testing of the resulting quantities.

This foregoing discussion is of course in contrast to the situation of polarised grammatical variation in English, which is not generally seen in these terms. We shall however discuss this issue in 4.8 below, in the light of recent argumentation.

Ashby (1992) also analysed variation in the use with indefinite reference of *on ~ vous* in his 1976 Tours corpus. The pronouns *nous, on* and *vous/tu* are involved in a process of variation and change whereby *nous* with definite 4th-person reference has largely been replaced by *on*. At the same time, *on* with indefinite reference ('they', 'you' or 'people' in English) varies with *vous* and *tu*, depending of course on the formality and intimacy of the speech situation. Ashby's results regarding *on ~ vous* were similar to those discussed in Sections 4.2 and 4.4 above in showing relatively non-sharp patterns of variation: the sharpest difference was between 38% use (46/122) by older males of *on* (the standard variant), against 83% use (121/145) by younger females. Ashby himself stated (1992:154–5) that his 'distributions suggest that the variation between *on* and *vous* is a stable sociolinguistic 'marker' [*sic*] in the sense [of] a linguistic feature subtly signalling a social distinction, rather than an ongoing change'. The term 'indicator' rather than 'marker' seems more apt here, but clearly the point at issue is the participation, stressed in preceding sections, by all speaker groups in the use of this grammatical variable.

Ashby's results contrast quite strikingly with those reported by Coveney (2000a) on variation between *nous* + 4th-person verb-form and *on* with definite 4th-person reference, illustrated as follows, both translatable as 'when we're asleep':

(21)   quand nous sommes en train de dormir ~ quand (nous) on est en train de dormir

The second variant, expressing 4th-person reference through the use of *on* + 3rd-person verb form with or without a preceding doubled 4th-person pronoun, is overwhelmingly more frequent than the first in everyday spoken French. Indeed, using results taken from the Picardy corpus referred to previously, Coveney found that only eight out of 30 speakers in his corpus whose speech he analysed used *nous* + 4th-person verb form at all. This provides a sharp contrast with *ne*, used at least once by 29/30 of the speakers sampled in the same corpus. Clearly the replacement by *on* of *nous* is in *oïl* French largely complete if Coveney's results are representative; in contrast to the variation between indefinite *on* and *vous* reported by Ashby, which appears to show a still continuing process of change. On the basis of his findings on *nous*, Coveney suggested that *nous* may now be a hyperstyle variable. The evidence for this suggestion is rather indirect, since there are available no fully comparable interspeaker and intraspeaker figures from the same corpus that show *nous* used in formal as well as informal style. An interspeaker calculation might for instance compare the results of Boutet (1994), who reported zero use of *nous* + 4th-person verb in a corpus drawn from interviews with factory workers, with use of *nous* by the WC speakers in Coveney's corpus. Hyperstyle variation would then imply more style variation than the presumably rather small social-class difference between Boutet's and Coveney's results, but no cross-stylistic figures are available to make possible a robust claim concerning the possible hyperstyle value of *nous*.

However this may be, if we assume, as seems plausible, that *nous* does indeed show hyperstyle variation then this French variable seems to be of the 'vestigial' type alluded to in Section 4.2 above, that is the type of variable that is in the process of leaving a speech community and which, on account of its restricted level of use, shows little interspeaker variation. Trudgill (1999a) draws attention to the problems associated with quantifying interspeaker differentiation in embryonic and vestigial variables; in both cases tokens may be insufficient to confirm impressionistic judgments of the incipient value (in the case of embryonic variables) of the perceivedly incoming variant. A corresponding problem attends the quantification of vestigial variables; as stated above, Coveney's Picardy corpus is by no means small, but a much more extended quantification would be required to confirm reliably whether the type of outgoing variable that *nous* + 4th-person verb form appears to be, does indeed show restricted interspeaker differentiation combined with considerable style shift. We leave until Section 4.9 below a fuller discussion of this issue as it concerns intraspeaker variation.

4.6.3 Non-polarised grammatical variation in English

The corresponding English situation, i.e. that regarding grammatical variables not subject to sharp patterns of variation, is rather unclear. The example of the deletion of the English complementiser 'that', shows there does exist at least one area of English variable syntax that is not subject to stigmatisation. Examples of the 'that' variable are as follows:

(22)   the woman [that] I saw yesterday

(23)   he said [that] he would

Several researchers have quantified variation between standard 'that' and non-standard zero realisation of this variable; the study that is most directly relevant to the present discussion is that of Kroch and Small (1978), whose results were drawn from a corpus of speech recorded from a phone-in programme broad-cast from Philadelphia, USA. This study appears to be the only one that can be called variationist, in the standard sense of comparing the language of two socially differentiated speaker groups in a spoken mode; most studies of the (that) variable have compared realisation rates across contrasting written styles. The study of Kroch and Small compared the speech of callers with that of the 'hosts' or respondents in the radio studio, and found a mean that-realisation rate of 43.3% across the studio respondents, compared with 29.8% for the callers. We may call this is a sociolinguistic result, since one can plausibly assume that the studio respondents would be MC speakers, bearing in mind the fact that respondents of this kind are generally regarded as professional special-ists upon whose expertise callers wish to draw (cf. Behnstedt's results on interrogatives, discussed above). If we regard this is as essentially a WC–MC result, it is plain that the differentiation pattern contrasts quite sharply with that shown in Table 2 above (3rd-person verbs without -s in US and UK English). This result also goes against Kroch and Small's explanation (1978: 48) of the greater use of 'that' by MC speakers: 'the standard language [...] favours the most direct correspondence between propositional form and surface syntax', presumably because presence of 'that' marks explicitly the relation between the matrix verb and following complement. This argument from logic is of course reminiscent of those discussed in Section 4.3 above, particularly regarding multiple negation. Nevertheless the argument seems incongruous if one bears in mind the low sociolinguistic value of variation in (that); it appears that linguistic explanations of the social value of grammatical variables in English are doomed to fall wide of the mark. However this may be, Kroch and Small's findings confirm one's intuitions concerning the limited sociolinguistic value of (that); indeed, this variable recalls those that may be more usefully thought of as being used productively in formal speech rather than deleted in informal. This especially true of (that) realised as a *wh-* complementiser or relative pronoun, as in: 'the woman whom I saw' or 'the house which is on the corner'. As stated above, French *nous* and *ne* appear also to be variables of this type; it would likewise be interesting to have available intraspeaker data on (that), so as to establish whether the variable has hyperstyle value.

Regarding the relation between variation and change in (that), Smith (2000) compared realisation rates between the radio speech section of the London-Lund corpus of English (1959–61) and his own corpus of radio speech, recorded in 1998 and drawn from a relatively formal BBC radio political discussion programme called 'Any Questions?'. Smith found a rate overall (i.e. for all syntactic contexts aggregated) of 44.2% realisation in his 1998 corpus, against 59.3% in the London-Lund corpus. We again note an association between a non-polarised grammatical variable and a slow rate of change. These two results may be argued to present difficulties of direct comparability, given that Kroch and Small's findings are from US English while Smith's are from the UK. Against this we can point to the results shown in Table 2 above, on 3rd-person verbs without -*s*, and again mention the high degree of non-localisation that English grammatical variability shows. It may be therefore that this comparison of Kroch and Small's results and those of Smith gives a reasonably reliable indication of the relation between variation and change for this variable.

4.6.4   Beyond the variationist method

In addition to those listed above in Table 8, there are of course a number of grammatical variables in French that appear not to have been the object of variationist analysis, and that may well differentiate speaker groups in the polarised way seen in English. Some are these are listed below, with the standard variant first:

1. use of the indicative where the subjunctive is required standardly:

e.g. il faut que j'aille au marché ~ il faut que je vais au marché 'I must go to the market'

2. use of stranded constructions where fronting is standard:

e.g. les assiettes sur lesquelles il y avait des crasses ~ les assiettes qu'il y avait des crasses dessus 'the plates that had dirt on them'

3. non-standard subject-verb concord where subject and verb are separated in a cleft sentence:

e.g. c'est moi qui suis le plus fort ~ c'est moi qu'est le plus fort 'I'm the strongest'

4. use of the conditional tense in conditional clauses where the imperfect is standard:

si ça m'avait intéressé ~ si ça m'aurait intéressé 'if that had interested me'

We are in the regrettable position of not knowing the frequency of these grammatical variants relative to others such as negation and interrogation, for lack of any quantification yet performed. If we assume that the variants listed above are rather rare, and hence difficult to quantify in a corpus of manageable size, a perhaps more fruitful method of measuring variation in grammar would be that developed by Biber (1988, 1995) which seeks to exploit what the author refers to as a Multi-dimensional (MD) framework of analysis. The dimension relevant here is the concentration on a large number of linguistic features that vary across text types. For English in his 1995 study, Biber included 16 grammatical and functional categories, ranging from tense and aspect markers through subordination features to negation, comprising a total of 67 features. Similar numbers are analysed for the other languages examined. Thus the MD method studies linguistic features in bundles, to overcome the problems of comparability raised by the structural differences between the very different languages studied. Clearly a cross-linguistic analysis is not pertinent in relation to the present discussion; but Biber's essentially asocial approach to register variation (rather than intraspeaker variation, since written texts are also included) could perhaps be adopted, at least so far as methodology is concerned, as complementary to the variationist sociolinguistic perspective. An MD analysis proceeds by looking first at a dimension along which a set of texts varies; for example, the 'involved' dimension as opposed to the narrowly informational. A basic postulate is that linguistic features co-occur in a text in bundles, because they share involvement in the linguistic expression of a speaker or writer along a stylistic or register dimension. Thus an informational text will be highly nominal and will feature longer words as well as a high token/type ratio, indicating a widely varied vocabulary.

An adaptation that relied on a simple count of raw numbers of non-standard grammatical variants having a similar dimensional function as they co-occur in a text, would clearly go some way to remedying the low token numbers that preclude a robust quantification of grammatical variation. Coveney (2000a) refers to what he calls 'co-varying features' as those which 'tend to occur in the same utterance as the variant in question, but which cannot reasonably be supposed to exert an influence on the choice of that variant'. Thus Coveney found several examples of *nous* + 4th-person verb co-occurring with *ne*, and cited Laberge's (1977: 135) finding that *nous* co-occurred both with *ne* and with formal lexical alternants such as *habiter* and *demeurer*, where the everyday equivalent is *rester*; all of these verbs are translatable as 'to live' or 'to reside'. It is clear from this that a quasi-MD approach draws upon items from the different levels of linguistic analysis: from morpho-syntactic items, and from lexical items that are full as well functional. In addition, this approach adopts a simple counting procedure that focuses on one set of variants only. This is more or less the approach employed to quantify variable lexis in the Dieuze corpus; we describe and discuss the results and methodology below in Chapter 6. In the mean time, we may remark, firstly that a similar method adapted to variable grammar remains to be applied to French; and secondly that the MD approach, at least adopted in this rather crude way, will mask differences between the socio-stylistic value of variants in the absence of a more narrowly focused approach designed to group together variants having formal and/or functional properties in common.

4.7 Summary

In the preceding sub-sections we have discussed patterns of interspeaker grammatical variation in French and English, in terms of their probabilistic distribution across a wider or narrower range of social groups, outlining the various factors that may be responsible for the apparently rather highly contrasting patterns seen in French and English. We start from the straightforward observation that some French grammatical variables are subject to less unfavourable evaluative judgments than certain English variables. This inference refers to the relation between the behavioural and evaluative axes of language variation: we again cite Eckert (1989:248): 'Labov's original (1966) findings in New York City clearly lined up socioeconomic class, style, sound change, prestige, and evaluation on a single axis.' Non-standard variants that are not subject to a high degree of unfavourable evaluation will not show sharp differentiation patterns, most notably along the dimensions of social class and style. The sound change (or grammatical change) dimension is related in that a change which is in the process of spreading through a speech community is often the object of unfavourable evaluation, often simply because it disturbs the conservative orientation of many speaker groups, and thus will shift from 'indicator' to 'marker' status. From this viewpoint we can speculate that indicators are variables that are potential markers. As suggested previously, it may be that whenever the differential use of a variable reaches the point of distinguishing two or more social groups sufficiently sharply, the groups will come to be aware of the difference. Their awareness will then be reflected in their socio-stylistic behaviour.

These considerations relate to the patterns of grammatical variability in that the lack of sociolinguistic salience shown by variables such as English (that) and some French interrogative structures may be explicable in part by reference to their relative diachronic stability, although it must be said that diachronic evidence on recent changes in French interrogatives is not clear from a comparison of Behnstedt's and Coveney's results (shown in Tables 5 and 6). The corresponding case is provided by Ashby's results on *ne* deletion shown above in Table 10, which appear to show a consistent mapping between patterns of variation and the way in which they indicate future change. We can only accept the corollary of this, namely that English grammatical variables showing sharp variation patterns are in process of relatively rapid change, by leaving aside the other factors that induce speakers to form the negative evaluations responsible for patterns of the type shown above in Table 3 concerning English 3rd-person verb forms without -*s*. These evaluations appear to be prompted by an acceptance on the part of MC English speakers of the normative view concerning the ready corrigibility of low-level grammar (cf. Matthews 1981:7, cited in 4.3 above).

We return to our original proposition, nuanced as follows: (some) variable grammar in French is distributed socially in a way that seems not to correspond to (much) variable grammar in English. The significance of this is as stated above: the considerable stigmatisation that grammatical variation attracts in English appears to show that the standardisation process has been applied successfully to the grammar of that language in way that it has not, or not wholly, in French. This is most emphatically not for any lack of standardising initiatives in France. In the following section we will need to qualify this proposition to fit the two French grammatical variables examined in this chapter from the viewpoint of intraspeaker variation. Specifically, Table 2 above, showing variable ne-retention rates, shows little dramatic difference between speaker groups; the table also shows rather low rates of ne retention generally. We now consider how this pattern relates to the intraspeaker dimension of variation.

4.8 Intraspeaker variation in grammar

Subsidiary to the issue of interspeaker variation in grammar discussed in preceding sections, is the question of the relationship between it and intraspeaker variation. We call this issue subsidiary, by no means because it is less important or interesting, but because the dearth of results showing patterns of intraspeaker variation in grammar precludes the formulation of more than tentative conclusions, to an even greater extent than is true of those sketched in the preceding section.

The few results available in French (e.g. Behnstedt 1973; discussed in relation to Table 5 above) suggest that some variable grammatical items may correspond in their sociolinguistic function to English variable pronunciation, since the 'core' results shown in Table 5 have the non-polarised patterns characteristic of much variation in the English sound system. This is true along the intraspeaker as well as the interspeaker dimension. The rather scarce findings reported in English often reveal sharp patterns of style variation in grammar, reflecting perhaps the higher degree of consciousness that certain intermediate speaker groups possess of the socio-stylistic value of grammatical variants. Table 11 below provides an instance of this pattern.

This table shows the information given in Table 3 above concerning treatment of 3rd-person verb forms in Norwich only; however, Table 11 expresses the information through use of the standard verb form. The additional dimension of information here concerns intraspeaker variation. The most striking result in this display is that shown by the UWC and LMC speakers; the former in particular have a quite dramatic shift between the formal and informal styles, while the LMC group show a degree of style shift that is lower than the UWC speakers, but is still substantially higher than that of any other group. In a sense

Table 11. Percentage of 3rd-person verbs with -s in Norwich, by social class and speech style (adapted from Trudgill 1997: 105)

Social class	% -s	
	Informal	Formal
UMC	100	100
LMC	71	95
UWC	25	62
MWC	20	28
LWC	3	13

this is classic finding, in showing higher degrees of variation in the speech of intermediate social groups. What is of particular interest here is obviously the interpretation of these results; explanations are customarily formulated in terms of the linguistic insecurity of intermediate social groups; or of the fact that they have a wider social range of interactants than speakers above or below them in the social-class hierarchy. This latter factor is connected to the weaker, more loosely-knit social networks within which intermediate social groups are commonly reported as interacting; linguistic change is held to proceed through these weaker network ties, while strong ties are associated with the maintenance of linguistic norms, whether vernacular or overtly prestigious (cf. Milroy and Milroy 1985, 1992). The results shown in Table 11 relate to Trudgill's Norwich survey conducted in the late 1960s, reported in Trudgill (1974). Reporting on the results of a subsequent study he had conducted of linguistic changes that had come about in Norwich in the intervening period, Trudgill (1988) makes no mention of change in present-tense 3rd-person verb forms. Furthermore, although Trudgill does not discuss these results from the viewpoint of variation and change, the fact that he saw fit to reproduce them in a recent paper (1997) and without any caveat as to their current validity, suggests a perception on his part that no substantial change has taken place in the intervening period.

We discussed above in Section 4.6.2 the relation between variation and change in grammar, and we may note here the suggestion of Ashby (1991:9) that change in grammar tends to be slow relative to phonology. It appears more plausible therefore that the large degrees of LMC and UWC style shift in Table 11 are due to speakers' evaluative attitudes towards a stable socio-linguistic variable. With regard to the relation between variation and change in grammar, Cheshire (1997:5) has suggested recently that morpho-syntactic variation in English is distributed in cognitively prominent sentence types such as interrogatives and negatives, which have 'a more direct connection to the context of face-to-face interaction than others' by virtue of their involving the hearer more closely than less prominent structures; Cheshire argues that these latter are more susceptible to penetration by standard grammatical forms. Grammatical variation in English may therefore be more tightly constrained in its situational and social variation than phonological variation, by reason of its localisation in prominent, high-involvement speech acts. If true, this suggests a more complex relation between the intraspeaker and interspeaker dimensions where grammatical variation is concerned. As suggested above in 4.3, grammatical variation in English may serve to signal aspects of a speaker's social identity in a way that is a different from most variable pronunciation features; this greater salience may be due to the lesser frequency of grammatical variables.

In addition to the localisation of non-standard grammatical variants in some syntactic contexts rather than others, Cheshire (1997:6) mentions the 'serial effect' that tends to produce a string of standard or non-standard variants in a particular stretch of discourse. This notion is allied to that of co-occurrence discussed previously. Grammatical variation may also be tied more closely than variation on other linguistic levels to the different types of discourse that are associated with formal and informal speech styles, in the sense that a more involved type of discourse will make use of syntactic structures and sentence types that will in turn favour certain non-standard grammatical variants. This is in line with Cheshire's suggestion that non-standard grammatical variants are maintained in more prominent sentence types such as negatives, which may be found in more intimate styles of discourse if one assumes that disagreement is more readily tolerated between intimates. It is unclear whether interrogatives, the other sentence type mentioned by Cheshire, are more frequent in informal styles; Milroy (1987b:42) notes that '*direct* questions — that is, requests for information which are syntactically realized as interrogatives — are rather uncommon in everyday interactions between peers', (emphasis in original). Certainly it is intuitively clear, as discussed at length by Milroy (1987b:41–51), that interrogatives can be perceived as threatening in formal situations, in part no doubt because of the use of direct questions as a means of control in classrooms and other institutional settings. The corollary to this might be the greater acceptability of direct questions in informal speech events. We explore further the relation between variable grammar and discourse in the following sections in connexion with deletion of *ne* in French; as well as in Chapter 6 as it concerns variation in lexis. We have already noted in the previous chapter the influence of discourse structure upon articulation rates.

4.9 Intraspeaker variation in *ne*

Evidence of intraspeaker variation in French is largely anecdotal. The type of variation that can be called 'micro-style' variation; i.e. intraspeaker variation within what a researcher may for convenience have designated a single speech style, has been reported by several scholars: clearly, no speech event is uniform in this respect, and Ashby (1981a) has commented on this aspect of stylistic variation, albeit only anecdotally. Ashby compared realisation rates of variable French liaison in the first and second halves of the interviews he conducted, finding slightly lower rates in the second half, when informants were no doubt more relaxed, and felt less need to employ a formal speech style.

As mentioned above, Coveney (2000a) suggested that *nous*+4th-person verb form may now be a hyperstyle variable. Coveney (1996:88–9) suggested further that hyperstyle grammatical variation in French may characterise the behaviour of *ne*; he reported a massive style shift in his corpus by a 35-year-old intermediate-class male informant, the director of one of the holiday camps where the data was being recorded. This informant was interviewed by Coveney on two occasions clearly distinguished by their formality, the subject-matter discussed, and indeed separated in time: on the first occasion, recorded in his office, the informant was explaining the way in which the camp was organised; the following morning, when the second part of the interview was recorded, the informant and fieldworker were strolling in the grounds of the camp and chatting less formally. Between a 50% ne-retention rate in the first part of the interview and 11.4% in the second, the shift is quite sharp, and exceeds the largest degree of interspeaker variation apparent in Coveney's results, shown in Table 1 above (20.4%, between the oldest and youngest speaker groups). Coveney suggests (1996:89–90) that 'although we clearly need more information about the social and stylistic differentiation of *ne* in various communities, it seems possible that it is [...] a "hyper-style" variable'. Coveney (ibid.) goes on to draw a parallel between hyperstyle variation in French and that reported in Tehrani Persian by Jahangiri and Hudson (1982), and noted by Bell (1984) as the only reliable example he found in his comprehensive survey of the sociolinguistic literature. Ashby (1981b) also reported large degrees of style shift in *ne* by three speakers in his Tours corpus between formal and informal speech styles. Coveney (ibid.) proposes a comparison in the following terms, which we have discussed in the previous chapter in connexion with the influence upon French speakers' sociolinguistic behaviour of the spelling:

> Contemporary France and Iran might be thought to have little in common, but perhaps one significant sociolinguistic similarity helps to account for the fact that hyper-style variables are found in both societies: formal styles, which reflect the conservative written language, seem to involve, in certain respects at least, a quite different type of linguistic behaviour than informal styles in both French and Persian. Bell reports that Persian variables are losing their inter-speaker variation (1984: 156). As the loss of the French negative particle nears completion, we might expect that the same process would take place [...].

Evidence supporting this proposition of Coveney's regarding the impending loss of interspeaker variation in the use of *ne*, and its corresponding acquisition of hyperstyle value, is provided by the fact that the use of *ne* now appears to be 'no longer part of the vernacular linguistic system which is transmitted from generation to generation by the normal processes of acquisition' (Coveney 1996: 90). Evidence in support of this is provided by the fact that pre-school French children show near-zero use of *ne*, acquiring the negative particle only when they start attending school and come increasingly into contact with written French. Below we present some results deriving from a quantitative study of intraspeaker variation in *ne*, with the aim of throwing new light on the issue of the hyperstyle value of the negative particle.

4.9.1   Variation in *ne* in the Dieuze corpus: Identification difficulties

Results concerning the variable treatment of ne are presented below in Table 12. Before discussing results, we examine briefly the issue of tokens excluded because of invariance and other factors.

It is worth remarking firstly, in the context of the light that methodological issues can throw upon changes proceeding in colloquial French, that the figures in the 'N' columns in Table 12 below refer, not to all tokens of omissible *ne*, but to those which were capable of being unambiguously identified as occurring at loci of variation. One principal context which presents identification difficulties is that where *ne* potentially follows a lexical item having a terminal /n/ and precedes a vowel-initial word. This is of course because *ne* reduces to /n/ prescriptively before a vowel, as in:

(24)   on (n') a pas de responsabilités
     'you have no responsibilities'

At the same time liaison is near-invariable in *on*, so that the /n/ is almost always pronounced. Coveney (1996: 66) remarks that 'it does not seem possible systematically to distinguish a liaison [n] and an [n] representing ne'. The preceding example (from the Dieuze corpus) reduced, so far as it is possible to determine without recourse to instruments, to the following form: *on a pas de responsabilités*. However, following the practice of Coveney, who himself followed that of Sankoff and Vincent (1980) and Ashby (1976), tokens were excluded in this context in view of the difficulty of determining with certainty the presence of *ne* in the absence of the availability of instrumental analysis. As Coveney remarks, speakers may occasionally signal the presence of *ne* in these contexts in a relatively easily perceptible way, perhaps most often through a lengthened /n/, but no such instances were noted in the Dieuze corpus. Two further ambiguous instances are as follows:

(25)   jamais on (n') irait taper sur quelqu'un
       'we'd never go and hit anyone'

(26)   on (n') est pas dans un lycée technique
       'we're not in a technical school'

It was the author's impression that a lengthened /n/ was present in these utterances, both of which occurred in interview style, but the tokens were nevertheless excluded in the absence, as noted above, of a reliable means of identification. A similar difficulty of identification occurs after other /n/-final negative items such as *rien, aucun* and *personne*, as well of course as any /n/-final word preceding *ne*+vowel-initial word. This problem is worthy of mention because of its sociolinguistic interest; as a result of the pronoun's frequency, preceding *on* is by far the commonest locus in the Dieuze corpus that presents this identification difficulty. This of course reflects the virtual absence, discussed above in connexion with Coveney's results (2000a), of the expression of 4th-person reference through the use of *nous*+4th-person verb form in everyday spoken French. These excluded tokens represent some 8% (214 tokens) of the total analysed.

We may mention further that several tokens were excluded because, again in the absence of instruments, it proved impossible to distinguish between /l/ and /n/ in sequences such as (from the Dieuze data):

(27)   mon père i(l) (n') a pas voulu qu je l fasse 'my father didn't want me to do
       it'

The proximity of the place of articulation of /l/ and /n/ accounts perhaps for this identification difficulty. The presence of background noise was also a factor in these cases.

4.9.2   Other excluded tokens

Aside from identification problems, the further issue influencing the decision to exclude loci is that of invariance. Pre-formed sequences such as *n'importe* and *ne serait-ce*, where the speaker clearly has no choice regarding the use of *ne*, were rare in the corpus; the issue of invariance presented itself rather in connexion with invariable absence. Clear examples are those such as *ça va pas!* or *ça va pas, non?*, perhaps suitably translated into English as 'Forget it!', 'No way!' or 'You're joking!'. These sequences appear to offer speakers no choice over the presence or absence of *ne*, and were therefore excluded. More numerous examples concern reflexes of *je sais pas* 'I don't know', which reduce to [ʃepa] or [ʃɛpa] or even [ʃːpa]. These forms were used by several speakers, without literal force, for various pragmatic purposes: to mitigate, and sometimes as a particle expressing indifference, with the pragmatic force of *peut-être*, as in:

(28)   tu peux me l donner demain [ʃɛpa] moi
       'you can give me it tomorrow maybe'

Given the relative ease of identifying in context the difference between tokens of [ʃɛpa] used as a negative response to a direct question and those used epistemically, these latter were excluded from the quantification given below. It seems defensible to exclude these for the further reason that their use appears is idiolectal rather than sociolinguistic, some speakers using them considerably more than others. It should be borne in mind however that their exclusion contributes in some measure to the quite considerable variation in tokens numbers between individual speakers, an issue we discuss in detail below.

It may be pointed out finally in this connexion that several speakers tended to alternate between a radically reduced form of *je ne sais pas* such as [ʃɛpa] in conversation style, and the fuller reflex *je sais pas* [ʒə sɛ pa] in interview, thereby displaying style shift between the forms that appeared to be more readily available to them than the seemingly now highly formal *je ne sais pas*.

A further potentially categorical locus concerns the sequence *pas mal*, literally of course 'not bad' but now perhaps lexicalised to the equivalent of *bien* or *beaucoup* for some speakers. Following Coveney (1996:69), instances of *pas mal* were included as potential loci for use of *ne* where the literal force was clearly translatable as 'not bad', as in *il est pas mal* 'he's / it's not bad', rather than as equivalent to *beaucoup*, as in *on avait pas mal discuté* 'we talked a lot'. Elliptical sequences with no verb (*pas mal*) were of course excluded, as containing no locus for variation.

We turn now to a discussion of the results for *ne* in the Dieuze corpus.

4.9.3 Patterns of variation in *ne* in the Dieuze corpus: Linguistic factors

Table 12 below shows percentages of *ne* retention in a sample of sixteen Dieuze informants. Most immediately observable here are the near-zero levels of retention for all speaker groups, broadly irrespective of speech style. Nevertheless, rather modest degrees of style shift in the expected direction by the female groups stand in fairly sharp contrast to the treatment of *ne* by both male groups, who show negligible or indeed negative style shift. These results are of course in conformity with many others in the literature that show especially female speakers' linguistic behaviour approximating more closely to the conservative standard in more formal styles. Certainly the fact of the younger males' producing just two tokens of *ne* out of a potential 570 is quite striking. To this extent the results are in line with expectations: nevertheless, where they do occur, degrees of use of *ne* and of style shift are very modest, and this can be explained in various related ways. One explanation refers to the development of communicative competence in the Dieuze speaker sample, who can plausibly be assumed to have had no substantial experience of highly formal, principally public situations of the type that have been reported as triggering very high rates of *ne*: sermons and lectures, for instance (Pohl 1975:21). Another way of explaining these low degrees of style shift is to suggest that the majority of the speakers did not feel that the two speech styles were sufficiently differentiated in formality for high rate of *ne* to be suitable in interview style. Against this it can be pointed out that large degrees of style shift have been found in the corpus for variation in lexis (discussed in Chapter 6) and some phonological contexts, principally those discussed in the previous chapter. The obvious conclusion is that stylistic competence emerges at different rates on the different levels of linguistic analysis; this is endorsed by the near-zero rates of style shift observed in the corpus for variable liaison (discussed in Chapter 5).

Nevertheless several speakers did feel impelled to employ *ne* more frequently in the interview style, and the phenomena of interest underlying these figures are both linguistic and social. It will become apparent that the linguistic – social division is not in fact tenable, but for convenience we retain it here. Turning first to the linguistic factors associated with style shift, several researchers have noted (Coveney 1996; Moreau 1986) that deletion of *ne* when it follows a subject NP, as it overwhelmingly does in the Dieuze corpus, is constrained linguistically by the nature of the NP; broadly, a preceding subject pronoun, either conjunctive or disjunctive, favours deletion, while a more complex lexical NP subject promotes realisation of *ne*. Thus of the 46 instances

Table 12. Observed frequencies (N) and percentages of *ne* retention (%) in the Dieuze speaker sample

Gender / Age	Interview		Conversation	
	%	N	%	N
Males 16–19				
JM	0.9	1/109	1.4	1/72
BR	0.9	1/116	1.4	2/144
BB	0	0/70	0	0/41
ES	5.0	2/40	6.6	3/45
Group average	1.2	4/335	1.9	6/302
Females 16–19				
VN	0	0/60	0	0/126
SH	4.6	3/65	1.2	1/78
EM	4.6	4/86	0.9	1/103
CN	7.7	10/129	1.2	2/164
Group average	5.0	17/340	0.8	4/471
Males 11–12				
CF	3.3	2/60	0	0/97
AR	0	0/29	0	0/112
JB	0	0/45	0	0/55
BW	0	0/50	0	0/122
Group average	1.1	2/184	0	0/386
Females 11–12				
SP	0	0/46	1.3	1/73
SM	0	0/41	0	0/71
NG	3.2	2/62	4.6	3/65
CY	8.3	6/72	1.9	1/53
Group average	3.6	8/221	1.9	5/262
All groups	2.9	31/1080	1.1	15/1421

of *ne* realisation shown in Table 12, 34 were preceded by a 'heavy' subject such as a lexical NP with or without a following relative; a demonstrative such as *celles*; or a disjunctive pronoun such as *eux*. Of the remaining 12 tokens of *ne*, 11 were preceded by a clitic pronoun, and the remaining one was associated with an imperative sentence.

We shall discuss the interrelation of linguistic and social factors by concentrating chiefly on the use of *ne* by one speaker, the older female informant CN. This informant is suitable because she was talkative, and hence produced a copious volume of speech in both styles, with several interesting examples. She also produced style shift in the expected direction. The instances of insertion of *ne* that she produced are also representative of those produced by other members of the speaker sample. Of the ten tokens of *ne* produced by CN in interview style, three followed a clitic, while seven followed a non-pronoun subject: either a lexical NP:

(29) les profs n'ont pas la loi
      'the teachers aren't in control'

(30) les parents ne savent pas
      'the parents don't know'

(31) parce que [l]es sujets ne nous plaisaient pas trop quoi
      'because we didn't like the subjects much'

(32) les cours n'étaient pas comme ici
      'the lessons weren't like here'

demonstrative plus relative:

(33) mais celles qui n'ont pas l permis i [*sic*] doivent s débrouiller toutes seules
      'but the girls who haven't got a driving licence have to manage by themselves'

disjunctive pronoun:

(34) et eux n'acceptent pas les Continentaux
      'and they don't accept the Continentals'

or inverted negative item:

(35) personne ne l'a encore fait
      'nobody's done it yet'

The negative particle was clearly perceptible in (35) as [nə], providing an exception to the type of identification difficulty discussed in 4.9.1 above.

In addition to the seven non-pronoun NP loci that triggered *ne*, only one other associated with *ne* was observed in CN's speech in the interview; this was:

(36)   une prof qui faisait rien
       'a teacher who did nothing'

Clearly there is an association here between a tendency to use lexical or other non-pronoun NPs and the nature of the speech situation; if CN's production is representative, non-pronoun NPs are rare in speech that is not highly formal. They are certainly rare in the two styles recorded in Dieuze. A figure of eight non-pronoun subjects out of 129 potential loci for insertion of *ne* is rather spectacularly low (6.2%), but a comparison with CN's speech in conversation style is even more revealing: out of 164 potential loci, only three (1.8%) can be unambiguously interpreted as potential lexical NPs, and none of these triggered *ne*. These were as follows:

(37)   celui d'avant i marchait pas
       'the one in front wasn't working'

(38)   je faisais celle qui comprenait rien quoi
       'I pretended not to understand'

(39)   je dis: 'Madame, les X marchent pas'
       'I said, Miss, the X-key doesn't work'

Regarding example (37), we can remark again that the syntax is in line with the tendency in French, frequently noted (e.g. Harris 1988:231–2), for clitic pronoun subjects to occur even where there is already an NP subject leftwards in the string. To reiterate, this process is said to have come about as a result of the non-contrastive character of most French present-tense verb paradigms, owing to the fact that five out of the seven verb forms that mark person are homophonous. Harris argues that this homophony has resulted in the cliticisation of the conjunctive personal pronouns, at least in non-formal speech, so as to ensure contrast of person. He states that:

> [...] we may regard French *ils aiment* [izɛm] 'they love' as one polymorphemic word (subject-prefix + stem) in exactly the same way as one regards Latin AMANT, or Old French *aiment*, as one polymorphemic word (stem + subject suffix).'

Against Harris's view, it must be pointed out that an interpretation of *ils aiment* as 'one polymorphemic word' is contradicted by the fact that the sequence can be interrupted, although only by other pronouns and of course *ne*. With regard to use of *ne*, the result of this very frequent retention of the clitic subject pronoun before the verb is perhaps that irrespective of the presence of a preceding NP subject, speakers are overwhelmingly operating with the quasi-fused clitic + verb sequence, and that this is a constraint that greatly disfavours the use of *ne*. It is clear from CN's use in interview style of full NPs without pronoun doubling that this constraint can be overridden where greater degrees of self-monitoring are required, and where the form which is perhaps the default ([NP] + clitic + verb) is felt to be inappropriate. Similarly, (35) above could well in more informal speech have been organised using clitic + verb: *il (n') y a personne qui l'a encore fait,* i.e. as a sequence beginning in principle with a subject clitic, even if in everyday speech the pronoun in *il y a* is rather rarely realised. From a sociolinguistic viewpoint, it appears likely that forms of the NP + clitic + verb type, because of their surface pleonastic structure, are the object of disapproval by teachers and others concerned with exerting normative pressure.

Example (38), *je faisais celle qui comprenait rien quoi*, is quite closely comparable to *celles qui n'ont pas l permis*, the example produced by CN in interview style (33). Although the second utterance has the sequence *qui + ont*, which Coveney (1996:80) reports as a context favouring *ne* retention in his corpus as a result of the juxtaposition of vowels consequent on deletion, the syntax of the two sequences is otherwise similar. We may suggest therefore that these two sequences are sufficiently comparable to illustrate the operation across the two speech styles of audience design in a straightforward sense; the adaptation of an utterance in response to the perceived status of the addressee.

Regarding the factors influencing use of *ne* after a clitic without preceding NP, Coveney (1996:56) has the example of *ne* inserted to repair a miscomprehension, and we may recall the precisely parallel case observed in the Dieuze corpus and discussed previously in relation to articulation rates; this was as follows, again produced by CN:

(40)   CN: je m foule pas
       FW: comment?
       CN: je n me foule pas.

A further example appears to have been influenced by the 'serial effect' that has been reported as tending to produce a string of standard or non-standard variants in a particular stretch of discourse (Cheshire 1997:6):

(41) et eux n'acceptent pas les Continentaux comme i disent / i ne veulent
      que des Corses
      'and they don't accept Continentals as they call them / they only want
      Corsicans'

This is the full form of example (34) given above. It is seems likely here that the
relative proximity of the first locus for *ne* has influenced the second. A further
factor may be the higher probability of *ne* retention associated with *que*;
Coveney (1996:76) reports 34.9% retention before *que*, compared with 16.6%
before *pas*, while Ashby (1981b:678) has 59% compared to 33%, a roughly
similar ratio.

The third instance of *ne* occurring after a clitic is as follows: *et l'année
dernière i n'avaient pas euh* (pause). This instance seems recalcitrant to explanation in terms of the surrounding discourse; we mentioned in 4.9.1 above the
identification difficulty concerning sequences such as *i(l) (n') a pas voulu*,
where some speakers appeared to insert /n/ rather than the /l/ of the pronoun.
CN's utterance was very clear and showed an unambiguous token of *ne*. The
explanation advanced by Coveney (1996:81) may be applicable here; he noted
a higher retention rate (30%) than the average (18.8%) in his Somme corpus in
the sequence *ils avaient*, and suggested that such sequences 'involve a more or
less obligatory liaison if *ne* is omitted, and it may be that speakers feel that this
would highlight the absence of the negative particle, which is still, of course,
considered a non-standard feature'.

In the following sections we examine in more detail the embedding of *ne* in
discourse, from the viewpoint of micro-style variation and audience design.

4.9.4 Issues connected with speaker choice: Token numbers

It will be seen in Table 12 above that numbers of tokens of *ne* per speaker are
somewhat lower than those reported by some other researchers (Coveney
(1996:86) has an average of 105 tokens per speaker), and this is partly due to
the frequency of excluded tokens of epistemic [ʃɛpa] and of *on* + vowel-initial
word sequences, discussed above. The mean number of tokens per speaker in
both styles in Table 12 is $2501 \div 32$ or some 78. It can be seen further that the
value for N varies across speaker groups, individual speakers and styles. This
variation is in line with that observed for the other levels of linguistic analysis
studied in the Dieuze data (phonology and lexis), and is probably caused in part
by the elicitation methods used. Especially younger children (and perhaps above

all younger boys) do not in their spare time stand about chatting sedately, respecting the rules of turn-taking and politeness as observed by adults; the younger boys especially often talked over one another, making comprehension difficult. Several of the younger informants became restless during the peer conferences and ranged around the room, interfered with the recording equipment, or engaged in activities near the equipment that caused a good deal of background noise, thereby making sections of the recordings very indistinct or even inaudible. So in spite of their value in eliciting spontaneous and often very informal data, the peer-conference recordings were no doubt less effective than more sophisticated methods (perhaps most notably a radio microphone) in capturing considerable volumes of clear speech. Informants were also advised to turn off the tape-recorder in the peer conferences when periods of silences intervened. As stated previously, the first ten minutes of the informal recordings were excluded from study, on the assumption that informants would have become less constrained by the presence of the recording equipment after this lapse of time. All of these factors contributed to the reduction of the volume of speech recorded in conversation style; for the analysis of variable phonology, this was not crucially important, but it is evident that the result is rather modest tokens numbers for *ne* for many informants, and especially for the younger groups. Nevertheless it can be seen that the mean number of tokens per speaker in conversation style is appreciably higher than in interview (89 against 68) and this suggests that speakers were more relaxed in the conversations; that is, they experienced the conversations as being less formal speech events.

Turning to the interviews, each lasted between 30 and 45 minutes, and it can be seen that tokens of *ne* analysed for each speaker group vary quite considerably. Although individual responses to the interviewer's questions varied a good deal, one at least of the older females (CN) produced notably more tokens than many other of the older speakers, and to some extent this reflected the older females' style of interaction in interview (and indeed conversation) style, which was in general more cooperative than the other groups'; the older and younger males were often content with informative but brief answers to the interviewer's questions and comments, while some of the younger females appeared to be slightly intimidated by the interview conditions, and hence often responded rather minimally. These differences in discourse style across the speaker groups are pertinent to a consideration of the discourse patterns influencing the rates of *ne* deletion indicated in the figures shown in Table 12; we discuss these patterns in the following section. Firstly however we consider a theoretical issue underlying the relative paucity of tokens of *ne* available in the Dieuze data.

We mentioned in Section 4.1 that *ne* is comparable to omissible phonological variables in its frequency and lack of involvement in propositional meaning. Again, what obviously distinguishes *ne* is its situation in variation at the syntactic level, and through syntax to discourse; a low-level example has already been discussed above, that of [ʃɛpa] used as a discourse particle. This instance raises the question of the level of analysis at which a speaker's choice is operating. Again, a comparison with variable phonology is illuminating. A basic axiom of the variationist approach is that speakers 'locate themselves socially in a multi-dimensional space, as an "act of identity"' (Hudson 1996: 207) through the probabilistic use of phonological variants, among other means. The substantial amount of evidence amassed so far indicates that speakers do this in a regular and predictable way, so that only a relatively restricted number of tokens of any phonological variable needs to be quantified for a reliable analysis to be performed for a given speech style. Milroy (1987b: 134) suggests a target of some 30 tokens per speaker, per variable in the linguistic environment of interest. This figure is arrived at on the basis of '[...] general statistical laws; if the number of tokens is lower than 10, there is a strong likelihood of random fluctuation, while a figure higher than 10 moves towards 90 per cent conformity with the predicted norm, rising to 100 per cent with 35 tokens.' (Milroy, ibid.). This statistical view suggests that sociolinguistic behaviour on the variable phonological level proceeds largely outside a speaker's conscious control, and can thus be compared with other types of quasi-conscious behaviour that are amenable to relatively straightforward quantification and have a distribution in the relevant population that can be modelled statistically.

This proposition appears not to be tenable in regard to variation in *ne*, or at least to a lesser extent. This is because variation in the use of *ne* is closely tied to factors that are influential at the discourse level of analysis, perhaps most notably to topic and to *ne*; by this latter term is meant the attitude adopted by a speaker towards the topic under discussion. Holmes (1997: 207) points out the need to bear in mind that the analysis of any stretch of linguistic behaviour is a snapshot, and that speakers are continually engaged in a process of construction of their identity that leads them to present different aspects of this identity in response to various motivating factors: 'gender [to which we may add all social] identity is constantly being constructed, and people may reinforce norms at one point, but challenge and contest them at others'. This quotation is designed to illustrate what is meant below by a speaker's subversive tone or orientation. The underlying assumption here is that tone is most saliently manipulated at the levels of grammar and lexis, but it is worth noting that the use of a vowel or consonant in an unexpected context, or a salient phonological stereotype (Chambers and Trudgill 1998:75), can also serve to subvert or reinforce the tone of an exchange in a way that is closely comparable to what occurs on the more salient linguistic levels. The issue of the influence of topic will be discussed in Chapter 6 in connexion with lexical variation in the Dieuze data.

In connexion with variable *ne* deletion, the point at issue here is that the various factors influencing speech production do not necessarily line up: the topic under discussion may be serious, but the tone subversive and the speech situation informal. Correspondingly, a speech situation may be informal but the tone serious. Leaving aside the question of conversational tone, we shall see in Chapter 6 that the influence of topic raises considerable problems of comparability in the Dieuze data on the level of variable lexis, and puts serious difficulties in the way of any attempt to set up Labovian-type lexical variables having two or more variants. We examine in the following section, from the point of view of its influence upon *ne*-deletion rates, how the tone of a narrative can work against the topic and style. We note here however that the issue of token numbers, referred to initially in this discussion, is relatively unimportant for the reasons connected with topic and to *ne*; clearly, a reasonably adequate number is required for a reliable quantification of *ne*, but in view of the unpredictable nature of the variation in topic and tone found in the Dieuze corpus it is unclear whether differentiation in these factors across a very large corpus would ever even out sufficiently to give a fully representative picture of the use of *ne* as it interacts with discourse through its situation in syntax. We do not however wish to imply by this that other studies have been over-inclusive in their analysis of tokens of *ne*; their results justify the methodology employed, and in any event no previous study has attempted to quantify intraspeaker variation in *ne*. We shall see in Chapter 6 that the issue of the size of the corpus analysed is relevant also to the study of lexical variation.

4.9.5 Relation between discourse and intraspeaker variation in *ne*

Several researchers have remarked the influence of topic upon rates of *ne* deletion; Sankoff and Vincent (1980:302–3) noted that the rare cases of use of *ne* by their Montreal informants tended to occur when the topic was a serious one, such as religion or education. As pointed out previously, a principal difference between the two speech styles in the Dieuze data is that while both interview and conversation styles were broadly devoted to discussion and narratives, the topics discussed in the two styles varied considerably, and conversation style was often characterised by an emphasis on the affective aspect of the topic under discussion, with interviews tending to be more narrowly focused on the informational dimension of variation. We shall see below that as well as lexis, intraspeaker variation in *ne* is also mediated through the factors of topic and tone, but in ways that appear to be even more complex than what obtains in lexis.

At first sight, the audience design account of the psychosocial motivations that propel style shift would appear to apply to *ne* in quite a satisfactory way. As stated previously, formal situations calls for speech that derives from the 'standard' or prestige end of the social-class continuum of language varieties. Linguistic items in these varieties derive prestige, either because their use is associated with social groups whose behaviour is highly prized, and/or because they are associated with the standard written language. The French variable *ne* is clearly of the latter type, whose clear representation in writing can be presumed to enhance its socio-stylistic value. As noted in the last chapter, however, the Dieuze elicitation methods resulted in rather high rates of style shift at the levels of some variable phonology and of lexis. We have seen that degrees of style for *ne* are very modest, but the typical case of CN discussed above demonstrates that shift across the two styles reflects, through a somewhat more frequent use of NP subjects in interview than in conversation, a concern on the informant's part to issue decontextualised information to an interlocutor who did not share the same knowledge base. Correspondingly, the more frequent use of clitic subjects in the conversation style reflects the more extended nature of the discussions and narratives that took place; for example, at one point in a conversation CN and her interlocutors engaged in a comparison of their experiences when taking driving lessons that lasted some 15 minutes. Clearly, an extended discussion implies more frequent use of pronoun subjects to the extent that the participants will tend to be aware of the identity of the referents. By contrast, discussions in the interviews generally covered more topics in less depth.

Following on from the issues discussed above is the indirect relation, mediated through discourse structure, between rates of *ne* deletion and audience design. In 4.9.3 we discussed the cases of the use of *ne* by CN in interview style, suggesting that the nature of the speech situation was such as to work against the strong constraint that induces speakers to produce the clitic + verb sequence as perhaps the default form. We suggested immediately above, more specifically, that the perceived lack of shared knowledge between fieldworker and informants was responsible, through the more frequent use of NP subjects, for higher rates of *ne*. We turn now to use of *ne* in the conversation style, again referring principally to instances produced by CN.

Two examples illustrate the 'metaphorical' use of *ne* in formal style quite clearly. The first concerns CN, who in the course of discussing a fellow pupil who was quite seriously overweight, remarked:

(42)   elle ne peut pas bouger
       'she can't move'

The use of *ne* here appears to reflect a concern on CN's part to adopt a serious, compassionate tone, and this was endorsed by the intonation and 'warm' voice quality employed. An even more striking example was produced by EM, another older female. She was describing in conversation style her close relationship with a female cousin who lived in another village some distance away, and with whom she regularly exchanged very long letters. At one point she remarked on the intimacy of the letters; she customarily discussed with her cousin any topic, however personal:

(43)   comme si les kilomètres ne nous séparaient pas
       'as though we weren't miles apart'

Clearly, we cannot state with certainty which factors account for the use of *ne* in a given sequence, but we may note here the conversational tone adopted by the speaker, who clearly is taking the subject very seriously, and the use of *ne* where its deletion would jar with the almost solemn effect aimed at.

We can draw a parallel here with the concept of 'metaphorical code-switching' formulated by Blom and Gumperz (1972) in order to account for switching between codes practised by bilinguals, of the type which cannot be explained by a change in situational factors but which is prompted rather by the desire to 'convey special communicative intent' (Li 1998:156). Clearly, any comparison between an instance of intra-language style-shift and what is happening in cross-language code-switch is problematic, perhaps most notably in regard to the level of salience that obtains in each case. A related question is whether the formal and informal varieties of French are separate for their speakers in a way that is true of clearly delimited languages. But as Milroy (1987b:171) suggests, 'although bilingual or bidialectal switching is a more clearly visible process than monolingual style-shifting, the psychosocial dynamics underlying these different kinds of intraspeaker variation are similar'. It is possible to quarrel with this proposition in its application to every respect in which style-shifting and code-switching are comparable, but the quotation emphasises the aspect of intra-sentential style-shifting and code-switching that is of interest here: the psychosocial motivation responsible for the selection of a given language, dialect or variety fragment. It appears plausible that the motivations propelling instances of style-shift referred to here as 'metaphorical' are similar to those associated with metaphorical code-switching. Certainly the formulation cited above, referring to the wish to 'convey special communicative intent', captures very well the motivation underlying insertion of *ne* in the instances discussed immediately above. Schiffrin (1985, 1987) has perhaps the most comprehensive treatment of the analysis of discourse variation using quantitative methods.

At the same time, we should reiterate here the caveat regarding numbers of tokens of *ne* present in the Dieuze corpus. We have suggested that variation in topic and tone has contributed to the diminution of intraspeaker variation in *ne* in the corpus, within the context of low rates of retention overall. However, while there were no examples of *ne* retention in a less serious tone in conversation style, serious discussions in interview style by no means always, or even often, called for retention of *ne*. We suggested also that because of the unpredictable nature of variation in topic and tone, the scaling-up of a corpus might not necessarily give a different picture. This is however a speculative statement that empirical results might contradict. One the one hand, the issue here is one of representativeness; we can suggest that the analysis of a larger corpus drawn from a socially wider speaker sample may yield insights regarding the relation between the intraspeaker use of *ne* and micro-style variation capable of being extrapolated to the speech community that is being modelled. On the other hand, the Dieuze results discussed above are suggestive rather than robust; but they certainly give the rather negative result that the relationship between speech style, and the factors that influence it, notably topic, tone and the relationship between the locutors, is by no means uniplex, as the two-dimensional displays used throughout this most of book might seem to indicate.

4.10 Conclusion to the intraspeaker analysis of *ne*

The results, data and argumentation presented in the previous sub-sections can be summarised as follows: a Labovian analysis of intraspeaker variation in *ne* needs to be supplemented by qualitative, discourse-analytic methods. This is because of the situation of *ne* in grammar, which in turn is indissociable from the discourse level. Several of the stylistic effects produced by the Dieuze informants in conversation style through their use of *ne* (those given above are representative) contradict a simplex formal–informal analysis of style variation. Micro-style variation, present of course in both of the broad styles discussed here, is reflected in the use of *ne* through a reduction in degrees of style shift, since the 'formal' episodes in conversation style call for the use of *ne* quite frequently relative to interview style, albeit within the context of very little *ne* retention overall.

In the context of the relation between variation in grammar and its location in discourse structure, we may refer again to the suggestion of Cheshire (1997:5) to the effect that morpho-syntactic variation in English, such as non-standard subject-verb concord, is found in cognitively prominent sentence types such as interrogatives and negatives, which have 'a more direct connection to the context of face-to-face interaction than others' by virtue of their involving the hearer more closely than less prominent structures. Thus variation in English grammar appears also be more tightly constrained than in phonology, by reason of its localisation in prominent, high-involvement speech acts. If true, this reinforces our suggestion of a rather complex relation between the intra-speaker and interspeaker dimensions where grammatical variation in French *ne* is concerned. From the point of view of variation in its relation to change, Cheshire argues that low-involvement sentence types are more susceptible to penetration by standard grammatical forms than less prominent constructions.

From this latter point of view, diachronic deletion of *ne* in French is of course a process that is largely complete; or if still in progress, now proceeding rather slowly. One consequence is that the interspeaker value of *ne* is rather limited. Nevertheless we can draw a parallel with Cheshire's hypothesis by pointing out that the insertion of *ne* in everyday French is associated with constructions such as lexical NPs, which can be assumed to be cognitively prominent by virtue of their relative complexity and infrequency. Speakers can often if they wish avoid such constructions through NP doubling, as we have seen above. But the 'productive use of *ne*' (Sankoff and Vincent 1980) remains available as a stylistic resource. What we have attempted to highlight here is the rather complex nature of the various components of style, as well as of their interactions with the syntactic constraints influencing the choices speakers exercise in their use of *ne*. The Dieuze results, on account of showing very low levels of *ne* retention, cannot be said to provide reliable evidence of the hyper-style value of the variable. Nevertheless we have seen a striking instance of the relation between the limited interspeaker value of *ne* and its salience as a stylistic resource.

CHAPTER 5

Variable liaison

5.1 Introduction

We examine variable liaison in a separate chapter, because this area of French variation is a special case, and its uniqueness demands separate treatment. From a linguistic viewpoint, although it concerns the variable pronunciation of consonants in certain contexts, liaison is not solely a phonological phenomenon, but also responds to input from syntax and morphology. The linguistic phenomenon of variable liaison thus defined appears also to be unique to French: no other language seems to have the prescriptively variable pronunciation of spelling consonants, although as we shall see English does have an 'intrusive' consonant whose behaviour bears a resemblance to one type of variable liaison in French.

The social distribution of variable liaison is also unusual; it is mostly used by middle-class speakers in formal speech styles, and its accurate (as against hypercorrect) use seems to be dependent on a high degree of literacy. This uneven distribution raises a question of comparison: are there areas of variation in English or other languages, on the levels of grammar or lexis, that bear comparison with variable liaison? We discuss this more fully in a later section.

Firstly however, we define the various types, or phonetic realisations, of liaison, and subsequently we distinguish and describe the four different categories of liaison. We then present some findings that provide insights into variable liaison, some from the variationist viewpoint, others using qualitative methods. Subsequently we consider whether these findings throw any light on the relationship between variable liaison, and variation on the other linguistic levels discussed in this book.

5.2 Definition of liaison

Liaison is the pronunciation before a following vowel, in certain syntactic contexts, of a word-final consonant that is silent in the other relevant phonetic contexts, i.e. before a consonant or a pause. Thus for example, the French liaison consonant /z/ is silent in the plural definite article *les* before a word beginning with a consonant, as in *les livres* 'the books' /lelivʀ/ or before a pause, as in *lis-les* 'read them' /lile/, but pronounced before a vowel, as in *les églises* 'the churches' /lezegliz/.

The only exceptions to this pattern are the set of words beginning with so-called *h aspiré* or 'aspirate h' and vowel-initial numerals. We discuss these cases in more detail below.

5.2.1   Liaison consonants

The liaison consonants found in French are the following, underlined in the orthographic examples:

(1)   /z/ as in *nous avons* 'we have', *allez-y* 'go there', *deux ans* 'two years'
      /n/ as in *on est à trois* 'there are three of us', *un ennemi* 'an enemy'
      /t/ as in *c'est impossible* 'it's impossible', *grand écran* 'big screen'
      /ʀ/ as in *dernier acte* 'last act', *aller en ville* 'go into town'
      /p/ as in *beaucoup aimé* 'liked a lot', *trop aimable* 'too kind'
      /k/ as in *sang impur* 'impure blood', (from the *Marseillaise*); *long hiver* 'long winter'

It can be seen that various orthographic letters represent the six liaison consonants. The first three, /z/, /n/ and /t/, are common in everyday speech, while the second three are rather rare; /k/ especially is rather seldom heard, being found above all in collocations such as *long hiver*.

5.2.2   Liaison avec enchaînement

When a liaison consonant is pronounced, it usually also undergoes *enchaînement* or linking to the following vowel. Thus contrary to what the spelling indicates, the phrase *les églises* will syllabify as follows (a full stop indicates a syllable boundary): /le.ze.gliz./. This is known as *liaison avec enchaînement*. In some cases *enchaînement* and *liaison avec enchaînement* are phonetically identical, as in the two following oft-quoted phrases:

(2)   petite amie   /pə.ti.ta.mi./ 'girlfriend'
      petit ami   /pə.ti.ta.mi./ 'boyfriend'

In the first phrase, the second /t/ in *petite* links to the /a/ in the following word. This /t/ would of course always be pronounced, as it marks the gender of *amie*. Therefore this phrase illustrates *enchaînement* but not liaison. In the second phrase, because final /t/ is not pronounced before a consonant or pause, there is liaison as well as *enchaînement*.

It is generally accepted that spoken French (unlike English) is characterised by an open syllable structure of the following pattern: CV.CV. *Enchaînement* adds, through the process of forward resyllabification, to the already high proportion of syllables in French that are inherently open; that is, *enchaînement* opens syllables in connected speech when speakers attach a consonant to a vowel in the following syllable or word. Evidence is readily available to substantiate this proposition; the following list provides concrete evidence of this tendency of word-final consonants to cross word boundaries. These examples are all taken from the Dieuze corpus, and were produced by children aged 11–12. *Enchaînement* can be heard in adult speech, but is more clearly detectable in the speech of children, who frequently pause for breath between or even within words, and *enchaînement* (with or without liaison) takes place across the pause, as these examples show:

(3)   ils sont bien (pause) n-organisés   [isɔ̃bjɛ̃ # nɔʁganize]
      'they're well organised'

      sa deuxiè- (breath) me-année   [sadøzjɛ # mane]
      'his second year'

      ils doivent-euh (pause) t-intégrer   [idwavtø # tɛ̃tegʁe]
      'they have to join'

      les personnes-euh-z-âgées   [lepɛʁsɔnøzaʒe]
      'the old people'

5.2.3   Liaison sans enchaînement

Liaison normally occurs with *enchaînement*, but it also occurs without. One example given by Encrevé (1988: 32–35) is the sentence: *J'avais un rêve* 'I had a dream', where instead of the sequence of open syllables resulting from *enchaînement*: [ʒa. vɛ. zœ̃. ʁɛv.], the liaison consonant /z/ in *'avais'* is attached to the preceding vowel, as in [ʒa. vɛz. œ̃. ʁɛv.]. The liaison consonant may also be followed by a glottal stop: [ʒa. vɛz. ʔœ̃. ʁɛv.]. This type of liaison is characteristically used by public figures such as politicians and broadcast journalists. An amusing example of liaison without *enchaînement* being used to provide a meaningful contrast is the following, where a politician, interviewed on the radio, was commenting on the numerous ministerial posts held by François Mitterrand during the Fourth Republic:

> (4) …et quand Monsieur Mitterrand était ministre, et Dieu sait qu'il l'a [bo.ku.pe.te.], pardon [bo.kup.ʔe.te.]…

The humour turns here on a pun, which in turn depends on the syllable boundary in [bokupete], consequent on the non-pronunciation or pronunciation respectively of the non-linked liaison consonant /p/ in beaucoup: 'When M. Mitterrand was a minister, and goodness knows he farted a lot (*beaucoup* [Ø] *pété*), I beg your pardon, was [it=a minister] a lot [*beaucoup* [p] *été*). We discuss the social distribution of *liaison avec enchaînement* in more detail below.

5.3   Liaison categories

Table 1 below provides a summary description of three of the four types of liaison we discuss here; in addition to the 'invariable', 'variable' and 'erratic' categories (shown in the columns), we also examine *fausse* 'false' liaison because of the sociolinguistic interest it provides. Table 1 also shows (in the rows) the four grammatical categories into which each of the three main types of liaison fall. Examples are given in italics. The 'special cases' row refers to the idiosyncratic and non-productive cases: set phrases (*accent aigu* 'acute accent' etc.), *h aspiré* (explained below) and numerals. *Fausse* liaison is not exemplified in Table 1, but to anticipate the discussion in 5.3.3 below, it occurs where an intrusive liaison consonant is inserted, i.e. where none is present in the spelling. We refer to it below as 'incorrect liaison'. In contrast, the insertion of an 'erratic' liaison consonant appears in most cases to be influenced by spelling. So far as the relation between spelling and pronunciation is concerned, we can draw a parallel (developed in 5.3.3 below) between English 'linking' and intrusive' /r/ on the one hand, and 'erratic' and 'incorrect' liaison on the other.

5.3.1   Invariable liaison

The large and productive category of invariable liaison forms is exemplified in the noun–invariable and verb–invariable cells in Table 1 below, which include combinations such as:

> determiner + noun (*les églises* 'the churches', *un ami* 'a friend',
> *deux ans* 'two years')

and:

> personal pronoun + verb (*ils ont répondu* 'they replied')

These forms are invariably made, at least by speakers of metropolitan French; De Jong (1993) has reported non-liaison in Canadian French in *ils* + verb-form, whereby for instance *ils ont* may be pronounced [ijɔ̃] or [jɔ̃]. Table 1 also shows, in the special/invariable matrix, examples of the non-productive set phrases where liaison is invariably made. These phrases are residues from an earlier state of the language, when liaisons were made more frequently than now. As the table suggests, by no means all liaison forms fall into the invariable category. Encrevé has estimated that this category of invariable liaison accounts for some 48% of all liaisons made in everyday speech, although this figure would of course depend on the number of variable liaisons made by individual speakers; this number will in turn be conditioned by sociolinguistic factors, which we examine in more detail below.

Invariable liaison has a parallel in English, where the liaison consonant /r/ in a word like 'hear', which is silent before a consonant or pause, is pronounced before a vowel. Thus in the sequences: 'I can't hear the noise' or 'I can't hear', no /r/ is pronounced, whereas in 'I can't hear a noise' /r/ reappears.

5.3.2 'Erratic' liaison

In contrast to liaisons made by all speakers irrespective of sociolinguistic factors, a further liaison category is labelled by prescriptive grammarians as *interdite* or 'forbidden'. These are shown in the third column of Table 1. Encrevé calls this category *'erratique'*, reflecting the fact that liaisons of this type occur unpredictably and sporadically, or are regarded as errors. However, it may be more accurate to call some liaisons of this type 'hypercorrect', since they are likely to be made by speakers who are unsure of the prescriptive rules governing variable liaison, and who are led by the influence of spelling into making a liaison where the standard language requires none. An example of seemingly hypercorrect liaison is pronunciation of the liaison consonant /t/ in a singular noun before a vowel-initial verb, as in *le soldat* [t] *est parti* 'the soldier left'. The further major examples of hypercorrect liaison are after *et* and before numerals: thus *les* [Ø] *onze* is prescribed, not *les* [z] *onze* ('the elevens', e.g. number eleven buses).

Table 1. Classification of liaison forms (adapted from Encrevé 1988:47)

	Invariable	Variable	'Erratic'
Noun	determiner + noun, pronoun, adjective: *vos enfants* 'your children' *deux autres* 'two others' *un ancien ami* 'a former friend'	plural noun + predicate, adjective: *des soldats anglais* 'English soldiers' *ses plans ont réussi* 'his/her plans succeeded'	singular noun + predicate, adjective: *un soldat anglais* 'an English soldier' *son plan a réussi* 'his/her plan succeeded'
Verb	personal pronoun + verb: *ils ont compris* 'they have understood' *nous en avons* 'we have some' verb + personal pronoun: *allons-y* 'let's go' *ont-ils compris?* 'have they understood?'	verb + complement: *je vais essayer* 'I'll try' *j'avais entendu* 'I'd understood' *vous êtes invité* 'you can come' *il commençait à lire* 'he started to read' *c'est un village* 'it's a village' *on est oblige* 'we have to'	et + complement: *et on l'a fait* 'and we did it'
Uninflected		uninflected monosyllabic words: *en une journée* 'in a day' *très intéressant* 'very interesting' uninflected polysyllabic words: *pendant un jour* 'for a day' *toujours utile* 'always useful'	
Special cases	fixed locutions: *comment allez-vous?* 'how are you?' *les États-Unis* 'The United States' *de temps en temps* 'from time to time' *tout à coup* 'suddenly'	aspirate h: *des héros* 'heroes' *en haut* 'upstairs', 'on top' article etc. + relevant numerals: *la cent huitième* 'the 108th' *en onze jours* 'in eleven days'	

These remarks concerning hypercorrection do not apply to an erratic liaison made before a word in the *h aspiré* lexical set, where liaison is prescriptively blocked; for example before *hall* 'hall', vestibule', *haricot* 'bean', *héros* 'hero'. Words in this set are not in fact aspirated (Carton (1995: 40–1) uses the term *h disjonctif* 'disjunctive h'), and the three examples cited are pronounced [ol], [aʁiko], [eʁo]. However, words in the *h aspiré* set behave as if they had the initial aspirate consonant [h]. The consequence is that liaison does not occur before the words in the *h aspiré* set. Thus in the singular, *un hall, un haricot, un héros* are pronounced: [œ̃ol], [œ̃aʁiko], [œ̃eʁo], not [œ̃nol], [œ̃naʁiko], [œ̃neʁo]. In the plural, *les halls, les haricots, les héros* are pronounced: [leol], [leaʁiko], [leeʁo], not [lezol], [lezaʁiko], [lezeʁo]. The sociolinguistic interest of the *h aspiré* set is that many speakers regularise some forms, such as *haricots* and *Hollande*, so that alongside the prescribed forms *les haricots* [leaʁiko] and *les Hollandais* 'the Dutch' [leɔlɑ̃dɛ], [lezaʁiko] and [lezɔlɑ̃dɛ] are now common. It may be that speakers wish to mark plurality additionally by pronouncing the [z] in these instances. At the same time, frequent *h aspiré* words such as *haut* 'top' and *hors* 'out of' show no tendency towards regularisation. A form like [lezaʁiko] will of course be regarded by prescriptivists as a *liaison interdite*, characteristic of lower-class speech.

5.3.3 'Fausse' or 'incorrect' liaison

In contrast to erratic liaison, so-called *fausse liaison* takes place when a liaison consonant is inserted where none is present in the spelling. This category is not shown in Table 1. As was mentioned above, the use of hypercorrect liaison seems to be motivated largely by linguistic insecurity. By contrast, *fausse liaison* (we will use the term 'incorrect liaison' henceforward, despite its prescriptive overtones) seems to be prompted by several, quite different motivations, only some of which have a sociolinguistic input. Some examples seem to be straightforward performance errors, as in the case of the senior civil servant, working as an administrative official at the French National Assembly, part of whose job was to register new deputies after a legislative election (Hare 1990: 69). One element of this task was to check the identity of deputies: as he put it in the course of being interviewed by an academic researcher:

(5) je vérifie que ce soient bien [t] eux qui aient été élus
     'I check that they are in fact the ones who have been elected'

This type of liaison is interesting from a psycholinguistic viewpoint. One can hypothesise that it results from a slip of the tongue, a metathesis that displaces a consonant from its intended place. Without undue mentalism, we can speculate that an initial version of the phrase was:

(6)   je vérifie que ce soient [t] eux qui aient été élus

Subsequently the *bien* is inserted and assumes the liaison consonant associated with *soient*. A highly educated speaker in a formal interview will be very likely to realise the variable liaison in *ce soient eux*, indeed anyone who uses two optional subjunctives in this context (*soient* and *aient*) will be likely to use the liaison too. Therefore it seems very implausible that an incorrect liaison of this type results from ignorance of the prescriptive liaison forms.

A more straightforward example from the sociolinguistic point of view, is the following incorrect liaison apparently motivated by the desire to hyper-correct. In the Dieuze corpus, a 16-year-old girl produced the following utterance when speaking to the researcher:

(7)   je trouve que les hommes politiques sont trop [z] ages
'I think politicians are too old'

In this example *trop* [z] *âgés* was pronounced [tʀozaʒe]; formal style would have called for [tʀopaʒe], and informal for [tʀoaʒe]. The insertion of the liaison consonant [z] was presumably prompted by the desire to mark plurality; of course no plural marker is required after the invariable adverb *trop* in the standard variety. An additional influencing factor may be the rarity of the liaison consonant /p/. The infrequency of this type of liaison makes its study in a quantitative framework difficult, but Gadet (1997a: 51) cites a similar example, which concerns a pupil of school age talking to a well-known journalist in a live television interview, an event that is likely to elicit very formal speech. The pupil produced the following incorrect liaison:

(8)   l'école réunit mille [z] élèves 'the school has a thousand pupils'

Here the motivation seems similar to the previous example. The 1986 *Petit Robert* has a comparable example:

(9)   les chemins de fer [z] anglais 'English railways'

The above examples seem to be motivated quite differently from the incorrect liaison forms more commonly cited. These latter are known popularly by various terms that are untranslatable without an extended gloss: *'cuirs', 'velours', 'pataquès'*, *'des liaisons mal-t-à-propos'*. They all have in common the insertion of an intrusive liaison consonant, as in: *donne-moi* [z] *en* 'give me some'; *moi* [z] *aussi* 'me too'; *il faudra* [t] *aller* 'we'll have to go'. In these cases, one can argue that the intrusive [z] and [t] are inserted to avoid the need to juxtapose two vowels, or perhaps, in the first example, on the analogy of *donne-nous-en* 'give us some'.

We can draw a parallel here between this type of incorrect liaison and 'intrusive r' in English, where the consonant is absent in the orthography but inserted pre-vocalically, as in: 'draw [ɹ] ing', or 'law [ɹ] and order'. The motivation for the realisation of 'intrusive r' in these examples seems to be similar to what motivates incorrect liaison of the *donne-moi* [z] *en* type, namely, as suggested above, the avoidance of two vowels in sequence; more precisely, the desire to preserve a regular consonant-vowel alternation. Nevertheless, it is worth pointing out that intrusive 'r' in English is quite tightly constrained phonologically, and can only appear after certain vowels: one can say 'India [ɹ] and Pakistan', but not 'free [ɹ] and easy' (Lass 1984:71).

Incorrect liaison (in English and French) is of course represented by prescriptivists as proper to low-status speech, and stigmatised accordingly, but a form akin to incorrect liaison has become canonical in French in such inverted interrogative constructions as *a-t-il*, as well as in the phrase (cited by Grevisse 1986:50) *entre quatre* [z] *yeux* 'between us two' (sometimes written *entre quatre-z-yeux*).

5.3.4 Variable liaison

Between invariable liaison forms which are always pronounced and those which are regarded as forbidden, lies a large area of variation consisting of those liaisons which are traditionally referred to as 'optional' (*facultatives*). The more neutral term used by Encrevé is simply 'variable'. Variable liaison is conditioned by the interaction of linguistic factors, which we discuss below, and sociolinguistic factors. The linguistic factors concern the phonetic properties of the liaison consonant; and the closeness of the syntactic link between the two units involved.

The middle column of Table 1 above illustrates the various grammatical categories of variable liaison, some of which are commoner than others. Common examples of variable liaison are as follows:

1. Between a verb (generally a frequent one such as *aller* or *être*) and a complement. Thus one may hear *c'est un village* 'it's a village' pronounced either [sɛtɶ̃vilaʒ] or [sɛɶ̃vilaʒ].

2. After invariable words (typically conjunctions, adverbs and pronouns, such as *mais* 'but', *depuis* 'since', *pendant* 'in' or 'during', *toujours* 'always' or 'still', *quand* 'when', *très*, 'very', *trop* 'too'). Thus, *quand il arrive* 'when he arrives' may be pronounced as [kãtilaʁiv] or [kãilaʁiv]; *très intéressant* 'very interesting' as [tʁɛzɛ̃teʁɛsã] or [tʁɛ̃teʁɛsã].

The set of words involved in variable liaison in everyday speech is fairly small, and consists largely of function words such as determiners, pronouns, short, frequently-occurring adjectives and adverbs, and parts of the verbs *aller* 'to go', *être* 'to be' and *avoir* 'to have', used as auxiliaries or as full verbs. However, the potential number of words that can realise liaison in more formal speech is very large, since for example any adverb ending in the *-ment* suffix is a potential liaison site; as is any verb form with an ending containing a liaison consonant (*-aient*, *-ont*, *-ent* for example); and any plural noun ending in a pronounceable *-s*.

We now examine briefly the purely linguistic constraints that condition liaison.

5.3.4.1   *Phonetic factors influencing variable liaison*

At least one researcher (Ashby 1981a:50) found that those variable liaison consonants which are articulated with less force are pronounced more often, other things (syntactic factors) being equal. This means that /t/, a voiceless plosive and hence the type of consonant that requires the greatest amount of articulatory effort, is the least likely of the three frequent liaison consonants to be realised. Of the other two, /n/ requires less force in its articulation than /z/, and is correspondingly more frequently pronounced. A further, non-phonetic explanation of the higher frequency of /n/ and /z/ is that they are more frequent in invariable liaison than /t/.

5.3.4.2   *Syntactic factors influencing variable liaison*

Invariable liaisons are made generally between words that are closely linked syntactically. This is the case, for example, between articles and nouns, e.g. *les enfants*, and between verb form and clitic pronoun, as shown in verb/invariable cell in Table 1. French is a language which overwhelmingly has definite and indefinite marking. Articles and nouns are therefore closely associated within the same phrase, in this case a noun phrase consisting of article + noun. Similarly, a clitic pronoun is by definition inseparably tied to its associated verb form.

By contrast, liaison between phrases is variable. Many more combinatory possibilities exist on both sides of a phrase boundary, as between for example a verb phrase and its complement. Manifestly, this is because the sense of a statement can be expressed in more than one way. Thus, 'I'd like to go' could be rendered: *j'aimerais y aller, je voudrais y aller: j'aurais envie d'y aller*, and so on. The syntactic links between the various verb phrases and their complements are therefore weaker than that between article and noun. Liaison within phrases tends therefore to be invariable and liaison across phrases variable. However, it must be emphasised that this is a tendency; several of the variable liaison contexts involve 'intra-phrasal' liaison: *très intéressant, soldats anglais*, etc. Thus De Jong (1988) has pointed out that generative models of syntax fail to predict invariable as against variable liaison when applied to empirical data. De Jong suggests that this is because other linguistic factors are influential: notably word category, word length, the phonetic nature of the liaison consonant, and whether the consonant follows another, as in *hommes* pronounced [ɔmz] if the variable liaison is made.

It should further be pointed out that there is variation within variable liaison. This is illustrated by an utterance containing four potential liaisons, discussed by Gadet (1997a: 52):

(10)   des [z] hommes [z] illustres [z] ont [t] attendu 'famous men waited'

The first liaison, *des hommes*, is defined as invariable, the other three as variable in varying degrees; Gadet describes *ont attendu* as 'fairly frequent in everyday speech', *hommes illustres* as 'rather rare', and *illustres ont* as 'exceptional elsewhere than in elevated speech'. Thus it seems that broadly, the weaker the syntactic link across a liaison site, the more 'elevated' the liaison. This brings us to sociolinguistic factors.

5.3.4.3   Sociolinguistic factors influencing variable liaison

We take it as axiomatic that variable liaison is an overtly prestigious feature of French pronunciation. It is found most frequently in the more formal styles of speech of educated speakers, broadly when they are paying most attention to their speech production; although as we will see below, this latter statement needs qualification. Relatively few speakers control variable liaison fully, and it appears to be dependent on a high level of education and literacy; it is very likely that speakers need to be aware of the relevant liaison consonants in spelling to feel confident in producing all and only the prescribed variable liaison forms. Typical speech events where high realisation rates of variable liaison are likely are politicians' public speeches and serious broadcast journalism. Newsreaders, who are almost always reading from an autocue even though their speech may appear spontaneous, produce a large number of variable liaison forms. Many political speeches and news bulletins share the characteristic of being scripted; we can say that these speech styles are akin to the reading styles of socio-linguistic interviews, discussed in Chapters 2 and 3. We have seen that reading styles generally trigger formal speech. But the tone of the speech event is also an important factor; thus for example, in Jacques Chirac's first presidential New Year address to the French nation on 31 December 1995, the realisation rate of variable liaison was very close to 100%, and contained such notable instances as the pronunciation of [ʀ] in *léguer: pour garder et léguer* [ʀ] *à nos enfants…* 'to guard and bequeath to our children …' Similarly, the speech made by André Malraux on the occasion of the installation of Jean Moulin's ashes in the Panthéon is famous as much for the liaisons it contains as its highly emotional tone: one notable liaison made by Malraux is normally regarded as erratic and hypercorrect: *accent* [t] *invincible.*

We may reasonably suggest that Chirac and Malraux wished to emphasise the solemnity of these speech situations. A solemn occasion is clearly a formal one, and one characteristic of formal situations is the stress laid upon the distance between the participants. On a solemn occasion, this distance finds extreme expression; each participant is as it were a solitary member of the gathering, and this is reflected in highly formal language. Plainly however, not all public occasions are solemn, or even necessarily formal. This is shown by a study of the variable liaison rates realised by Charles de Gaulle (Encrevé 1988:258). Encrevé found that these rates varied between 9% and 100% over ten public speeches. He points out that these percentages were calculated not from entire speeches but from extracts; this might be seen as a methodological shortcoming, but Encrevé concludes from this that any public speech (we may add, any stretch of speech, public or private) contains much 'micro-style' variation. In other words the tone of a speech may vary considerably: from solemn, to jocular, to intimate, to facetious, to sarcastic, and so on. In this sense we again define 'tone' as the speaker's attitude to what s/he is saying. As we saw in the previous chapter, tone finds expression at all levels of linguistic variation, and we can regard variable liaison in this type of public speech event as a kind of manipulative tool, used by professional public speakers to create or diminish the distance between themselves and their audience. This is why we need to qualify the statement, made above, that high rates of variable liaison are the result of a high degree of self-monitoring on the part of a speaker; this is true, but politicians may also monitor their speech so as to produce lower liaison rates, with a view to emphasising solidarity with their audience.

In the next section we examine several corpus-based studies of variable liaison from the viewpoint of the light they throw on the relation between variation and change in liaison. Although this relation is not the principal focus of this book, we will see below that the unusual nature of liaison as an area of variation also produces idiosyncratic results in diachronic change.

5.4 Variationist studies of liaison: Problems of comparison

Corpus-based, quantitative studies of variable liaison are not very numerous, and this is understandable given that liaison involves syntactic factors as well as phonological. Thus for example, while some liaison forms are quite frequent, others are rare, and the researcher has to confront the problems of frequency, discussed in Chapter 4, which often arise in the analysis of variable grammar. However, a few researchers have studied liaison using quantitative (if not always variationist) methods. We briefly review some of them here, before trying to conclude whether any consistent results have emerged.

Ågren (1973)

Ågren examined variable liaison using a corpus of formal speech drawn from some 40 hours of radio discussion programmes; the speakers were journalists, politicians and authors. Ågren was not concerned principally to examine social variation, or to distinguish between variable and invariable liaison, but rather to study the influence of linguistic factors on the frequencies of the different variable liaison forms. However, he did distinguish between casual and careful styles in his data, observing higher realisation rates in careful style for most liaison categories. Clearly, this finding is unsurprising, but Ågren's study was the first to confirm the status of liaison as a prestige variable through the analysis of a large corpus of spontaneous language data — 8,441 tokens. The overall realisation rate in Ågren's corpus was 61.6%.

Malécot (1975)

Malécot described patterns of liaison in a corpus of spontaneous speech, obtaining his data by recording surreptitiously the speech of a sample of his acquaintances, upper middle-class Parisians. He examined the influence both of linguistic and extra-linguistic variables; of the demographic variables studied, no sex-related variation was observed, but speakers aged 20–29 were found to realise liaison forms more frequently than older groups. Malécot attributed this to the fact of the younger speakers' status as 'apprentice' members of the establishment, whence their desire to speak in a manner acceptable to their elders. He also studied the influence of certain rather unusual situational variables, such as topic and 'attitude', i.e. friendly, deferential, hostile, joyful, etc. but he found they had no significant influence on liaison rates. Malécot reported an average figure of 64% of liaisons realised, unfortunately without distinguishing between variable and invariable forms. He did however observe that in his data that the realisation rate for what he terms optional liaison was very low indeed. This finding may indicate that Malécot succeeded in capturing an informal speech style, although Ashby (1976), who studied *ne* in Malécot's corpus, reported high rates of *ne* retention. The conclusion to be drawn from this may be that variable liaison is more closely tied to style than to social class, although of course it does seem that a high degree of literacy is needed as a prerequisite to the full control of liaison.

Ashby (1981a)

Ashby, in a study undertaken in Tours, observed social variation along the dimensions of sex, age, and two social class groupings, lower and middle, in a sub-sample of 16 informants (thus with only two speakers per cell). His results are as set out in Table 2 below.

Table 2. Variable liaison in Tours (adapted from Ashby 1981a)

	Age 14–21		Age 51–64	
	(N)	%	(N)	%
WC female	293	34	293	19
WC male	203	17	386	25
MC female	527	24	622	45
MC male	408	43	450	48

Table 2 has the classic findings of lower use of liaison forms by younger and working-class speaker groups, with the exception of the working-class females. Surprisingly, all of the female speaker groups show lower realisation rates than the corresponding male groups, again except the younger working-class females, who realise more liaison forms than their corresponding sex, age and social class groups. Ashby speculated that this apparently aberrant pattern was attributable to too broad a social class categorisation into 'working' and 'middle', and that this female group would be better assigned to the upper working-class or lower middle-class. The average score for all groups in this speaker sample is 34%.

Ashby's results show a fairly consistent age-grading effect that to some extent confirms the impressionistic perception of variable liaison as a prestige area of variation that is proper to older middle-class speakers. This impression is strikingly illustrated by an anecdote recounted by Nicholson (1909:95); a young actress was rebuked by a playwright for making the variable liaison after plantées in: *les fleurs, nous les avons plantées* [z] *ensemble* 'we planted the flowers together' The playwright reproached the actress as follows:

(11)   Vous n'avez pas le droit de faire de pareilles liaisons à votre âge. Cette affreuse 's' vous vieillerait de dix ans!
       'You musn't use such liaisons at your age. That dreadful 's' will age you by ten years!'

Encrevé (1988)

We have already mentioned that Encrevé studied *liaison sans enchaînement* in the speech of French politicians; he also compared realisation rates of *liaison avec enchaînement* using apparent-time methodology, studying recordings of the speeches of French heads of state over a period 1928–81. He found that variable liaison was in decline over this period; he also found a decrease since the beginning of the 1970s, between the last speeches made by de Gaulle and those of Giscard d'Estaing and Mitterrand made in the 1980s.

A further valuable finding that Encrevé reported was that invariable liaison is not subject to variation (1988:49). This statement may seem absurdly tautological, but one needs to bear in mind the tendency of traditional and even descriptive grammarians to establish liaison categories without systematic observation of speech corpora. Encrevé's summary classification of liaison forms, shown in Table 1 above, is based on a fuller taxonomy drawn up by Delattre (1956) who, however, based his classification on the impressionistic observation of educated Parisian usage. Delattre's taxonomy is the standard reference point that has been used by many scholars studying variable liaison. However, Encrevé based his conclusion concerning invariable liaison on the observed fact that only two out of 5,029 possible invariable liaisons, defined as such by Delattre, were not made in the corpus Encrevé studied.

As well as studying the speech of politicians, Encrevé also analysed the liaison forms in the data collected by Laks in 1975, in his study of a small group of Parisian lower-working-class adolescents. He found that out of 1,082 possible liaisons, all 508 invariable liaisons were made, while astonishingly, only 17 of the remaining 576 variable liaisons, or 3%, were made.

Green and Hintze (1990, 1992)

Green and Hintze also studied upper middle-class *oïl* French informants, using a speech corpus systematically controlled for age and sex. Their sample was composed of eight informants, four male and four female, divided into two age groups; 35–40 and 55–65. Their studies were concerned primarily to examine the effect on the use of liaison of linguistic factors not previously considered, notably rhythm boundaries and the glottal stop. Green and Hintze observed sex-related variation in their sample, with females using significantly fewer liaison forms; but no significant age-related variation was reported, perhaps unsurprisingly in view of the rather narrow age spread in their speaker sample. The overall realisation rates they reported, combining both variable and invariable liaison, were very high: 71.75% for women, 81.25% for men.

De Jong (1991)

De Jong studied variable liaison in the speech of a sample of 45 informants recorded in Orléans in 1969. He considered that the corpus was composed of careful speech, as speakers' responses were elicited by an interviewer using a questionnaire. The social parameters De Jong considered were age, class and sex. He reported an overall liaison rate of 49.2%, and found little difference between men and women (46.9% against 50.8%) or between the age groups. However, De Jong but he did find that social class differences were statistically significant, which is unsurprising in view of the large difference in liaison use between the highest class (UMC) and the lowest (LWC): 61.6% against 29.6%.

Armstrong (1993)

Armstrong studied variable liaison in the Dieuze corpus that we have already discussed in connexion with some phonological variables and with *ne*. This speaker sample used very little variable liaison except after monosyllabic adverbs and prepositions such as *très* 'very', *dans* 'in', *moins* 'less', *chez* 'in' (the house of), *tout* 'all' (adverb), etc. Liaison after the 3rd-person verb form *est* was almost categorically absent, except after full noun phrases, as in for example *mon frère est en Troisième* 'my brother's in Fourth Year' [i.e. aged 15 or 16 years].

It is unsurprising to find little variable liaison in the speech of a sample of children and adolescents speaking in two rather informal styles; what is interesting is the gross mismatch in the realisation of variable liaison between the Dieuze speaker sample and that recorded by Laks and analysed by Encrevé. This is most strikingly illustrated by the figures in Table 3 below. These show both social and stylistic variation in the realisation of liaison after *quand*, or rather the lack of variation along these dimensions, in a sub-sample of 16 of the Dieuze informants. As mentioned in Chapter 3, this sub-sample was chosen according to the relatively large volume of speech produced by each informant. It can be seen nevertheless that token numbers are in no case large.

What is most immediately striking about these results is the lack of systematic variation along the usual sociolinguistic dimensions. Certain speakers, irrespective of their age or sex, do not, on the basis of these findings, make the liaison after *quand*. Broadly, a speaker in this sample who makes a liaison after *quand* will realise the liaison regardless of speech style. We might conclude from this that the two styles are not distinct in terms of formality to trigger variation in *quand*; but it seems more likely that in this sample, those speakers who have acquired liaison after *quand* have not yet achieved the communicative competence necessary to enable them to style-shift using liaison. The only speaker who might be argued to be showing this competence is SM, a 12-year-old girl, whose speech we have already had occasion to discuss. A further question relates to the sociolinguistic factors that have caused only some speakers to acquire liaison after *quand*; is it the more 'literate' speakers who do so? In any event no clear social-class correlation was found that might explain the seemingly random variation shown in Table 3, although it was the researcher's (untested) impression that pupils who responded more positively to the inculcation of literacy (like SM) used variable liaison forms more frequently. The justification for the rather heavy reliance on the speech of SM is that, in Hudson's term (1996: 112), she was a 'skilled' speaker who produced several stretches of language that are very interesting for our present purposes. At the same time, she showed variable linguistic behaviour in broad conformity with her gender- and age-group. We reproduce below an interesting example of a stretch of elevated speech that occurred in conversation style, again produced by SM. We have already discussed this fragment in Chapter 3, in connexion with the influence of reading styles on intraspeaker variation. This was a fable in the style of La Fontaine, entitled *Le moustique et l'écrevisse* 'The mosquito and the shrimp' which had been composed in French-language classes by SM and one of her classmates, presumably with their teacher's help. It was to be performed at a school concert. SM's recitation from memory is notable for its variable liaisons; two extracts containing liaisons are as follows:

Table 3. Total numbers (N) and percentage realisation in the Dieuze speaker sample of liaison (%) after quand, e.g. in: *quand il arrive* 'when he arrives'

Gender / Age	Interview		Conversation	
	(N)	%	(N)	%
Males 16–19				
JM	2	0	10	0
BR	22	100	9	100
BB	9	100	2	100
ES	6	100	5	100
Females 16–19				
VN	2	100	12	100
IR	8	12.5	7	14.3
EM	11	100	10	100
CN	6	100	20	100
Males 11–12				
CF	11	100	6	100
AR	8	100	10	100
JB	4	100	–	–
BW	3	0	2	0
Females 11–12				
SP	7	0	5	0
SM	6	100	13	84.6
NG	19	100	5	100
CY	2	0	6	0
All groups	147	78.2	136	76.5

(12)   Un moustique des plus piqueurs
       S'en allait_avec une troupe de promeneurs
       [...]
       Bien que ce ne soit pas_une couronne
       Mais_un bouquet de fleurs[1]

However one might wish to categorise these liaisons in terms of the taxonomy proposed by Gadet (1997a: 52) and discussed in 5.3.4.2 above, the point at issue here is that liaisons after *allait, mais* and *pas* were totally absent in spontaneous speech in the Dieuze corpus. We may note firstly, that this extract shows that the 11–12 female Dieuze informants at least are in contact with formal instruction regarding variable liaison. The interesting question raised by this extract concerns the extent to which SM may have internalised and generalised the rules governing variable liaison on the basis of having memorised three tokens. As mentioned above, SM gave the impression of unusual linguistic competence for her age, and she is the only informant in Table 3 to show style shift in the expected direction. This tantalising glimpse into the communicative competence of an individual emphasises that variable liaison is part of a supralectal overlay whose mastery seems quite highly dependent on individual competence. We discuss this supralectal aspect of variable liaison in more detail below in Section 5.6.

A further interesting aspect of the results shown in Table 3 is the dramatic contrast between the realisation rates for *quand* in Dieuze, and those reported by Encrevé in Paris. Encrevé (1983, 1988) analysed variable liaison in the corpus recorded by Laks in Villejuif, at that time a mainly working-class district of Paris. Laks's speaker sample was a group of male lower-working-class adolescents; perhaps the most non-standard speakers one could find, the true custodians of the vernacular. It is inconceivable that Encrevé excluded liaison after *quand* as a variable form in Laks's data; therefore the realisation rate in this context must have been close to zero, since variable liaison was realised only 17 times in all in Laks's corpus, and twelve of these liaisons were after *dans* and two after *est.* It is also inconceivable that *quand* occurred so rarely as to be negligible. Further, it seems very unlikely that liaison after *quand* counted as being invariably present in Laks's very non-standard data. So we can conclude that

---

1. A translation of the first couplet has been given above, but for convenience, it is repeated here: 'A mosquito of the biting-most sort / Went out with a troop of strollers …' Translation of the second couplet: 'Although it is not a crown / but a bouquet of flowers'.

liaison after *quand* was almost never made in Laks's data. In contrast, as we saw above, the realisation rate for this context in the Dieuze data is 77.4%. Liaison was also variable in the Dieuze data in *dans, tout, chez, très* and *moins*. These lexical items occurred even less frequently than *quand*, and were distributed in a similarly erratic pattern, rendering them even less amenable to quantitative analysis. Nevertheless, *dans* did occur in sufficient numbers to allow the calculation of a realisation rate of 91.8% (N = 110 for all speakers in both styles). Aggregating the occurrences of *tout, chez, très* and *moins* for all speakers in both styles (N = 42) gives a realisation rate of 83.3%. Liaison after *dans, tout, chez, très* and *moins* must also have been near zero in Laks's data, as argued above.

In itself this contrast is not very surprising, since most of the Villejuif informants were victims of inner-city deprivation, and integrated into a sub-culture that involved activities such as petty crime. School was very much excluded from this culture. By contrast, most of the Dieuze informants were successfully 'socialised' into middle-class values, and this of course implies regular attendance at school. Nevertheless the interest of this contrast lies in the fairly direct comparability of two groups of young people, very different in their response to mainstream values, and the way in which their respective responses are reflected in their grammar.

Smith (1996, 1998)

Smith (1996, 1998) compared realisation rates in the corpus of radio speech recorded in the early 1960s by Ågren (see above) with his own corpus, recorded in 1995–6 from *France Inter*. He found a decline in variable liaison in five out of the six grammatical categories he studied, and an overall decline from 61.6% in Ågren's data to 46.8% in the *France Inter* data. Table 4 below shows the liaison rates in Ågren's and Smith's corpora in the six categories.

The six grammatical categories studied by Smith were as follows:

i.   after forms of *être*;
ii. after forms of *avoir*;
iii. after forms of the semi-auxiliary verbs *falloir* 'must', *pouvoir* 'can' and *devoir* 'must';
iv. after the negative particle *pas*;
v.   after polysyllabic adverbs and prepositions, e.g. *pendant* 'in', 'during', *toujours* 'always', *extrêmement* 'extremely';
vi. after plural nouns.

Table 4. Variable liaison in Ågren's (1960–1) and Smith's (1995–6) corpora

Category	1960–1		1995–6	
	(N)	%	(N)	%
être	3858	87.9	1301	78.8
avoir	1140	51.4	411	28.0
semi-aux	851	50.2	407	25.8
pas	965	23.1	379	21.4
poly. adv.	988	40.3	234	12.8
pl. nouns	639	26.6	309	22.0
Totals	8441	61.6	3041	46.8

What is interesting about the display in Table 4 is the range of disparities between the degrees to which liaison has declined across the six categories. We can see that by far the most frequent category, *être* in its various forms, is also quite stable, if in slow decline (87.9% > 78.8%). This is probably a reliable result given the large number of tokens analysed by each researcher. Smith suggests that the frequency of *être*, and especially the 3rd-person singular form, as in *c'est intéressant*, may enhance the stylistic value of this category in a formal situation; conversely, in everyday speech the non-liaison after the frequent *est* may be important cumulatively as an informal marker. Correspondingly, although *avoir* in its various forms is a very frequent verb, it may be less salient sociolinguistically because the frequent 1st- and 3rd-person singular forms *ai* and *a* contain no liaison consonant. Against this, it has to be said that there is no clear correlation between frequency and stability in the other four categories.

5.4.1 Liaison in Montreal French

The case of variable liaison in Montreal French is interesting because it illustrates the striking ways in which a language variety can diverge from its standard language. The long isolation of Canadian French from the influence of hexagonal French explains the distinctiveness of some of the features found in the Canadian varieties. De Jong (1993) studied liaison in Montreal French, comparing the Sankoff-Cedergren corpus of 1971, described in Sankoff and Cedergren (1971) and the similar Montreal corpus recorded in 1984. His broad finding is in line with that reported for other sociolinguistic variables in Montreal: much higher rates of non-standard linguistic behaviour. In liaison this means that some forms are invariable in metropolitan French but variable in the Montreal variety. Thus as mentioned above, the pronoun *ils* may be pronounced [iz], [ij] or [j]: *ils ont* may have the pronunciation [izɔ̃], [ijɔ̃] or [jɔ̃]. This phenomenon does not seem to have been reported in metropolitan French. Even when the liaison after *ils* is made in Montreal, the standard pronunciation is now [iz] for all speakers, irrespective of their social class. Similarly, De Jong reports variable liaison after the pronoun *on* in Montreal, where this liaison form appears to be invariable in metropolitan French.

The above examples show the familiar pattern of non-standard linguistic processes, advanced in Canadian French, that are less advanced in the metropolitan varieties, or even barely present. A more exotic example is the case of the 1st-person verb form *suis* in Montreal; De Jong found that the use of liaison after *suis* had declined among middle-class speakers between 1971 and 1984, while its use had increased among working-class speakers. The explanation may be that liaison after *suis* is realised with the consonant [t] in Montreal, rather than the standard [z]. The middle-class speakers, whose awareness of metropolitan French was heightened during the 1970s and 80s as exposure to standard European French grew, were increasingly conscious of the non-standard value, from the Parisian viewpoint, of a form like *je suis* [t] *en train de le faire* 'I'm doing it'. This example endorses the suggestion advanced by Kroch (1978:18–19) concerning the strategies that more mobile middle-class speakers have available for adopting prestigious features so as to distinguish their speech from that of the working classes: they can resist connected-speech processes (CSPs) such as consonant-cluster simplification, vowel centralisation and schwa deletion; and they can adopt linguistic features from outside the immediate speech community.

Having presented various findings from the work of linguists who have used corpus-based methods to study variable liaison, we now consider whether the patterns presented above allow us to make a judgment as to whether liaison is declining among French speakers generally.

5.5   Variation and change in liaison

What is striking about the results given above is the widely different liaison rates for the different speaker groups. The situation regarding variable liaison is probably similar to variable *ne* deletion (Coveney 1996:64–5): differences between results reported by various researchers are no doubt due to the considerably different social characteristics of the groups studied, as well as the different speech styles elicited by the various researchers. Some consistent patterns do emerge from these results — little sex differentiation, older and middle-class speakers using more variable liaison forms — but in general, not enough directly comparable data are available to enable us to make any very confident assertions about the possible future directions of change in liaison. Ashby asserted (1981a: 56) that his results indicated the progressive loss of liaison, but it seems more prudent to conclude that the rather irregular patterns that he found in the speech of a small speaker sample should preclude any strong claims being made.

A further problem complicating the study of any possible decline in variable liaison is the lack of a baseline in the form of reliable historical evidence. As we mentioned above, Encrevé's classification of liaison forms shown in Table 1 is based on a fuller taxonomy drawn up by Delattre; but this classification is not based on systematic observation. Therefore we cannot be sure whether differences between Delattre's classification and later findings represent genuine change, or simply result from inaccuracies perpetrated by Delattre. This is the difficulty attending Encrevé's observation (1988: 48) that one of the few recent changes in liaison is after uninflected monosyllabic words (*très, trop, dans, quand*, etc.). Encrevé suggests that these forms have changed category fairly recently, from invariable to variable.

The results reported by Encrevé and Smith, based on the public speech of politicians and journalists, are more robust; it seems clear that variable liaison is in decline in the speech styles used by these groups of speakers. Here again, however, we are faced with the problem of direct comparability; does the decline of a linguistic feature found in the highly formal speech of highly educated speakers reflect a parallel decline in the wider speech community? Some linguists assert (notably Bell 1982, 1984) that media speakers tailor their language in response to their perceived audience: the principle of 'audience design' discussed earlier. It is not clear exactly how radio journalists form such an accurate picture of the sociolinguistic profile of their intended audience, but Bell (1982) has provided very solid evidence that radio journalists do operate audience design in this way. Bell distinguishes between stylistic variation in situations where speakers have direct, face-to-face feedback from their addressee(s), and those where the relationship is indirect. The example of the latter situation that Bell discusses extensively is variation between two New Zealand radio stations, the broadcasts of one of which were aimed at a relatively cultivated audience, the other rather more 'down-market'. Bell found very clear correlations between each radio station's target audience and the treatment of certain linguistic variables by the radio announcers employed on the respective stations. When speaking on the less prestigious radio station, announcers used more non-standard linguistic forms than those employed by stations whose target audience was presumed to be more cultivated.

Thus it is rather difficult to establish what conclusions are to be drawn concerning the status of variable liaison from the evidence provided by Encrevé and Smith. On the one hand, it appears that public speakers such as radio journalists produce an approximation to the mix of linguistic forms they think their audience expects to hear. On the other hand, of course, serious radio journalists are commonly regarded as the custodians of the standard language. We are not suggesting that politicians and broadcast journalists are at the forefront of linguistic change, with the rest of the speech community following; it does not seem very plausible that many speakers want to imitate the language they hear on the broadcast media, nor that most linguistic changes originate in these formal, highly-planned varieties. The most prudent guess regarding the relationship between public speakers, their audience, and linguistic change, is probably that serious broadcast journalists are at once the guardians of the standard language, and participants in variation and change within it. The standard language is of course subject to change like every other language variety; language in the serious spoken media is more formal than most, but still reflects, with a time lag, changes that are proceeding in more casual speech. This explains the large numbers of letters received by the BBC, and by *France Inter* and *France Culture*, complaining about the 'sloppy' pronunciation and non-standard accents of radio and TV announcers, written by listeners who expect media speech to conform closely to the standard. Thus it is probably true that variable liaison in the wider speech community is in the later stages of a slow decline, as the indirect evidence provided by Encrevé and Smith shows.

5.6 The stability of liaison

We suggested immediately above that variable liaison may be in slow but steady regression. We stated above also that the highly idiosyncratic character of variable liaison has interesting consequences for the way in which changes operate upon it, and we now examine this issue.

Historically, liaison is a linguistic residue, consisting of the maintenance in pre-vocalic position of word-final consonants that have been lost in the other phonological contexts (pre-consonant and pre-pause). It is debatable whether we can consider liaison as forming part of a process of variation and change that is resulting in the near-total loss of word-final consonants in French. This process has been taking place over a considerable period; indeed, over the history of the French language. One might therefore expect any remaining change to be slow; alternatively, liaison may be regarded as a more or less stable residue, unaffected by an otherwise general process of change. In any event, variable liaison consonants are probably better thought of as being inserted syllable-initially, rather than deleted word-finally, as we argue below. Moreover, Smith's (1996) study of diachronic change in variable liaison offers an interesting alternative argument to one of simple progressive loss; we now present and discuss this view.

One of the most striking features of variable liaison is its quite large degree of linguistic arbitrariness. The loss of word-final consonants in pre-consonantal and pre-pausal positions proceeded in a phonologically natural way for quite a long period in the history of the French language; it appears that the loss of word-final consonants before another following consonant was more or less complete by about 1300, the end of the Old French period (Price 1984:46). This process is natural in that word- and syllable-final consonants are articulated weakly, and the trend to reduce consonant clusters also appears be a natural process. Moreover, from the hearer's point of view word-final consonants are more difficult to perceive; at least, it is difficult to distinguish phonetically fairly similar consonants such as /p, t, k/ from one another, and communicatively, therefore, the cost of articulating them may often outweigh the benefit (leaving aside functional factors such as the marking of semantic features word-finally). The loss of word-final consonants before a pause seems also to be a natural process from the articulatory point of view, but when this began to happen at a later stage in the history of French, probably by the beginning of the 17th century, it met with a good deal of resistance from prescriptivists. This contrasts with the earlier situation regarding the loss of word-final consonants before another consonant; the difference is that the 17th century was the time when the French language was beginning to undergo intensive codification at the hands of grammarians. By this time many words had acquired a double or triple pronunciation depending on whether they were pronounced before a consonant, pause or vowel; a survival of this stage is the French numeral *six*, which today of course is still pronounced [si], [sis] or [siz] depending on the following phonological context (consonant, pause or vowel).

The net result of this turbulent period was linguistic uncertainty regarding the pronunciation of word-final consonants, resulting from the partial success of the grammarians in restoring certain consonants in all phonological contexts, and from the confusion inherent in a situation where some words have more than one pronunciation. The situation was ready for the imposition or consolidation by upper-class speakers of a linguistically arbitrary system; one that is not transparently rule-governed, but can only be learnt through long immersion in the appropriate milieu. Clearly, the motivation for developing or maintaining such a system is to be able to distinguish members of the group from non-members. We can draw a parallel between variable liaison and any in-group code whose function is to mystify non-initiates. For instance, teenage slang and verbal games such as *verlan* have much the same function. However, there is a crucial difference between the codes used by marginal groups such as adolescents or ethnic minorities, and variable liaison: the latter is (or was) an area of variation used by the powerful to exclude the socially ambitious. A closer parallel might be the complicated English lexical set referred to previously and distinguished by the back vowels [ʌ] and [ʊ], which in southern/standard English give the minimal pairs 'putt' and 'put', 'pus' and 'puss'; these are not predictable from spelling, as these examples show, and are probably difficult to learn unless one grows up in the right environment.

Variable liaison is therefore both largely linguistically unmotivated and unpredictable. From a synchronic perspective the phenomenon appears to be unmotivated phonologically, since one can argue that on the one hand, non-realisation of liaison is governed by ease-of-articulation factors, while on the other, realisation of liaison conforms to the 'maximal onset principle' which is claimed to correspond to a speaker's preference for consonant-initial syllables. On the phonetic level, informal styles appear generally to be characterised by less linguistic substance, and weak syllable-final consonants such as /l/ and /r/ often elide in everyday French. From this point of view liaison is distinctive also, since liaison consonants are syllable-initial and it seems more plausible to describe variable liaison as the insertion of consonants in careful style, rather than as a deletion phenomenon in informal speech.

From an acquisitional viewpoint, Garmadi's (1981:64–72) distinction between what she terms the *norme* and the *sur-norme* 'supra-norm' seems pertinent in relation to variable and invariable liaison; the *norme* refers to a core lect, primary in terms of order of acquisition and more or less common to all members in a speech community, admitting of course of some degree of overlap, while the *sur-norme* corresponds to a supralectal overlay acquired at a secondary stage by an elite who have achieved a high degree of literacy. Variable liaison would seem to be characteristic of the *sur-norme*, both in terms of its being acquired at a relatively late stage, and its dependence on a high level of literacy.

From the social viewpoint, variable liaison is controlled confidently only by the educated middle classes, and used by them mainly in formal styles. From this point of view, to a certain extent it resembles certain stereotypically upper-class phonological variables, like the vowel alternations mentioned above or the English aristocratic pronunciation (now in recession) of 'off' as [ɔːf], or of 'house' as [hais]. Further parallels can be sought in the English 'shall/will' shibboleth, or the absence of a word-initial glottal stop in Scots and Irish dialects, where one is present in emphatic RP: hence 'an [ʔ] apple' (RP), but 'an apple' (Scots), giving the effect of 'a napple'. Here again, however, regional origin is probably more relevant in these examples than the degree of literacy achieved.

Furthermore, the uniqueness of variable liaison is precisely its variable use: the use that conveys social/stylistic information. So whereas an English upper- or upper-middle-class speaker will realise [ɔːf] and [hais] consistently, the equivalent French speaker's use of liaison will be variable. A closer parallel still might be the variable habit of English upper-class speakers of referring to themselves by using the impersonal pronoun 'one'. But no other area of variation, in any language, seems to be very closely equivalent to French variable liaison. Encrevé has suggested that variable liaison is an 'inverted sociolinguistic variable', because variation is actually encouraged in middle-class/formal speech; in contrast to many other variables, where middle-class speakers largely succeed in suppressing variation in their speech compared to working-class speakers, who show more variation. This is no doubt overstating the case, since we have seen that working-class speakers do use variable liaison to some extent. But this does not detract from the highly unusual character of the phenomenon. A further possible formulation is in terms of the socio-linguistic notion of the stereotype (Chambers and Trudgill 1998: 75), a linguistic feature of whose social/stylistic value speakers tend to be highly aware, and which may be characteristic either of standard or non-standard varieties.

How do these considerations relate to the possible disappearance of variable liaison? We said above that variable liaison is largely arbitrary from a linguistic point of view, and hence difficult to learn without direct experience of the appropriate social milieu. This means that upper-class speakers can use the variable confidently as a badge of identity, and can also define what variable liaison forms are to be used. The attitude of upper- or upper-middle-class speakers towards prescriptively correct linguistic forms is generally more relaxed than that of their immediate social inferiors, the lower-middle classes, perhaps because upper-class speakers interact in more exclusive social circles; hence they notoriously take little heed of what outsiders think of their behaviour. Moreover, the social behaviour of the upper classes is almost by definition the 'best' behaviour, to be emulated by the socially ambitious. So far as language is concerned, these latter groups need to rely on education, and books more generally (including etiquette books) to learn the current version of the standard language, or any other form of socially 'correct' behaviour.

The recent history of variable liaison shows its unusual character: broadly, it ebbs and flows in response to large-scale social conditions; in particular, in response to the relationship between the upper-middle and lower-middle classes. Smith (1996: 22–3) points out that in the 19th and early 20th centuries, the bourgeoisie (the upper-middle class living on inherited income) used liaison more sparingly than the class below. Smith cites Nicholson (1909: 82) to this effect: '[…] it is only the class of people intermediate between the educated and the illiterate who link [i.e. use variable liaison] profusely'. Nicholson speculates further: 'To this perhaps is due, in some measure, the growing tendency among the educated towards a more sparing use of liaison in familiar and colloquial speech'. Smith draws a parallel between a linguistic feature that is the property of a small, privileged group, and a commodity on the stock market; when the commodity becomes too widely available, its value falls. Correspondingly, when a linguistic feature comes to be widely used, by groups other than the most prestigious, the latter group must find other forms with which to differentiate itself from those below it. This formulation is of course reminiscent of Bourdieu's (1982) notion of the 'linguistic market'.

Thus Nicholson is probably not quite accurate when he refers to the 'most educated' groups as using liaison less than their social inferiors; the bourgeoisie might indeed have been more educated than the petite bourgeoisie, but as we have suggested, education is not necessarily (or was not then) the key to mastering a prestigious area of linguistic variation. Parallels in English are the aristocratic use (now seemingly defunct) of forms which, when used by other social groups, are perceived as being uneducated; for instance, the use of 'ain't', or of non-standard 'don't', as in 'Port don't do the liver any good' (Powell 1966: 39). A closer parallel still is in English upper-class attitudes to spelling-pronunciation, as exemplified by the scornful attitude of Wyld (1906: 366), a socially highly-placed historian of the English language, who remarked of pronunciation that relies on spelling: 'careful speech is always vulgar'. Wyld would berate his students for not using upper-class, non-orthographic pronunciations such as 'weskit' for 'waistcoat', or 'forehead' to rhyme with 'horrid'.

From about the late 1960s onwards, the attitude of the French upper-middle class towards the standard language has undergone further changes, again as a result of the way French society has evolved (when referring to this period we need to use the term 'upper-middle class', as the bourgeoisie in the 20th century are now more or less equivalent to the English 'middle classes'). We have already seen (Smith 1996, 1998) that variable liaison in formal radio speech has declined between the early 1960s and 1996. Smith argues that this decline reflects the changes consequent principally on the social upheavals of the 1960s and 1970s, typified most spectacularly by the 'events' of May 1968. He suggests that although no substantive change in the French economic structure has taken place during this period, most notably in terms of the distribution of wealth and income, important symbolic social changes have come about. After Italy, France continues to have the highest ratio of inequality (15:1) between the highest and lowest 10% of wage-earners in the OECD group of countries; at the same time French decision-makers now feel the need to adopt a consensual rather than a directive approach, and to emphasise solidarity rather than hierarchy. Social divisions, between the middle and working classes, men and women, young and old, have become blurred during this period, even though economic divisions are as sharp as before, or even sharper, as Smith points out (1996: 133–4). Therefore it is to be expected that a linguistic variable such as liaison should decline during this period, given that it is so stereotypically a middle-class phenomenon.

In the intervening period, between about 1900 and the 1960s, the use of variable liaison saw an increase, with some liaison forms that had fallen into disuse being reintroduced: *voyons un peu* 'let's just see', *nous sommes arrivés* 'we've arived', *ils doivent aller* 'they have to go' (Encrevé 1988:259, citing Martinon 1913). Again, this seems to be a case of linguistic change tracking social change, as Smith again argues (1996:27). The French 19th-century bourgeoisie had previously avoided certain liaison forms so as to distance themselves from the petite bourgeoisie, and this reflected their sense of social, and hence linguistic, unassailability. The crucial change in the early and mid-20th century was the increasing importance of education as a 'legitimating' element. Those who direct France are still drawn largely from the upper middle-classes, but the possession of inherited wealth and titles is no longer generally seen as sufficient qualification for accession to the commanding heights of French industry or administration. Social privilege now requires the sanction of a high degree of educational attainment, typically in a *Grande École* (prestigious French higher-education establishment recruiting the administrative and technical elite through competitive examination). This is because education, including to the highest level, is commonly perceived as being in principle open to all. There is of course in reality still a very strong correlation between the social-class background of students and their chances of admission to a *Grande École*. According to this view, propounded notably by Bourdieu and Passeron (1970), the educational system has two functions: firstly to perpetuate upper-middle-class domination, and secondly to conceal the first function. Thus in the pre-1960s period, we can hypothesise that the high levels of variable liaison used by middle-class speakers responded to an association in the public mind between educatedness and the equitable access to power and wealth.

In the previous paragraphs we have tried to show that over the past 150 years or so, variable liaison, rather than declining steadily, has ebbed and flowed in response to large-scale social changes: or perhaps has ebbed and flowed against a background of slow decline. Clearly, we cannot predict whether variable liaison will eventually disappear or not, any more than we can predict how French society will evolve further. On the one hand, it seems likely from our current perspective that educated French speakers will continue to perceive this area of variability as a valuable sociolinguistic resource, useful for marking formal speech styles. On the other hand, the 'asterisk-heap' of linguistic history is piled with forms that now seem ludicrously formal: in English, 'whom' is now extremely stilted in speech; in French, interrogation through subject-clitic inversion (*quand pars-tu?* 'when do you leave?) is suffering a similar fate. We simply cannot foretell the future of variable liaison.

5.7 Prospects for liaison sans enchaînement

Finally, within the context of variation and change in liaison we may consider *liaison sans enchaînement*. As was mentioned above, Encrevé (1983, 1988), carried out an apparent-time study of variable *liaison sans enchaînement* in political discourse. He suggests that the use of this type of liaison is increasing, at least among educated speakers, basing his assertion on systematic observation of its increasing use in political discourse over the past fifty years, as well as on impressionistic observation of his peers, i.e. educated Parisians. Encrevé suggests various reasons for the emergence of this type of liaison:

1. the high degree of literacy among those who practise it, implying that knowledge of the written form of a word, which suggests a closed syllable, may induce a speaker to close syllables in speech;

2. knowledge of English and German, with their greater preponderance of closed syllables;
3. the increasing use of the *accent d'insistance* ('intensive stress'), a rhetorical device which displaces the main stress from its normal place on the last syllable of the intonation group, and which may be accompanied by the closure of the preceding syllable, as for instance in: *c'est impossible* (stressed syllable underlined).

Encrevé points out that the increase in the use of *liaison sans enchaînement*, if it continues, will to some extent change the syllabic structure of spoken French, to the extent that the number of closed syllables will increase. However, at the moment the phenomenon appears to be confined to the public speech of a rather small number of highly educated speakers, and it seems unlikely to spread much beyond this community.

5.8 Summary and conclusion

The idiosyncratic nature of French liaison consists of its greater variability in standard rather than non-standard varieties; also, one may add, in the fact that it is a linguistic resource which is highly dependent on literacy and hence not available to an entire speech community, but rather chiefly to the educated elite. For this relatively limited number of French speakers, those who control it fully, variable liaison has a very high socio-stylistic value. The linguistically and socially highly constrained nature of variable liaison means that it does not comfortably fit into the analytic framework that we have sought to develop here: that which seeks to explore the sociolinguistic function, for an entire speech community, of variation on the different levels of linguistic analysis considered in relative isolation from each other. Thus for example, as an insertion rather than deletion phenomenon it shares properties with grammatical variables such as the elision of *ne*. Liaison seems to be a highly unusual case; at least if we draw the relatively limited but intuitive comparison between its prominence in French and parallels in the other major, Western standardised languages.

Chapter 6

Variation in the French lexicon

6.1 Introduction

The remarks made at the beginning of the Chapter 4, concerning the difficulties associated with quantifying grammatical variation, may also be applied to variation on the lexical level. The frequency issue associated with the study of grammatical variation is also present in lexis, as we shall see. In addition, the problem of semantic equivalence raises issues connected with the socio-stylistic distribution of variable lexis that do not appear to have been treated by scholars working in variation; in particular, the intraspeaker level seems not to have been studied by a direct comparison of linguistic behaviour, although Lodge (1989) obtained interesting interspeaker results through a variationist attitudinal study. As before, in this chapter we discuss these issues using illustrative variable language data analysed in the Dieuze corpus.

6.2 Previous studies of variable lexis

Rather little variationist research has been devoted to French lexis, or indeed to lexis in general. Perhaps the most substantial research programme devoted to style variation in lexis is that associated with Biber (1988, 1995), which however focuses principally on the functional aspects of style variation by comparing variation across speech and writing. Biber sees on the one hand 'production circumstances' (i.e. situational context), and on the other communicative functions as the principal factors influencing variable lexis, and indeed language in general. Production circumstances include scripted vs. unscripted communication, personal vs. impersonal, proximal vs. distant, interactive vs. unidirectional and others; communicative function has to do broadly with the ideational–affective polarity of an interchange. From a sociolinguistic viewpoint, Biber's view of the relation between social and register variation is broadly that middle-class speakers have in the nature of things occasion to use, and therefore access to, a wider range of 'elaborated' registers than working class speakers. Biber does however recognise elsewhere in his work (Finegan and Biber 1994) the existence of purely symbolic linguistic variants which are involved in register variation and serve no functional purpose, and whose function is to signal formality of register through the fact of their deriving from prestigious social varieties. Nevertheless the variationist paradigm is one which is largely orthogonal to Biber's enterprise.

Sankoff, Thibault and Bérubé (1978), in an early study of variable lexis in the large Sankoff-Cedergren corpus of Montreal French (Sankoff and Cedergren 1971), defined a threefold object of their analysis as 'the alternation among partial synonyms in a number of well-defined syntactic contexts, the logical and semantic relations between these forms, and the interaction between individual variability and the socio-economic differentiation of the speech community' (p. 23). We will examine most of these issues in this chapter. The analysis of Sankoff et al. which is relevant here, and which approximates to a variationist or least correlationist study of variable lexis, shows social-class differentiation in the use of Montreal French words meaning for instance 'paid employment' and 'task'; with MC speakers showing greater use of high-value variants such as *ouvrage* 'paid employment' while WC speakers had higher rates of use of non-standard variants such as *job*.

In the same corpus, Martel (1984) reported correlations between age and level of education and the differential use, on the one hand of lexical variants characteristic of Quebec French and on the other of standard French (i.e. non-localised, non-Quebec variants). Thus for example, Martel reported greater use of standard French *film* 'film', 'movie' among younger and more highly-educated speakers, while older speakers with fewer years of education showed greater use of the localised term *vue*. One can certainly think of this result as 'variationist' in that shows probable penetration of Quebec French by the standard variety, and aligns with the findings concerning /r/ in Montreal (Clermont and Cedergren 1979) which showed younger, MC females as the agents of the replacement from outside the community of the localised apical /r/ by the European French uvular variant.

Schenk-van Witsen (1981) reported gender-related differentiation in the use of lexis in a speaker sample recorded in Orléans in 1969–70. Rather than individual lexical items, Schenk-van Witsen focused on quantifying the use of lexical sets referring to areas of experience and modes of expression that previous scholars (Jespersen 1922; Lakoff 1975; Key 1975) had reported or suggested as differentiating men and women. Certain results were unsurprising, other less so: Schenk-van Witsen found that men referred to subjects such as sport, politics and business more frequently than women, while women talked more often about their house, family and friends. These differences seem unsurprising because the females in the speaker sample were mostly house-wives. On the other hand, women used more personal pronouns while men used more abstract nouns, place names, nouns of number and polysyllabic adverbs.

Variationist studies of lexis of actual usage are thus rare, but the few available afford interesting glimpses into the subject. Lodge's (1989) question-naire-based study elicited speakers' attitudes to the use of pairs of non-standard lexical items, and his results echoed remarkably accurately the results of many sociolinguistic surveys of actual behaviour: females and lower-middle-class speakers reported less use of non-standard lexis, students and retired people greater. Interestingly, lower-middle-class speakers reported less use than middle-class, another well-attested finding.

Lodge's (1989:427) remarks regarding variation in lexis generally and French lexis in particular are quite pertinent: he points out that while a consid-erable amount of research has been carried out on (especially Canadian) French variable phonology and grammar, '...less research has been devoted to variation in the lexicon. This is understandable given the recalcitrance of the lexicon to systematic analysis, but it does not abolish the interest which many features of the French lexicon present to the variationist.' The remarks concerning gram-mar made in Chapter 4 apply *a fortiori* to vocabulary: while any phonemic system is a more or less closed set, it is impossible to delimit the lexicon of a language. Further, as Lodge remarks (Lodge et al. 1997:32): 'Linguists have a rather perverse tendency to locate lexicology outside the central core of their discipline, probably because the thousands of words in a language cannot be embraced by 'rules' in the same way as its phonological or grammatical sys-tems.' Certainly, the relations between lexical items (words and phrases), by virtue of their involvement in various types of meaning, are of a complexity, as we shall see, that puts difficulties in the way of variationist analysis.

6.3   Lexical variation in the Dieuze corpus

French at first sight appears to possess a lexical resource which seems less copious in comparable languages, and which offers to the linguist the opportu-nity of analysing lexical data by transferring the sociolinguistic-variable concept to the lexical level. These data consist of the pairs of lexical doublets or alternants which are numerous in French, and which appear to reflect the particularly wide gulf between the standard and non-standard varieties of the language, wider perhaps than in other standardised Western languages. One example from this lexical set is the pair *voiture* (standard) and *bagnole* (non-standard), both of which have the equivalent reference expressible by English 'car', but each of which conveys different 'associative' meaning (cf. Leech 1981:18–19; problems of semantic equivalence are discussed below). One aim of the present analysis, then, is to investigate whether social and stylistic variation in the lexicon is more pronounced in French than on other linguistic levels. This notion seems plausible if one assumes that full lexical items have more cognitive prominence, and therefore potentially greater value as socio-linguistic markers, than phonological or syntactic variables. We have already seen that variation between the standard and non-standard (sets of) varieties is apparent in French to varying degrees at all linguistic levels, but as Lodge suggests (1993:256), in the course of a discussion whether contemporary French may be characterised by a form of diglossia: 'it is probably in the lexicon that style-shifting in French is indicated most obviously'. The presence of style shift in lexis manifestly implies variation along the interspeaker dimensions, notably of social class, age and sex. Whether by this 'obviousness' is meant sociolinguistic salience in respect of the speech community's awareness of it (as opposed to the linguist's) is not made clear, but the involvement in semantic content of full lexical words especially, in a way that does not obtain on the levels of variable phonology, morphology and perhaps grammatical words, makes this notion plausible. Put more simply, speakers are aware of words in a way they are not aware of phonological and morphological items. This is of course reflected in the fact that variation and change on the lexical level is a subject of interest to and comment by laypersons, as it is perceived to be the level most susceptible to comment without specialist knowledge.

A broader aim addressed here is the consideration whether lexical variation can profitably be examined in a quantitative paradigm.

6.4   Structure of the chapter

This chapter has the following broad structure: firstly, we describe issues relating to the methodology, that is the identification and analysis of the lexical data. Problems surrounding analysis of the data are discussed in tandem with the presentation of results. We examine interspeaker variation initially, and subsequently intraspeaker variation, and the issues associated with each of these axes will be considered in turn. Finally, we consider the sociolinguistic status of lexical variation in the light of the results emerging from the variable data presented here.

6.5   Identification and analysis of lexical variables in the Dieuze corpus

The starting point for the analysis discussed here was the questionnaire-based investigation conducted by Lodge 1989. The sources used to aid identification of the lexical variables (apart from the list of fifty lexical doublets used by Lodge, of which a sample is shown below) were: (i) the researcher's intuitions, reinforced by judgments found in dictionaries (principally the *Petit Robert* (1986) and *Nouveau Petit Robert* (1995) and the recent bilingual *Oxford-Hachette* (1997), as well as Merle (1986) and Hérail and Lovatt (1990); and (ii) cases of self- or other-repair or comments by informants on their own or their colocutor's use of non-standard lexis.

Table 1: Sample of lexical doublets selected by Lodge (1989)

Non-standard	Standard	Gloss
baffe (pop.)	gifle	'slap'
bagnole (fam./pop.)	automobile	'car'
bahut (arg. des écoles)	lycée	'secondary school'
se balader (fam.)	se promener	'to walk'
baratin (pop.)	discours abondant	'spiel'
blague (fam.)	farce	'joke'
bosser (pop.)	travailler	'to work'
bouffer (fam.)	manger	'eat'
boulot (fam.)	travail	'work'
bouquin (fam.)	livre	'book'
pèze (arg.)	argent	'money'
piaule (pop.)	chambre	'bedroom'
pieu (pop.)	lit	'bed'
pif (pop.)	nez	'nose'
pognon (pop.)	argent	'money'

Reproduced above in Table 1 is a sample of the fifty pairs that Lodge selected; they were chosen so as to avoid specialist slang and one should therefore expect that all of the words would occur in 'general' informal discourse. This is clearly an essential requirement. Given with the words are the style labels attributed to them by the *Petit Robert*, one of the standard French dictionaries. The *Petit Robert* definition is also provided. The list is reproduced to give readers unfamiliar with informal French lexis an impression of the extent of the phenomenon, which seems much less common in English (for instance) than in French.

6.5.1   Classification of lexical items

The list given above is very far from being exhaustive: 237 different items were observed in the Dieuze corpus, and are listed and glossed in the appendix. The style labels in Table 1 call for some comment. Bilingual dictionaries commonly employ a tripartite distinction between style labels; the *Oxford-Hachette* distinguishes between *familier* (colloquial), *populaire* (casual) and *vulgaire* (vulgar or taboo). This tripartition has been adopted here, despite its shortcomings (discussed more fully below). It is clear that style labels, among other features of dictionaries, lag considerably behind usage. For instance, the 1995 *Nouveau Petit Robert* retains for *pèze* the style label '*argot*'. A further point is that terms of *argot* or *jargon* (both translatable as 'slang' or 'jargon', judging by the *Petit Robert* definitions), originally the property of marginal social groups, are quite often adopted into the mainstream of a speech community. Calvet (1994:5) points out that everyday usage does not maintain any consistent distinction between *argot* and *jargon*, even though dictionaries attempt to do so: *argot* is defined by the *Petit Robert* as 'the language of criminals, of the criminal class', but also as a 'set of oral non-technical words affected by a social group', and *jargon* as 'an incomprehensible language' and 'language particular to a group and characterised by its complication and the adoption of certain words and phrases'. Indeed, it can be seen in Table 1, from the application to *bahut* of the style label *argot* that the *Petit Robert* does not use the label consistently in its own terms. Similarly, the attribution of the label *argot* to *pèze* seems rather puzzling in the sense of criminal or other in-group slang, in view of its current widespread distribution. Turning to the labels we apply in our analysis below, *familier* may be glossed straightforwardly as 'colloquial'. *Populaire* is a problematic term; literally 'working-class', its application to some of the items given above reflects the prescriptive orientation of the *Petit Robert*. Words thus labelled are in fact used by all social classes in casual styles. Unsurprisingly, *vulgaire* tends to be applied to scatological terms.

The cases of self- or other-correction referred to above are revelatory of speakers' negative attitudes towards non-standard lexis, and these attitudes are of course often in conflict with their usage. Two examples may be given to illustrate different aspects of this phenomenon. In one conversation, a young male speaker used the exclamation *putain* (all items discussed in this chapter are glossed in the appendix); immediately afterwards he said as if to himself:

(1)   j'ose pas dire le mot parce que c'est en train d'nous enregistrer
      'I can't say the word because it's recording us'

(The verb *oser*, generally 'to dare', seems to be used here in its regional sense of *avoir le droit* 'be allowed to'). The above utterance is characterised by several non-standard features in pronunciation and grammar: deletion of *ne* in *j'ose pas*; of /r/ in *parce que*; of schwa in *en train d'nous*...; assimilation following schwa deletion, resulting in [ãtʀẽnnu]; non-realisation of variable liaison in *c'est*+vowel-initial word. One can plausibly assume that the speaker was unconscious, or largely so, of the non-standard value of these phonological and grammatical forms; the contrast between this low level of awareness, and his highly conscious reaction to the socio-stylistic value of *putain* illustrates rather strikingly the issue alluded to above, the greater sociolinguistic salience of the lexical level.

A more elliptical example of a similar evaluative reaction to the same word was provided by an older female speaker in conversation style who, responding to a remark made by her interlocuteur, expressed her astonished reaction by producing the following utterance, beginning to say *putain* 'bloody [fucking, etc.] hell', but switching in mid-word to a much milder expression:

(2)   pu: [py:] eh ben dis donc 'bloody ... well, I say'

In the case of *putain* and other lexical items which attract the dictionary style label of 'vulgar', the evaluative reactions expressed by speakers are generally in line with their own use of these items; in other words, members of speaker groups that perform self-repair in the way exemplified above (younger and female groups) tend to avoid highly stigmatised items. Other examples of self-repair were observed for the 'vulgar' lexical items *con* and *merde*. This high degree of conformity between evaluation and behaviour is understandable in relation to items such as those discussed above, i.e. terms that refer to taboo areas such as proscribed behaviour, body parts and bodily functions. We discuss the value of style labels in greater detail below; but briefly, a tripartite categorisation was applied to the lexical data discussed here, between items labelled by dictionaries *familier, populaire* and *vulgaire*.

As observed in the Dieuze corpus, speakers' reactions to certain lexical items other than those labelled *vulgaire* are less amenable to relatively straightforward explanation. One striking example concerns the term *nul*, which the (1997) *Oxford-Hachette* labels *familier* although the (1986) *Petit Robert* attributes no style label, while the (1995) *Nouveau Petit Robert* labels *familier* the extended application of the adjective from inanimate to animate objects. The term is an adjective of pejoration, corresponding to English 'hopeless' or 'useless'. In conversation style, an older male was recounting a dispute between himself and a teacher, in the course of which the teacher had described a piece of work the informant had done as '*nul*'. According to the informant's account he had retorted:

> (3)   on dit pas 'nul'; on dit 'médiocre'.... 'you don't say "hopeless"; you say "mediocre"'

The attitude revealed by this remark recalls the mismatches, discussed by Trudgill (1972), between speakers' actual use of non-standard linguistic items and their attitude towards the items, as revealed by their estimated or 'self-reported' use. There is of course an important difference between Trudgill's finding and the attitude implied in the above example; the Dieuze informant can plausibly be assumed to have been indignant because he perceived the use of a colloquial lexical item (which the informant himself had used in conversation style) to be inappropriate in an exchange concerning a serious topic between two non-intimates who were furthermore unequal in terms of status and power. So much is fairly straightforward, but the wider issue of what one might term the motivation behind the perceived 'contamination' of lexical items having no obvious taboo value such as *nul* is rather less so, since until fairly recently the history of *nul* was totally respectable. One might hypothesise that children and adolescents are the principal innovators of terms of (especially) praise and blame (as suggested by I. and P. Opie 1959: 161); such terms may then come to be perceived as non-standard by virtue of their being associated with a social group which is often the object of disapproval by older people. If this is so, then what is striking in the above example is that the informant, himself a member of this former group, has internalised and expressed the widely-held evaluative attitude, while of course continuing to show use of non-standard lexis characteristic of his social group.

6.5.2   The issue of lexical frequency

Full lexical words are much less frequent in a given text than phonological or most grammatical elements, and if, as is often the case in a sociolinguistic study, one is attempting to establish statistically significant correlations, between on the one hand the treatment of a linguistic variable by a group of informants, and on the other an extra-linguistic variable such as social class or speech style, then reasonably large numbers of tokens of the variable are required in order to ensure statistical reliability. Guy (1980: 1–36) points out that at least ten tokens per variable per speaker are desirable in order to minimise the possibility of random fluctuation; this possibility decreases as the number of tokens observed increases above ten. One can easily see that figures of this order may well be difficult to achieve for individual speakers or even speaker groups for full lexical items, given their infrequency relative to phonological segments or grammatical words.

The solution to the frequency problem adopted here is to treat the set of variable lexical items as a group variable or 'metavariable', to use L. Milroy's term (1992: 168). Milroy coined this term to refer to the stops /p,t,k/ in Tyneside English, considered as a single area of variation where glottalisation and glottalling appear to be spreading through the three sub-variables, with /t/ as the most favoured environment. Thus, each individual lexical item is considered as a sub-variable comprising one standard and one (or more) non-standard variant.

Before we discuss these results, it may be mentioned that lexical alternants which are constrained on the level of collocation have been excluded from the present analysis. Thus the non-standard lexical items which are the object of study here, and which are listed in the appendix with English glosses, all have a standard equivalent, and each member of a standard/non-standard pair such as *voiture~ bagnole* will fit into a given string with equivalent denotational force: *j'ai garé la voiture~ la bagnole* 'I've put the car in the garage'. Collocational constraints, although they do exist on the lexical level, are relatively marginal compared to those arising in the attempt to distinguish the variants of variable French interrogative forms, for example (see Coveney 1996). An example is the alternation between *chose* and *truc*; it is not clear whether the collocation *les bonnes choses* 'nice things' can alternate with *les bons trucs*. Sequences such as these, which were not numerous, were therefore excluded from the analysis.

Table 2 below shows raw scores based on a simple count of the distribution of non-standard lexical items between speaker groups and across speech styles, in order to show a broad picture of the situation. These scores are presented assuming that all lexical items possess the same social/stylistic value, which they patently do not. We present a more finely-grained analysis in subsequent sections.

6.6   Lexical variation on the interspeaker dimensions

Table 2. Total numbers (N) of non-standard lexical items used by speaker groups in interview and conversation styles, numbers of different items used by each group (Range), and duration in minutes (Time) of recordings in each style

	Interview			Conversation		
	N	Range	Time	N	Range	Time
Males 16–19	125	46	196	679	155	191
Females 16–19	55	26	193	372	93	205
Males 11–12	106	16	153	200	46	169
Females 11–12	71	13	180	113	33	166
All groups	357	–	722	1364	–	731

Table 2 shows several sharp differences between groups and across styles in the use of non-standard lexis. Even this rather crude method of comparing numbers of tokens of non-standard lexis across groups and styles irrespective of the differential stylistic value of individual items, indicates some interesting (and familiar) patterns. The older males show by far the greatest use of non-standard lexis, both in terms of numbers of tokens and of the range of different individual items used. The shift across styles shown by this group is also very striking. The difficulties associated with handling lexical style shift in an accountable way will be discussed below, and only social variation will be examined in this section. In interview style, a very neat sex-related pattern is observable, with both female groups using fewer non-standard terms than the male groups. This result has not been tested for statistical reliability, for reasons that are discussed below, but it conforms to the sociolinguistic gender pattern (SGP) reported in many other studies and referred to in previous chapters. The present pattern shows females tending strongly to avoid non-standard lexical forms. In conversation style, the patterns which relate the speaker groups involve both sex and age; in the older groups, males use approximately twice as many terms as females (679:372), and this relation also obtains for the younger groups at a lower numerical level (200:113). Possible interpretations of this pattern are presented below.

Columns showing the duration in minutes of the recordings analysed have been included to show the relation between this factor and variation across styles and groups. Some 12 hours of recordings were analysed in each style for all speaker groups aggregated, and the 'All groups' row shows that the very similar figures in the 'All groups/Time' matrices contrast sharply with the very different figures for N for all groups in each style. For individual speaker groups, it is observable that the younger groups talk less; interviews were wound up when it became apparent that little more talk would be elicited, and the younger groups were less talkative in conversation style than the older. In conversation style, informants were told to switch off the tape recorder if conversation dried up; this happened more often with the younger groups, and one can assume that the relatively restricted use of non-standard lexis by the younger informants is related to some extent to the fact that they talk less than the older informants, judging by the measure used here; it may be that the younger speakers also found the speech situations more intimidating than the older speakers, with a corresponding effect on the degree to which the former groups monitored their speech. Nevertheless, the sex-related pattern mentioned above, which shows both male groups producing similar numbers of tokens in interview style, goes against the foregoing observations to some extent and shows that the amount of talk produced, measured in this admittedly imperfect way, bears only an indirect relation to numbers of tokens produced.

The results shown in Table 2 reveal two clear patterns: (i) in interview style, a very clear sex-related effect with age apparently unimportant; and (ii) in conversation, increasing use of non-standard lexis with age and, cutting across this pattern, greater use of non-standard lexis by males than by females in the same age group in both speech styles. The two facts of these rather sharp patterns of differentiation seen in both speaking styles, and of the large differences between the range of different items used by the four speaker groups in conversation style, raise interesting problems of interpretation.

In variable phonology, stylistic competence is beginning to emerge in preadolescents by the age of the youngest speakers in the Dieuze sample, 11–12 years. Labov (1970:288–9), sketching a proposed schema of the development of linguistic and communicative competence, asserts that it is only after the age of twelve or so, in 'early adolescence', that children begin to develop an awareness of the social and stylistic significance of language, followed by an increasing degree of control over the contextualised use of language. Romaine (1984:83–111) assembles a range of more recent evidence to argue that this awareness may emerge well before adolescence.

The variable phonological patterns observed in the Dieuze data appear to bear out Labov's suggested timescale. Thus the generally rather subtle patterns of age-related phonological variation discussed in earlier chapters are plausibly describable as an example of fine-grained age-grading in the development of stylistic competence on the phonological level, rather than as an effect of the elicitation methods used. That is to say, the rather modest (but generally statistically significant) degrees of style shift which the two younger age groups often show on the level of pronunciation, and which contrast with the larger degrees shown by the two older groups, suggest that by this age communicative competence in the younger speakers is beginning to emerge, rather than already fully in place, but that the elicitation methods used, notably the presence of the tape recorder in conversation style, is inhibiting the younger speakers from demonstrating their communicative competence (these two hypotheses are not mutually exclusive, of course). The former hypothesis is the more plausible in the case of the phonological level, since this level appears to be a more basic one than the lexical, both in terms of order of acquisition (phonology is acquired before most lexis, much of which is superimposed at a later stage), and of the arguably lesser degree to which phonology is accessible to self-monitoring. Thus the intrusion of an observer will interfere with phonology less than with lexis.

The question which confronts us in interpreting the results shown in Table 2 is therefore whether the age-related pattern seen in conversation style results from an effect of the observer's paradox, in this case the presence of recording equipment, or whether the younger speakers have not yet internalised the range of non-standard lexis which the older groups display. In other words, stylistic competence in the use of non-standard lexis may already be in place in the younger speakers, but the elicitation methods failed to access it. Alternatively, the pattern is a genuine case of age-grading, and the younger speakers have not yet internalised a large range of non-standard lexis, or competence in its contextualised use.

A third possibility is of course that the pattern is the result of chance. Owing to the infrequency of lexical items relative to phonological, numbers of individual lexical items per speaker are too small too permit the statistical testing of these results. The possibility that the results shown in Table 2 are due to random fluctuation cannot therefore be discounted, but the pattern shown in Table 2 is strikingly regular, showing a roughly geometrical progression in conversation style (1:2:4:8) from younger females through to older males. The sex-related pattern in interview style is also impressively symmetrical: it would be remarkable indeed if chance had produced these results.

To summarise, a tentative interpretation of the results shown in Table 2 allows of two possibilities. Because of the cognitive prominence of lexis relative to phonology and phono-syntax, for which a certain amount of text-internal evidence has been observed in the corpus (cases of self- or other-repair, or comments on the use of non-standard lexis), it may be that younger speakers were inhibited from displaying their full linguistic and communicative competence on the lexical level. Alternatively, that competence may not yet be fully in place in the younger speakers. In contrast to phonology, competence in lexis is dependent on 'ontological' or real-world knowledge which only age and/or experience can bring, and many of the lexical items used by the older speakers refer to areas of activity which are probably only dimly understood by most of the members of the younger groups.

The very clear sex-related pattern apparent in interview style, as well as that which interacts with the age effect in conversation, conform, as was indicated above, with the SGP reported in many studies; we have referred above to some of the more recent. The fact of the interviewer's being male is an additional possible influencing factor, if one accepts that according to Bell's audience design hypothesis, situational variation will be principally conditioned by the speaker's response to the status of his/her 'audience' or addressee, taking 'status' in a broad definition which also includes gender. Thus the females may have felt less at ease with a male interviewer, if one accepts this demographic polarity (male/female) as being capable of increasing social distance, with a consequent effect on the females' linguistic output. On the other hand, the gender-related differentiation seen in conversation style shows that even without the intervention of an outsider, the female groups, when interacting with their peers, show linguistic behaviour which is further from the vernacular than that of their male homologues, i.e. those who are similar in respect of age and social class. A more fine-grained analysis of the figures on lexis shown in Table 2 reveals further interesting differences between the speaker groups' behaviour, as Table 3 below shows.

Table 3 shows the same information displayed under the 'N' columns in Table 2, but expanded to indicate the use by the four speaker groups of items possessing different socio-stylistic values. To show this, the tripartite division mentioned above, between *familier, populaire* and *vulgaire*, has been adopted. As stated above, one shortcoming of these dictionary labels is that they date rather quickly. In addition, one is referring to the subjective judgments of lexicographers who are at least partly concerned to prescribe usage, or at least (in the case of bilingual dictionaries) to urge caution in the use of non-standard lexis for the benefit of language learners whose intuition in this respect may be imperfect. Furthermore, and perhaps most seriously, lexicographers assign style labels without reference to a rigorously defined speech community. This latter point will be further discussed below, when intra-

Table 3. Numbers (N) of non-standard lexical items used by speaker groups in interview and conversation styles, categorised by stylistic value

	Style label	Interview (N)	Conversation (N)
Males 16–19	Familier	120	399
	Populaire	4	153
	Vulgaire	1	127
	Total	125	679
Females 16–19	Familier	52	282
	Populaire	3	64
	Vulgaire	0	26
	Total	55	372
Males 11–12	Familier	105	167
	Populaire	1	19
	Vulgaire	0	14
	Total	107	200
Females 11–12	Familier	71	103
	Populaire	0	4
	Vulgaire	0	6
	Total	71	113
All groups	Familier	348	951
	Populaire	8	240
	Vulgaire	1	173
	Total	367	1364

speaker variation is examined. A further shortcoming is that this tripartition fails to capture the fact that stylistic values are in reality arranged on a continuum, not on a discrete scale. Therefore it needs to be borne in mind that the results set out above represent a schematised account of a situation which is not in fact tripartite, but continuous. This arbitrary division has the advantage of enhancing ease of presentation, and in justification it is also worth pointing out that any distinction between the members of a lexical set is very difficult to draw on principled grounds, and must contain a large arbitrary element. Thus a solution which is easy to apply methodologically seems justified. The style labels used are derived from one of the most recent medium-sized bilingual dictionaries to be published, the *Oxford-Hachette*, on the assumption that a recent dictionary will reflect current usage with a fair degree of accuracy, bearing in mind the limitations listed above.

Like Table 2, Table 3 shows some very striking inter-group differences, but on a finer level of detail. Perhaps most dramatic is the use by older males in conversation style of items labelled *vulgaire*; the figure of 127 tokens for this speaker group dwarfs those shown by the other three groups. This is also true of items labelled *populaire*. Use of *vulgaire* and *populaire* items gradually decreases across the other three groups, in contrast to the very sharp differences between these groups and the older males. The inter-group pattern observable in interview style contrasts rather sharply with conversation; the use of non-standard lexis by all speaker groups in interview style shows a similar distribu-tion across the three stylistic categories, with very little use of *vulgaire* and *populaire* items, and with the sex-grading discussed in relation to Table 2 very much the same in Table 3 for all groups within each stylistic category.

The much more frequent use of items labelled *vulgaire* by the older males is partially explicable by a very clear alternation in the distribution of *putain* as an exclamation. 53 tokens were observed for the older males, against 3 for the older females, 10 for the younger males and none for the younger females. This almost categorical sex-related pattern in the use *putain* is reflected in the distribution of the much milder exclamation *punaise*: no tokens were observed for either of the male groups; 10 for the older females; 3 for the younger females.

Intraspeaker variation will be discussed in detail in the following section, but it may be remarked here that only one word labelled *vulgaire* was used in interview style. This was *merde*, labelled by *Oxford-Hachette* as *vulgaire* when used as a noun, as it was in interview style, but *populaire* when an exclamation, as it almost always was in conversation. Indeed, use of lexical items from the three stylistic categories differs very considerably across speech styles, with lexis labelled *familier* accounting for 348/367 or 94.8% of the total number of tokens used in interview style, but representing 951/1364 or 69.7% in conversation. This brings us to the question of the legitimacy of comparing two speech styles on the lexical level.

6.7   Semantic equivalence across speech styles

We referred in the previous chapter to the difficulties of frequency and equivalence associated with transferring to the syntactic level the variationist methodology designed to analyse phonological variation, and the considerable literature these have produced, notably Labov (1978); Lavandera (1978); Romaine (1981). We have seen in previous sections of this chapter that, just as in the analysis of much grammatical variation, the attempt to quantify lexical variation raises problems of frequency, and hence of the statistical validity of results. Clearly, all lexical items, whether grammatical or full, do carry (although in widely varying degrees) both denotative and associative meaning, and in the analysis of syntactic variation, this fact again poses problems to a variable degree, as we saw previously.

On the level of full lexical items, the problem of equivalence presents itself in several forms. Syntactic variables mentioned previously give rise to serious semantic problems: in the case of the indefinite pronouns nous, *on* and *tu*, ambiguity as to reference; in the case of the *être~ avoir* auxiliary-verb alternation, ambiguity as to verb aspect. The problem of semantic equivalence as it relates to French lexical alternants concerns the need to determine whether either member of a standard/non-standard lexical pair such as *voiture~ bagnole* will be distributed across speech styles with equivalent denotational force, and whether the 'associative' meaning which each member conveys is such as to inhibit its distribution across styles. The term associative meaning is used by Leech (1981: 18) to subsume several types of meaning which are distinct from denotational or conceptual meaning. It is a useful term for the present discussion. Leech justifies the use of this umbrella term as follows:

> Reflected meaning and collocative meaning, affective meaning and social meaning: all these have more in common with connotative meaning than with conceptual meaning; they all have the same open-ended, variable character, and lend themselves to analysis in terms of scales or ranges, rather than in discrete either-this-or-that terms.

Leech points out that the various types of associative meaning share certain properties which distinguish them from conceptual meaning. In addition, the types of associative meaning may be so closely interwoven as to be inseparable: topic, emotional tenor and the relationship obtaining between the locutors all influence the formal–informal polarity of a speech situation where variable lexis is in question.

One might put this problem in the simplest terms by formulating the equivalence problem as it relates to lexis as follows: can one state that each member of a pair of lexical alternants has equivalent denotation, differing from the other member only in its socio-stylistic value? If so, one could assert that both *garçon* and *mec*, for example, denote 'human adult male', while *garçon* has the stylistic feature '+ formal', and *mec* ' – formal'. Such features are of course not binary but scalar, but we can set this aside for the purposes of the present discussion.

If it were possible to consider variable lexis in this way, the frequency problem would still remain, but in a different form. To resume the *garçon~ mec* example, *mec* occurred 71 times in conversation style in the Dieuze corpus, but once only in interview. Superficially, this appears to be a case of a very sharp style shift, and analogous to what occurs on the phonological level. Clearly, however, unlike phonological segments, lexical items are tied to topic, and therefore to the relationship between the locutors; and beyond this again to the types of discourse which are generally characteristic of formal and informal speech styles.

Thus several discussions in conversation style between older female speakers involved boys; who was dating whom and related matters. This discussion invoked much use of *mec*, which is clearly non-standard and has standard alternants, but raises a problem of comparison; unsurprisingly, the interviews constituting the relatively formal speech style do not include analogous discussions. We have already discussed in Chapter 3 the broad distinction between interview and conversation styles, expressed respectively in terms of 'ideational' and 'affective' orientation. The two styles certainly differ rather sharply in the topics which are discussed. Indeed, there is relatively little overlap in the use of non-standard lexis between speech styles, as Table 4 below shows. Thus Table 4 gives the distribution of individual lexical items across speech styles (not total numbers of tokens observed; each item in Table 4 was found at least once, and some very frequently).

Table 4. Distribution of individual lexical items across speech styles

	Familier	Populaire	Vulgaire	All
Conversation only	103	50	16	169
Both styles	37	4	1	42
Interview only	23	3	0	26
Totals	163	57	17	237

Lexical items are also broken down by stylistic value. Thus for example, out of the total of 237 individual lexical items observed, 169 were found at least once in conversation style only; of these, 103 were judged to be *familier*, and so on. It is apparent that *familier* is by far the largest category, representing 68.8% of the total number of items judged non-standard. Table 4 also shows that lexical items judged to be *populaire* or *vulgaire* occur rarely across both styles, and more rarely still in interview style only. It is also clear that by far the greatest number of lexical items occur in conversation styles only: 169/237 or 71.3%.

Furthermore, items occurring in both styles constitute a rather small proportion of the total: 42/237, or 17.7%. These distributional patterns raise rather serious problems of interpretation, which we examine below using specific examples. Therefore the 42 lexical items appearing in both speech styles are shown below in Table 5 below.

Table 5. Lexical items occurring in both speech styles, style labels, and numbers of tokens observed in each style

Lexical item and style label	Int	Conv	Lexical item and style label	Int	Conv
se balader (fam)	2	1	marcher (fam)	1	11
barbant (fam)	1	1	en avoir marre (fam)	5	22
bête (fam)	1	3	marrant (fam)	2	1
bled (fam)	2	4	mec (fam)	1	71
bordel (pop)	2	10	merde (vulg/pop)	1	17
bosser (fam)	1	4	patelin (fam)	2	1
boulot (fam)	3	3	plein (fam)	27	22
chouette (fam)	1	2	punaise (fam)	2	13
coincé (fam)	3	1	rigoler (fam)	4	23
cool (fam)	3	10	rigolo (fam)	7	1
s'emmerder (fam)	1	1	sacré (fam)	2	2
(s')engueuler (fam)	1	6	sinon	53	5
pas évident (fam)	5	1	sous (argent) (fam)	1	5
ex (fam)	3	1	super (fam)	3	19
des fois (fam)	86	27	super + adj. (fam)	2	23
foot (fam)	13	13	sympa (fam)	2	18
foutre (pop)	1	5	taré (fam)	1	4
s'en foutre (fam)	3	15	avoir la tchatch	1	1
en avoir rien à foutre (pop)	1	1	télé (fam)	13	27
louper (fam)	3	3	truc (fam)	48	99
machin (fam)	8	41	vachement (fam)	5	35

Table 5 shows the non-standard lexical items found in both speech styles in the Dieuze corpus. Style labels are also given above, except in one case where no attestation of the item was found in dictionaries or grammars: non-standard use of *sinon* (discussed further below). All of the items shown in Table 5 illustrate various aspects of the issues, adumbrated above, raised by the attempt to quantify stylistic variation in lexis.

Firstly, certain lexical items labelled *familier* are distributed more or less equally across styles, although in most cases very small numbers of tokens must preclude a definitive judgment on whether the items are, for the Dieuze speaker sample, stylistically unmarked. Thus the statistical problem discussed above in relation to social variation is also present on the stylistic dimension. Intuitively, however, items such as *foot, pas evident, plein, rigolo* and *télé* may plausibly be thought of as falling into the central category of the tripartition formulated by George (1993:157) between lexical items that he labels stylistically 'formal', 'neutral' or 'informal'. Thus quantification provides a useful insight into the stylistic value of these items for the Dieuze speaker sample. The usefulness of George's (or any) categorisation will be discussed below, but as George remarks (p. 156), the straightforward standard/non-standard distinction, which has been used in this chapter unquestioningly until now, is difficult to apply in a socio-linguistic situation which is subject to constant evolution. George refers to non-standard lexis as 'alternative'. It is clear that the concept of non-standard usage means little in the absence of an unchanging standard against which it may be measured, and this fact must also undermine any attempt to assign style labels without reference to a clearly defined speech community. Thus a term which is socio-stylistically 'neutral' for one speaker group, as for example *plein* clearly is for the Dieuze sample, may be informal for other social groups, and the style labels given above in Table 5, derived from the *Oxford-Hachette*, no doubt reflect the lexicographers' concern to deter language learners from offending native speakers with whom they are not intimate by using socio-stylistically marked lexis.

Thus the mismatch between the style labels used above, and the stylistic distribution of the words to which they are attached, is unsurprising in view of the prescriptive intent of the *Oxford-Hachette*. Many lexical items labelled *familier, populaire* or even *vulgaire* will have anodyne value when used by certain social groups, and/or in certain speech situations. Thus even George's attempt at a non-prescriptive categorisation of the socio-stylistic value of lexis is surely vitiated in the absence of a relatively rigorous definition of the speaker groups and speech styles in question, prior to the assessment of the socio-linguistic value of variable lexis. Nevertheless, it appears plausible that the *familier/populaire/vulgaire* hierarchisation (granting its schematic character) is valid in its own terms; that is, *merde* will be more stylistically marked than *punaise* in all French speech communities, but within each community, all terms in the hierarchy may have less force than in other communities. Thus the results presented in Table 5 show that a clearly defined speaker sample has behavioural and evaluative norms concerning variable lexis which cannot meaningfully be defined by reference to elusive, supra-local norms.

Turning to the lexical items in Table 5 which do show style shift, it is apparent that for most items, the equivalence problem discussed above hinders seriously the attempted quantification of style shift in lexis. The example of *des fois* 'sometimes' illustrates this: 86 tokens were observed in interview style, and 27 in conversation. This 'negative' shift is tied to the nature of the discourse in each style; in interviews, informants often described their activities over the school week and the weekend, and this involved much use of *des fois*. It is plain that this expression is stylistically neutral for the Dieuze speaker sample; the fact that it occurs more often in the more 'formal' style is a product of the nature of the discourse in that style, and must be explained using qualitative methods. Thus on the basis of the Dieuze corpus at least, one cannot consider *des fois* as a sociolinguistic variable. These remarks also apply to *sinon*, which was used, especially by younger speakers, non-standardly as a broad-spectrum linking word equivalent to 'and'. Thus when asked which school subjects they studied, younger speakers might well reply along the following lines:

(4) je fais anglais / sinon j'ai sport, math /
'I do English / and [lit. otherwise] I have sport, maths'

In this typical example, *sinon* is clearly not used in its standard, exclusive sense of 'otherwise'. Here again, the large 'negative' shift is explained by discoursal factors. However, quantification does prove useful in the case of *sinon* along the social dimension of age: 44 tokens were observed for the younger speaker groups, and 14 for the older. This non-standard use of *sinon* may therefore be one that is progressively eradicated under institutional pressure.

An analogous problem is posed by the ideational/affective polarity between interview and conversation styles discussed above, which is responsible for the large degrees of style shift seen in certain of the other items shown in Table 5; thus for example, the greater use of *cool, en avoir marre, super, super+* adjective (as in *super-bien*), *sympa* and *vachement* indicate the higher incidence in conversation style of relatively intense expressions of praise or blame, which are largely absent in interview style. The pungent expression of indifference conveyed by expressions such as *s'en foutre* and *en avoir rien à foutre* is also much more frequent in conversation style. Correspondingly, the frequent use of *machin* and *truc* in conversation relative to interview style appears to reflect the greater tolerance in peer group interaction of a certain degree of designative imprecision. This tendency may be partially explained by the fact that ontological knowledge is still developing in younger speakers, but the following example illustrates that the affective tenor of a speech situation may override considerations of precise designation. In conversation style, an older male was reproaching his best friend for not wanting to come to his birthday party, because another party was to be held elsewhere, and produced the following stretch of speech:

(5) si c'était toi qui fêtais ton anniversaire / et que / y avait la truc à machin
là / j'aurais   quand même pas été / même si ça m'aurait [*sic*] branché
'if you were having your birthday party and / there was the thingy at
whatsit / I still wouldn't go / even if I really fancied it'

The words *truc* and *machin* refer here respectively to *fête*, as the feminine article suggests (unless the speaker committed a performance error; no other smaller cases were observed in the Dieuze corpus), and to the name of the place where the competing party was to be held. Whether the speaker is deliberately disdaining to bring to utterance the precise equivalents of *truc* and *machin*, or whether this aspect of cognitive processing has been, as suggested above, overridden by affective considerations, this extract appears to endorse the point made above, namely that interview and conversation styles in the Dieuze corpus are broadly characterised by distinct types of discourse where different kinds of meaning are conveyed. An alternative explanation is the fact of shared knowledge held by the two speakers, which can obviate the need to for precise, decontextualised designation, and promote the production of 'restricted code' or heavily context-dependent language.

Thus it is clear that the involvement of (most) variable lexical items in the conveying of associative meaning precludes their being treated as Labovian sociolinguistic variables, in the Dieuze corpus at least, since this involvement inhibits their distribution across styles. Therefore we cannot assume that a lexical variable will be found in the speech of the Dieuze sample across the two speech styles in sufficient numbers to make variationist quantification meaningful. Lexical items which convey relatively intense affective meaning, such as *vachement*, and which therefore occur more rarely in the more ideational speech style, should thus arguably be excluded from an examination of lexical variation, in the Dieuze corpus at any rate. A much larger question is whether the unmitigated expression of emotion is rare in formal speech styles generally; this seems plausible given that formal speech tends to take place between non-intimates, and/or in situations characterised by an uneven power-solidarity distribution.

More frequent, functional set of alternants such as *beaucoup ~ plein* and *parfois ~ quelquefois ~ des fois* are clearly less problematic in respect of their susceptibility to quantification. The frequency of lexical items relative to phonological segments is of course low, as was previously mentioned, but if the corpus is sufficiently large, and has been stored in electronic form so as to make concordancing possible, this problem can at least be approached, as the lexical study reported by Sankoff et al. (1978) demonstrates. Nevertheless, this corpus consists of recordings in an informal interview style only. Examples of studies of frequent lexical items in English that show socio-stylistic patterning are Kerswill's (1987) quantification of variation in the pronoun system in County Durham, NE England, and Crinson's (1997) study of the variable use of by children of frequent adjectives and adverbs in Tyneside English (NE England). It is worth remarking that Kerswill's study again shows the social-regional patterning characteristic of so much UK English variation, in this case between pronouns that are conservative and localised and those that are standard and have a nationwide distribution (e.g. between 'thou' and 'you').

In a similar vein, we have seen that *plein* and *des fois* occur frequently enough in the Dieuze data to make quantification worth while, even though strong claims cannot be made in statistical terms. Other items such as *bagnole, balle, bouffer, connerie, frangin* etc. also show strong stylistic conditioning in their distribution (see appendix), and again if the corpus were large enough, it seems plausible that comparable speech events would occur often enough to treat such lexical items as sociolinguistic variables in the Labovian sense. This is to assume that a very large corpus would contain a distribution of types of discourse across speech styles which would be sufficiently equal to correct quirks such as the 'negative' shift shown for *des fois* and *sinon*. The statistical problem is even more acute in the case of the large number of lexical items observed in the Dieuze corpus that occurred only once in conversation style, and not at all in interview.

One may argue therefore that frequency is a purely methodological difficulty, and that there is no *a priori* reason to suppose that comparable speech events offering a choice between certain pairs of lexical alternants will not crop up sooner or later, if the corpus is sufficiently large, and constraints on the resources and time devoted to analysis are absent. This is of course speculation, and as suggested in Chapter 4 in connexion with intraspeaker variation in *ne*, quantification might well give results running contrary to impressionistic observation.

6.8 Summary and conclusion

We have seen that the attempt to quantify lexical variation raises several important issues. The quantification of social variation in lexis in the Dieuze sample reveals sex- and age-related patterns which are sharper than almost all of those seen in phonology. One may hypothesise that the greater cognitive salience of lexis, as well as the fact of age-grading, are probably responsible for these patterns. On the stylistic dimension, the very steep style shift shown overall and by the two older groups is closely tied to the different types of discourse, and hence meaning, typical of the two speech styles elicited. This latter fact shows that quantification gives glimpses into the nature of sociolinguistic variation of a quite different order from those revealed on the levels of phonology and syntax. Specifically, lexical variation is closely tied to topic, and hence to the relationship that locutors have contracted, in a way that variable phonology is not. Nevertheless, it may be possible to quantify certain variable lexical items, given a large enough corpus and sophisticated methods of analysis.

Two general conclusions relating to sociolinguistic theory emerging from the results presented here will now be outlined briefly.

One tentative conclusion which emerges from the results presented here relates to discussions in previous chapters concerning the expression of a speaker's social identity through the various linguistic levels: namely that speakers may be signalling more impersonal aspects of their identity (age, sex, social class) on the less meaning-related, more quantifiable linguistic levels of variable phonology, morpho-syntax and frequent lexis, while the differential use of unquantifiable lexis involves other more 'personal' extra-linguistic factors: 'tone ' or 'tenor' in terms of the speaker's attitude to the topic being discussed, the relationship between the speakers and the choice of topic, these last two closely linked. This conclusion goes somewhat against Bell's assertion (1984) that a speaker's choice of speech style is motivated principally by the status of the addressee, and suggests, as Labov remarks (1994: 157–8), that 'stylistic shifting responds to many independent variables and [...] no one of them can be considered as an "essential" or "controlling" factor'. 'Status' is used by Bell in the rather impersonal, demographic definition mentioned above, relating to social factors which are 'given' rather than to those which may have more immediate personal significance, and which relate to the discourse level of sociolinguistic phenomena traditionally handled by conversation analysis and politeness theory. It may be that aside from the methodological difficulties discussed above, variation between many pairs of full lexical items would be more fruitfully studied on this higher level. Certainly the results presented here have shown that a uniplex formal-informal dimension of speech style is not a tenable concept so far as most variable lexis is concerned.

A second general consideration relates to the status of lexical variation in a theory of variable linguistic structure. We have seen that the lexical set examined here is heterogeneous from several points of view: frequency, semantic weight, topic. Thus some less 'meaningful', or more 'grammatical' lexical items (*des fois, plein*) are amenable to quantification in a large enough corpus, so that they may be thought of as having a sociolinguistic status comparable to that of phonological variables. That is, they occur frequently enough to be quantifiable and have two or more variants, each of which has differing socio-stylistic value; and they may plausibly be assumed to be the common property of an entire speech community. Like phonological variables, these lexical items may thus be subject to diffusion throughout a speech community.

By contrast, other, less frequent items are so closely bound to semantic context as to make quantification difficult. They may moreover refer to areas of activity that are not common to the community. Therefore they may be unlikely to diffuse beyond sub-groups. In addition, many will be ephemeral. It is of course true that certain phonological and syntactic features are the property of clearly delimited regional/social groups. Nevertheless, the extremely heterogeneous nature of variable lexis, considered as an area of sociolinguistic variation, raises obstacles in the way of any attempt to formulate a coherent theory of the principles governing lexical variation.

On another level, even variable lexical items bearing some resemblance to sociolinguistic variables differ rather obviously from phonological variables in the difficulty they present in constructing a general theory to account for the adoption of variants. In variable phonology, non-standard speech processes tend often towards reduction, lenition and assimilation, despite frequent arbitrariness; in variable lexis, several quite disparate processes are responsible for the adoption or creation of non-standard lexical items. Some, like *quelquefois > des fois*, seem quite unmotivated, similarly to lexico-syntactic variables studied by other researchers: *avoir~ être* and indefinite pronouns in Montreal, reported respectively by Sankoff and Thibault (1980) and Laberge (1983). In other cases reduction is an important contributing factor, but against this, so is expansion in the form of (re)suffixation (e.g. *directeur > dirlo*). These two processes appear to have little or nothing in common linguistically. Linguistic 'inflation' or semantic weakening clearly has considerable influence in the adoption of non-standard lexis: casual speech (or casual speakers) appear to be in constant need of innovation in order to maintain intensity and vividness of expression. For instance, the term *génial*, whose pristine or at least earlier sense refers to genius, has weakened in everyday speech to convey warm commendation. This weakening process can be likened to the tendency for marked or emphatic grammatical structures to usurp the function of the unmarked. Historically, French negation has taken this route, since the negative adverb *pas*, originally used perhaps with literal, and certainly with emphatic force subsequently (Price 1984:252), came at an early period in the history of the language to accompany the negative particle *ne* to express negation. In everyday speech *pas* has of course now largely replaced *ne*. A contemporary example in French variable syntax is the use of what Coveney (1995) calls 'QU-final interrogative structures' such as *ça veut dire quoi?* 'what does that mean?' (cf. previous chapter): Coveney gives a thorough account of the rather complex array of linguistic and social constraints governing the use of this type of structure, designated SVQ in Coveney's notation. Despite the complexity of these constraints it seems legitimate to suggest that the often pragmatically marked form SVQ (echo-question), for some constructions at least, may for many speakers have largely replaced the unmarked form QSV (*qu'est-ce que ça veut dire?*).

Allied to the process of semantic weakening but different from it, is the shift of a word from one category to another (the French noun *classe* becomes an adjective, for example), a process which in this case illustrates what Lewis (1967:7) calls the drift from the descriptive to the evaluative use of a word. Thus the term *classe*, originally a descriptive term motivated by the desire to categorise, becomes an adjective expressing approval. An example of the shift from the descriptive to the evaluative in the direction of pejoration is the term English term 'adolescent'. Against these examples of change should be mentioned the stability of some non-standard lexis: words of pejoration such as French *niais* 'stupid' are attested over many centuries.

Space is lacking here to attempt a thorough-going taxonomy of the principles governing lexical innovation and change (and stability). In any event this is not the principal focus of this study. One useful preliminary distinction may however be that suggested by Calvet (1994:35), between variation which operates, on the one hand on the signifier (suffixation, truncation, alternation) and on the other on the signified (metaphorical shift, semantic weakening). In any event, the point at issue is that a rather untidy taxonomy would be likely to emerge from such an attempt, from which it might be difficult to derive a parsimonious theory of the principles responsible for lexical variation.

The essential problem is to establish whether 'chaque mot a son histoire', or whether it is possible to formulate general principles governing lexical variation and change. Clearly, at the most fundamental level lexical variation is the result of the arbitrary nature of the sign; the conventional character of the relation between signifier and signified (Saussure's *signifié*) makes possible variation and change on both aspects of the sign. Within this preliminary distinction, between variation operating on the signifier on the one hand and the signified on the other, it seems relatively straightforward to explain the principles governing variation operating on the signifier: truncation is akin to phonological reduction, and is of course common in the polysyllabic, Latinate lexis of French, while (re)suffixation, as well as slang systems depending on the transposition and addition of syllables, such as *verlan* and *loucherbem*, respond, at least in part, to the playful functions of language.

Non-standard variation operating on the signified, as well of course as variation in the standard language, responds to more complex constraints and implies semantic variation and change. We have already mentioned the shift from descriptive to evaluative use and semantic weakening: each of these processes can result in several types of semantic shift (to pejoration, amelioration, restriction, extension, metaphorical shift) and have been the subject of attempted classification by several linguists. Meillet (1912) established a threefold classification of the factors capable of bringing about semantic changes: linguistic, historical and social. Ullmannn (1962, Chapter 8) added a fourth, the psychological. It is principally the last two factors that seem responsible for lexical variation. More recently, Traugott (1989) has suggested that the fundamental tendency at the origin of all semantic (and therefore lexical) change is the shift from the objective to the subjective use of lexical items. Traugott suggests furthermore that this tendency is unidirectional.

It is manifest that semantic shift occurs in all language varieties, not only the non-standard. What remains to be established in general is the contribution that empirical studies of non-standard lexical variation can make to the task of classification discussed above; and in particular, whether a typology of lexical variation and change that is specific to non-standard language varieties can be formulated.

Chapter 7

Summary and conclusion

7.1 Summary of the issues discussed in this book

In previous chapters we have examined the distinctive ways in which French speakers express their social identity through variable language use. We have done this by examining in turn the linguistic levels of phonology, grammar and lexis, as well as the unusual case of variable liaison. Since we have already discussed our principal conclusions at some length, we confine ourselves here largely to summarising these, on each level in turn, considering subsequently the limitations of this study and further directions for research.

7.2 Variation in French phonology

Our central concerns in Chapters 2 and 3 have been the relations between social, regional and stylistic variation in the variety of French examined here. We have tried to explain the hyperstyle ratios in the corpora of language discussed by reference to the nature of the pronunciation features in *oïl* French indicating social identity. The results of the perceptual study described in Chapter 2 suggested that there are rather few pronunciation features in *oïl* French that show regional localisation. We suggested further that the features in French pronunciation indicating social (excluding regional) identity may be such as to create tensions between interspeaker and intraspeaker variation. This effect may be summarised in the following way:

There appears to be a dissonance in French between the interspeaker value of the nationally distributed phonological variables discussed here, and their intraspeaker value. As we have suggested in previous chapters, this may be due, on the one hand to the phonologically natural character of these variables, and on the other to their clear representation in spelling. The effects of this tension are apparent in both of the corpora studied here: less directly in the Dieuze corpus, in that the rather large degree of formality perceived by many of the informants in the interview style appears to have influenced their language production in the way formulated by Coveney (1996:89–90) and cited previously: 'formal styles, which reflect the conservative written language, seem to involve, in certain respects at least, a quite different type of linguistic behaviour than informal styles [...]'. To reiterate, we have suggested that formal styles reflect the conservative written language in the sense that these styles may be associated in the minds of many speakers with formal language instruction in the classroom; and with the inculcation of normed behaviour generally, by the teacher, the authority figure. At the same time, the Dieuze results are perhaps more significant in what they reveal of the effects of the elicitation methods used. That is, the quite large degrees of intraspeaker variation seem to show, as well as the probable relationship between formal styles and the influence of writing, referred to above, that variation between styles elicited by more direct 'audience design' methods, i.e. between unscripted speech styles differentiated by interlocutor, may be capable of producing larger degrees of style shift than methods depending on the direct influence of writing. This statement needs to be nuanced considerably, however; on the one hand, we have seen in Chapter 3 that very large degrees of style shift are associated with certain types of linguistic variables and certain types of discourse structure, and this is a finding that appears not to have received much attention in the variationist literature. On the other hand, the differing effect of elicitation methods used in sociolinguistic studies on degrees of style shift observed must remain a rather abstract matter, given that the relation between style shift elicited, by whatever method, and 'real' style shift, remains largely unknown.

The rather small degrees of interspeaker variation between the Dieuze speaker groups remain puzzling in view of what has been reported for comparable (young) speaker samples in other languages, and this is an area in need of further research using fresh empirical data.

The tension between interspeaker and intraspeaker variation mentioned above is apparent in a more straightforward way in Hansen's Paris results. Here, the influence of the spelling, accompanied by rather small degrees of interspeaker variation, brought about a hyperstyle ratio that differs from those observed in other corpora (exemplified by Trudgill's Norwich results) in being distributed evenly across the two social classes sampled. This suggests a rather highly successful imposition of spelling norms in France, and the French situation appears therefore conform to Bell's (1984) schema of hyperstyle variation, according to which the phenomenon is characteristic of societies where there is very marked discontinuity between reading and speaking styles.

7.3   Variation in French grammar

In Chapter 4 we considered some examples of variable grammar in French, suggesting that these may be unusual in having a rather wide social distribution, in contrast to the polarised pattern seen in some English variables whose distribution has been quantified. The French state of affairs is striking in two ways: firstly, it obtains not only for grammatical variables such as *ne* that can plausibly be thought of as causing speakers rather little cognitive processing cost, but also for more complex areas involving word order, notably variable interrogation. The major limitation of the results discussed here is their small number; once again, a fuller discussion suggesting more robust conclusions awaits a wider range of results, in French as well as in other languages.

The analysis of intraspeaker variation in *ne* showed that despite the inter-speaker patterning characteristic of this variable, similar to what was found for phonology, the negative particle is used to operate metaphorical style shift, or what Bell refers to in his audience design classification (1991: 126–46) as 'initiative referee design'. We can suggest that cases of initiative shift prompted by a change of topic and tone rather than addressee conform to this definition in the sense that a speech situation may be 'informal' in the sense of taking place between two or more intimates, and 'non-standard' in the sense of the locutors not being highly placed in class terms (as in the Dieuze conversational style). At the same time, much micro-style variation takes place in speech situations such as these, as the topic is modulated, and in response the key or tone used to discuss the topic modulates through the use of referee design. The negative particle *ne* seems to partake of the salience which is characteristic of grammatical variables, and which appears to be necessary for the operation of much initiative style shift. This is because, in Bell's phrase (1991: 126) 'initiative style shift is essentially a redefinition, by the speaker, of the relationship between speaker and audience.' Thus in initiative shift, speaker and hearer remain constant while the speaker initiates a shift that does not occur in response to the physical arrival of a further addressee. It seems likely that a salient linguistic item will generally be required to operate a shift of this kind.

What is striking in this connexion is the relation between the potential salience of *ne* on the intraspeaker level if variation, and the limited interspeaker value of the variable. The Dieuze results show no hyperstyle pattern in the variable realisation of *ne*, and this is unsurprising in view of the youth of the speaker groups sampled. At the same time, it is unclear whether speaker groups showing higher levels of use of *ne* would also show hyperstyle variation: clearly, a variable such as *ne*, which has limited interspeaker value by reason of its obsolescent character (few speakers use it at high levels), is also potentially valuable as a stylistic resource; on the one hand by virtue of possessing the salience that appears to be inherent in many grammatical items, as discussed in Chapter 4; and on the other hand, by reason of its very obsolescence. From this latter point of view, we can draw a parallel between *ne* and phonological stereotypes of the kind discussed by Chambers and Trudgill (1998:75–6). Chambers and Trudgill have the following remarks concerning phonological stereotypes:

> There is also a third possible stage [beyond those that produce indicators and markers]. At this stage, awareness of particular variants becomes even higher, and speakers become especially conscious of them. Their social and regional connotations become a part of common knowledge, and speakers are able to report on them without difficulty (although not necessarily accurately).

This quotation brings out the point that where at least some stereotypes are in question, it is the 'evaluative axis' of variation, referred to by Eckert (1989) and discussed in several places in this book, which is the most important. The crucial element that is implicit in Chambers and Trudgill's description and that distinguishes a marker from a stereotype, aside from the varying degrees of awareness that speaker-hearers have of each, is degree of use; knowledge of stereotypes is quite largely evaluative, since rather few speakers use them in everyday interaction. As discussed above, it remains to determine the implications for intraspeaker variation of this combination of a high level of consciousness of stereotypes, and their low level of everyday use, which seems to characterise *ne* as well as the stereotypes in phonology that Chambers and Trudgill discuss (the principal difference is that phonological stereotypes are generally used only by a distinctive social group — Chambers and Trudgill give the example of the Brooklyn /ʌy/ variable — while a variable like *ne* is used at low levels by almost all speakers). While the quantitative nature of much phonological variation appears to result in numerical relations that are quite consistent across many communities studied, the involvement in style variation of grammatical items, as shown in the case of *ne* in Chapter 4, appears inevitably to require input from the qualitative, discourse levels of variation. This suggests that the often sporadic use of salient variables in initiative style shift may rule out the consistent measurement of hyperstyle effects in grammar, even where the conditions appear to suggest that hyperstyle variation will take place, as in the case of *ne*.

7.4   Variation in French liaison

The essential aim of Chapter 5, in which variable liaison was presented, was to convey the very distinctive character of the phenomenon. On a general level, the use of variable liaison is in line with the tendency for speakers in higher social groups and more careful speech styles simply to use more linguistic substance. At the same time, the use of variable liaison does not conform to the strategy for the use of prestigious features formulated by Kroch (1978: 18–19) and discussed above, i.e. the avoidance of connected-speech processes such as consonant-cluster simplification, vowel centralisation and schwa deletion, since the linguistic motivation propelling the use of variable liaison, as discussed in Chapter 5, is not easy to define in ease-of-articulation terms. A further distinctive feature of variable liaison is the explicitness of its codification: for instance, the standard French grammar, *Le Bon Usage*, devotes some four pages to prescribing its employment (Grevisse 1986: 49–53) and entire pronunciation manuals have been written on the subject for the benefit of foreign learners of French (e.g. Capon 1963). Of course, it is customary for foreign learners of a language to be taught its standard pronunciation, but for a relatively limited area of the pronunciation, that is, the variable realisation of some but not all word-final consonants, to have caused so much scholarly and pedagogical activity as well as so much linguistic insecurity among native speakers seems unusual. As before, cross-linguistic parallels may be found in a wider empirical base.

A further unusual aspect of variable liaison may be its relationship to variation and change. As we have argued elsewhere (Armstrong forthcoming), the recent decline of variable liaison (Smith 1996, 1998) can be contrasted with the apparent stability of phonological variables such as /l/, /r/ and schwa; these latter are striking by reason of their national distribution and their capacity to mark, through their representation in the spelling, what Laks (1983) refers to as the 'social trajectory' of a speaker, perhaps most obviously through his or her orientation to the value of the attribute of 'educatedness'. We have been rather little concerned with language change in this book, but diachronic evidence (summarised in Armstrong 1996; and forthcoming) suggests that the tendency towards zero /l/, /r/ and schwa in contexts where this is most linguistically natural is in tension with pressure exerted by the orthography. We have of course developed this theme at some length in this book, in relation to synchronic patterns of variation.

In relation to patterns of change, one can suggest that a variable whose mapping on the orthography is transparent can be regarded by speakers as an indicator of educatedness which is not negatively perceived by and large; perhaps because considered as being widely available to all by reference to spelling pronunciation. A clear counter-example to this is variable liaison. We saw in Chapter 5 that the relation between spelling and liaison is to a considerable extent arbitrary, and hence difficult to learn without direct experience of the appropriate social milieu. Plural forms such as noun + adjective, as in *soldats* [z] *anglais,* do provide fairly clear exceptions, but even liaison forms which might be thought to map straightforwardly onto the orthography ($\langle p \rangle = /p/$) can give difficulty, as we saw in Chapter 5 in the example of *trop* [z] *âgés.* Hornsby, (1999) gives further examples from an adolescent speaker sample, such as *long* [t] *apprentissage* 'long apprenticeship' (prescribed liaison form *long* [k] *apprentissage*) that again suggest the difficulty experienced by some speakers (in this case young working-class) in relating orthography to prescribed form. From this perspective, the decline of variable liaison is a phenomenon that seems plausibly to be motivated by the wish to converge towards values that are perceived as clearly 'accountable', in conformity with Bourdieu and Passeron's (1970) model of the role of education referred to in Chapter 5. In relation to the contrasting cases of liaison and French variables whose mapping onto orthography seems quite clear, this model seems in need of modification in the direction of the greater transparency and accessibility of education in its effects upon language standardisation.

The decline of variable liaison is of interest therefore in the way it may be reflecting the evolution of French social structures as suggested above; the contrast between the respective stability of French schwa and liquid deletion on the one hand, and on the other the decline of variable liaison, seems to point to convergence towards conformity with spelling-pronunciation norms from both ends of the social-class continuum. We may draw a comparison between the current apparent recession in variable liaison, and the continuing decrease in the acceptability of 'marked' or 'hyperlectal' RP in English. These two phenomena seem fairly clear indicators of the symbolic social convergence or diminution of social difference discussed in Chapter 5, which is motivated perhaps by the desire to attenuate the effects of continuing economic difference. It is noteworthy in this connexion that most language changes continue to proceed from below, through the adoption by upper-class speakers of lower-class linguistic forms. At the same time we can hypothesise that social, economic and educational pressures will continue to be exerted 'upwards' upon socially less highly placed speakers in the direction of spelling-pronunciation forms.

7.5   Variation in French lexis

The principal interest of the results concerning variable French lexis in Chapter 6 is perhaps methodological. The fact that French possesses a substantial set of lexical alternants having different socio-stylistic value offers an opportunity to examine the practicability of a Labovian analysis of variation in lexis. The analysis reported here produced sharply differentiated interspeaker results, and this is perhaps unsurprising in view of the salience of the lexical level. On the intraspeaker level, the analysis in Chapter 6 showed quite clearly that Labovian, quantitative, variation of the type reported abundantly in phonology and some morpho-syntax occurs in frequent non-lexical words, but that full lexical words are recalcitrant to an analysis of this kind by reason of their involvement in their expression of the relationship between interlocutors through topic and tone. To reiterate, the analysis of lexical variation in a 'mega-corpus' (Poplack 1989) may prove to give quantitative results that conform with those found on the other linguistic levels.

7.6   Limitations of this study

Firstly, we must mention the limited application of the arguments presented here; we are unaware of the social, and especially stylistic, value in *oïl* French of most of the phonological and grammatical variables listed and discussed in the preceding chapters. The interspeaker results that are available give rather contradictory indications, some showing rather small degrees of variation (e.g. Landick 1995), some rather larger (Ashby 1981; Laks 1983). Intraspeaker results are required that will complement those discussed here, and in particular give indications of variation as it concerns a wider social spread of speakers and other linguistic variables. Results from other languages on variable grammar and lexis are also required to form a broader empirical base than that which we have been able to consult here.

Secondly, the discussions in this book have for the most part been conducted in the static terms that seem appropriate to a broad account of the intraspeaker axis of differentiation. However, as we suggested in our discussion of intraspeaker variation in *ne* in Chapter 4, following Holmes' (1997) account of a multi-layered analysis of language variation, the influence of situational context needs to be considered where a dynamic view of the ongoing construction of social identity is in question. A dynamic view of this kind is in principle inseparable from the intraspeaker dimension of variation. As Bell puts it (1984:161), 'audience design informs all levels of a speaker's linguistic choices — [...] the form of speech acts, pronoun choice, the use of honorifics, and quantitative style shift'. Thus on every linguistic level, a speaker's choice of speech style is motivated by the interaction between the respective status of speaker and addressee: in less abstract terms, when speaking, 'persons respond mainly to other persons, [...] speakers take most account of hearers in design-ing their talk' (Bell 1984:159). Furthermore, this process evolves continually on the 'micro-style' level. The aspect of audience design that Holmes has empha-sised in her multi-level analysis of New Zealand speech is its dynamic, inter-actional character; when talking, speakers are engaged in continually changing acts of self-presentation, which refer to all aspects of the speaker's social identity and which are of course conditioned partly by the corresponding status of the addressee. 'Status' is used by Bell both in the rather impersonal, demographic sense that the word often evokes, and which relates to social attributes which are 'given'; but of course social status refers equally to those attributes that may have more central personal significance, and which relate, through speech style, to the level of sociolinguistic phenomena handled by conversation analysis and politeness theory. The results discussed by Holmes and others, as well as those touched on in our discussion of *ne* in Chapter 4, have shown that a uniplex formal-informal dimension of speech style is not a tenable concept where a wholly integrated view of socio-stylistic variation is attempted.

By and large, a uniplex optic of speech style has been adopted here. This is inevitable in view of the broad aims of the present study, so that we do not suggest that the adoption of this viewpoint is a defect here. A multiplex view of socio-stylistic variation, of the type developed in English by Holmes, Schiffrin and other scholars, has yet to find ample expression in French. Indeed, studies of this kind (or of any kind) that include a cross-stylistic component remain rare. Despite its central importance in sociolinguistic theory, style remains, as Bell (1996) has labelled it, 'the neglected dimension'.

7.7 Directions for future research

Corresponding to the limitations outlined above are the lacunae that remain to be filled in what is known of sociolinguistic variation in French compared to other languages; hence the frequent references to insufficient knowledge in the preceding sections. Coveney (2000b:37) has identified five areas of sociolinguistic enquiry in need of more research in French:

- sociolinguistic surveys of variation in more areas (especially France, Belgium and Switzerland);
- the relationship between social (class-based) and regional variation;
- the extent to which social variation exists at the levels of phonology, grammar, lexis and discourse;
- the extent to which linguistic changes currently in progress suggest convergence or divergence of varieties in France (and elsewhere);
- code-switching and language choice among various bilingual and bidialectal communities.

The present study has attempted to provide some information on the first four of these areas. More empirical data is needed; the programme continues.

Appendix

The following list shows all of the non-standard lexical items observed in the Dieuze corpus discussed in Chapter 6, with a (mostly British) English gloss where one seems readily available; otherwise a 'neutral' translation is given. A standard English gloss is given alongside the non-standard translation where this may not be clear in context. Where a literal translation would be unilluminating, a comment (italicised) is provided. Style labels are also given, and lexical items not attested in the Oxford-Hachette have been assumed to be familier (abbreviated to 'fam' below). As discussed in Chapter 6, Section 6.5.1, *familier* can be glossed as 'colloquial', *populaire* ('pop' below) as 'casual', and *vulgaire* as ('vulg' below) as 'vulgar'. The distribution of the lexical items across the two speech styles is also given, in numbers of tokens observed for all speaker groups aggregated.

Lexical item	Gloss / comment	Interview	Conversation
s'amener (fam)	to turn up		8
aprèm (fam)	afternoon		1
assurer (fam)	to be up to it, to be capable		1
bagnole (fam)	car		11
se balader (fam)	to go for a stroll	2	1
balance (pop)	grass, police informer		1
balèze (fam)	hefty		3
balle (fam)	French franc		17
bandant (vulg)	interesting, exciting		3
barbant (fam)	boring		1
se barrer (pop)	to go away		1
(re)baston (pop)	(another) fight		6
bécane (fam)	bike		1
être une bête (fam)	to be up to it, to be competent	1	3
bidon (fam)	phoney		1

Lexical item	Gloss / comment	Interview	Conversation
bled (fam)	village	2	4
boîte (fam)	night-club	1	
boîte (fam)	place of work	4	
bonhomme (fam)	bloke		5
(re)bordel (pop)	(another) mess, shambles	2	10
borne (fam)	kilometre		7
bosser (fam)	to work	1	4
botter quelqu'un (fam)	to interest someone		2
boucan (fam)	racket (noise)	1	
bouffer (fam)	to eat		20
avoir les boules (pop)	to be scared		3
boulot (fam)	work	3	3
bouquin (fam)	book		2
bourré (pop)	drunk	1	
branché (fam)	trendy	1	
se brancher sur quelque chose (fam)	to be interested in something		3
brique (fam)	10, 000 francs		1
cafouiller (fam)	to go wrong (of a situation)	1	
cailler (fam)	to be cold (of the weather)		1
caisse (pop)	car		2
caisse *adjective* (pop)	drunk		2
calculat(rice) (fam)	calculator		1
cambrousse (fam)	the sticks, the boondocks		1
canon (fam)	pretty girl		3
carbu (fam)	carburettor		4
casse (pop)	burglary		1
se casser (fam)	to go away		3
caté (fam)	catechism class		1
charcuter (fam)	to bungle a surgical operation		1
charrier (fam)	to joke or tease		1

Lexical item	Gloss / comment	Interview	Conversation
chercher quelqu'un (fam)	to pick a fight with someone	1	
chiche (fam)	capable (also: 'I dare you!')		1
chiant (vulg)	annoying		5
chié (pop)	awful, terrible		1
chien (fam)	nasty	1	
chier	to shit		6
en avoir rien à chier (vulg)	*expression of indifference*		1
chiottes (vulg)	toilets		2
choper quelqu'un (pop)	to arrest someone		1
chouette (fam)	smashing, very good	1	
chouï (fam)	party		2
ciné (fam)	cinema		1
cinglé (fam)	crazy		2
cinoche (fam)	cinema		2
claqué (fam)	tired		1
classe *adjective* (pop)	very good		4
clope (fam)	cigarette		10
cocard (fam)	black eye		2
cogner quelqu'un (fam)	to hit someone	1	
coincé (fam)	stiff, uptight (of a person)	3	1
con (vulg)	stupid		31
connard (vulg)	stupid		1
faire une connerie (vulg)	to do sth stupid; to fool about		30
conversass (fam)	conversation		1
cool (fam)	cool, relaxed	2	10
couilles (vulg)	balls, testicles		4
crack (fam)	expert	1	
crado (fam)	filthy		1
craindre (fam)	to be no good		5
craignos (pop)	useless, terrible		1
crevant (fam)	tiring		2

Lexical item	Gloss / comment	Interview	Conversation
crevé (fam)	tired		4
criser (fam)	to throw a tantrum or fit		4
cul (pop)	arse		2
culot (fam)	cheek, insolence		1
décoincer (fam)	to relax		1
débile (fam)	awful, hopeless		1
déconner (pop)	to do or say stupid things		8
défoncé (pop)	high on drugs		4
se défoncer (pop)	to go all out, not to spare oneself	1	
dégueu(lasse) (pop)	disgusting		7
dégueuler (pop)	to throw up, vomit		1
se démerder (pop)	to wangle a solution to a problem		3
dingue (fam)	crazy		4
dirlo (fam)	director (of a firm)		1
s'éclater (pop)	to have a good time		1
embarquer quelqu'un (fam)	to arrest someone		1
emmerdant (pop)	boring, annoying		1
emmerder quelqu'un (pop)	to bore or annoy someone		4
s'emmerder (fam)	to be bored	1	1
enculé (vulg)	term of abuse		1
d'enfer *adjective* (fam)	very good		8
enfoiré (vulg)	term of abuse		3
s'engueuler (pop)	to have an argument	1	6
entraver (fam)	to understand		2
pas évident (fam)	not easy	5	1
ex (fam)	ex (-wife, -husband etc.)	3	1
fada (fam)	crazy		3
bonne femme (fam)	woman		8
fendant (fam)	very funny		1
la fermer (pop)	to shut up		1

Lexical item	Gloss / comment	Interview	Conversation
coup de fil (fam)	telephone call	1	
filer quelque chose à quelqu'un (fam)	to hand someone something		3
flic (fam)	police officer		3
flinguer quelqu'un (pop)	to shoot someone	1	
flip (fam)	pin-table		3
des fois (fam)	sometimes	86	27
foot (fam)	football	13	13
fortiche (fam)	strong or competent		1
foutre (pop)	to do or put	1	10
s'en foutre (fam)	*expression of indifference*	3	15
se foutre de quelqu'un (pop)	to make fun of someone		19
va te faire foutre! (pop)	bugger off!		2
en avoir rien à foutre (pop)	*expression of indifference*	1	1
foutre le camp (pop)	to clear off, to go away		2
foutu (pop)	broken, out of order		6
(bien, mal) foutu (pop)	(well, badly) done / made / built		2
frangin (fam)	brother		13
frangine (fam)	sister		8
fric (fam)	money		8
frite (fam)	slap		1
avoir la frousse (fam)	to be scared		1
faire gaffe (fam)	to be careful		3
gars (fam)	lad, chap		58
gazer (fam)	to go well		1
génial (fam)	very good		7
gerbant (pop)	disgusting		2
gerber (pop)	to throw up, vomit		3
gonflé (fam)	cheeky, insolent		1
gonzesse (pop)	girl, woman		20
gosse (fam)	kid, child		5

Lexical item	Gloss / comment	Interview	Conversation
gueule (pop)	face		25
gueuler (pop)	to shout		1
intello (fam)	intellectual	1	
(faire une partie de) jambes-en-l'air (pop)	(to have) a roll in the hay		2
keuf (pop)	police officer		2
loubard (fam)	lout, hooligan		2
louper (fam)	to miss (bus, train etc.)	3	3
machin (fam)	thingummy, whatsit	8	41
marcher (fam)	to work, to succeed	1	9
en avoir marre (fam)	to be bored, to have had enough	5	22
se marrer (fam)	to have fun	1	
marrant (fam)	funny	2	1
maton (fam)	screw, prison warder		3
matos (fam)	material, equipment		1
max (fam)	maximum		1
mec (fam)	fellow, chap	1	71
merde (vulg/pop)	shit (*noun and exclamation*)	1	17
meuf (fam)	woman		3
mob (fam)	moped, motorised bicycle		5
moche (fam)	ugly		9
mono (fam)	monitor (in a holiday camp)		1
naze (pop)	useless, out of order		2
nénette (fam)	girl, woman		8
fin *adverb* (fam)	completely		10
nullos (fam)	useless, hopeless		1
à l'oeil (fam)	free of charge		1
patates (fam)	potatoes		1
patelin (fam)	village	2	1
en perpète (fam)	for a long time		2
pétard (pop)	revolver		1

Lexical item	Gloss / comment	Interview	Conversation
en avoir rien à péter (pop)	expression of indifference		1
péter (pop)	to fart		6
péter (fam)	to puncture or break		7
piaule (pop)	bedroom		5
le pied (fam)	very good		4
au pif (pop)	by guesswork		3
pisser (pop)	to piss		4
piston (fam)	string-pulling, influence	1	
pistonner quelqu'un (fam)	to pull strings for someone	1	
plan (fam)	trick, fiddle, scheme		1
laisser quelqu'un en plan (fam)	to let someone down		1
se planter (fam)	to get something wrong		4
plaquer quelqu'un (fam)	to ditch someone (a girl friend / boyfriend)		18
plein de (fam)	lots of	27	22
pognon (pop)	money		1
se pointer (fam)	to turn up, arrive		8
polar (fam)	detective novel	1	
pote (fam)	friend		1
poulet (pop)	police officer		1
pub (fam)	advert(isement)		2
pull (fam)	pullover		2
punaise (fam)	*exclamation*	2	13
putain (pop/vulg)	*exclamation*		66
pute	prostitute		3
quéquette (fam)	willy, penis		2
se ramener (fam)	to turn up, to arrive		1
rentrer dans quelqu'un (fam)	to lay into, to hit someone	1	
restau (fam)	restaurant		1
rétro (fam)	rear-view mirror		1
rigoler (fam)	to laugh or joke	2	23

Lexical item	Gloss / comment	Interview	Conversation
rigolo (fam)	funny	7	1
sacré (fam)	very good	2	2
salaud (pop)	*term of abuse*		7
shit (pop)	hashish		5
shooté (fam)	drug addict		1
shooteuse (fam)	hypodermic syringe		1
sinon (fam)	*non-standard use*	53	5
skin (fam)	skinhead	1	
sports-co (fam)	team sports	1	
sous (fam)	money	1	5
super (fam)	very good	3	19
super + *adjective* (fam)	very	2	23
sympa (fam)	nice (of a person)	2	18
taper sur quelqu'un (fam)	to hit someone	1	
s'en taper (pop)	*expression of indifference*		1
taré (fam)	ill, sick	1	4
tarte (fam)	slap		1
avoir la tchatch (fam)	to be talkative	1	1
télé (fam)	telly, TV	13	27
pas terrible (fam)	not very good	1	
se toquer de quelque chose (fam)	to be crazy about something	1	
toubib (fam)	doctor		1
transfo (fam)	transformer		1
avoir la trique (vulg)	to have a hard-on		2
tronche (fam)	ugly mug, face		1
troque (fam)	bistro, café		3
trop (fam)	'too much', very good		5
trou de cul (vulg)	arsehole		1
avoir la trouille (pop)	to be scared		2
trouillard (pop)	coward		3
truc (fam)	thingummy, whatsit	48	99

Lexical item	Gloss / comment	Interview	Conversation
la vache (fam)	*exclamation*		2
vachement (fam)	very, a lot	5	35
valser (fam)	to go smash		1
vélo (fam)	bike	1	
(re)virer quelqu'un (fam)	to throw someone out (again)		4

References

Ågren, J. 1973. *Etude sur quelques liaisons facultatives dans le français de conversation radiophonique*. Uppsala: Uppsala University Press.

Alpin, R. 1993. *A dictionary of contemporary France*. London: Hodder and Stoughton.

Armstrong, N. 1993. *A study of phonological variation in French secondary school pupils*. PhD thesis. University of Newcastle upon Tyne.

Armstrong, N. 1996. "Deletion of French /l/: linguistic, social and stylistic factors." *Journal of French Language Studies* 6 (1): 1–21.

Armstrong, N. 1998. "The sociolinguistic gender pattern in French: a comparison of two linguistic levels." *Journal of French Language Studies* 8 (2): 139–58.

Armstrong, N. Forthcoming. "The influence of spelling pronunciation in *oïl* French: an indication of social convergence?" In *French accents: phonological, sociolinguistic and learning perspectives*, Hintze, M.-A., Judge, A. and Pooley, T. (eds). London: AFLS/CiLT.

Armstrong, N. and Boughton, Z. 1999. "Identification and evaluation responses to a French accent: some results and issues of methodology." *Revue PArole* 5/6: 27–60.

Armstrong, N. and Unsworth, S. 1999. "Sociolinguistic variation in southern French schwa." *Linguistics* 37 (1): 127–56.

Ashby, W. 1976. "The loss of the negative morpheme *ne* in Parisian French." *Lingua* 39: 119–37.

Ashby, W. 1981a. "French liaison as a sociolinguistic phenomenon." In *Linguistic symposium on the Romance languages (9th)*, Cressey, W. W. and Napoli, D. J. (eds), 46–57. Washington, DC: Georgetown University Press.

Ashby, W. 1981b. "The loss of the negative particle *ne* in French: a syntactic change in progress." *Language* 57 (3): 674–87.

Ashby, W. 1984. "The elision of /l/ in French clitic pronouns and articles." *Michigan Romance Studies* 1(11): 1–16.

Ashby, W. 1991. "When does variation indicate linguistic change in progress?" *Journal of French Language Studies* 1 (1): 1–19.

Ashby, W. 1992. "The variable use of *on* versus *tu/vous* for indefinite reference in spoken French." *Journal of French Language Studies* 2 (2): 145–57.

Ashby, W. 2001. "Un nouveau regard sur la chute du *ne* en français parlé tourangeau: s'agit-il d'un changement en cours?" *Journal of French Language Studies* 11(1).

Bauvois, C. 1996. "Parle-moi, et je te dirai peut-être d'où tu es." *Revue de Phonétique Appliquée* 121: 291–309.

Behnstedt, P. 1973. *Viens-tu? Est-ce que tu viens? Tu viens? Formen und strukturen des direkten Fragessatzes im Französischen*. Tübingen: Narr.

Bell, A. 1982. "This isn't the BBC: colonialism in New Zealand English." *Applied Linguistics* 3: 246–58.

Bell, A. 1984. "Language style as audience design." *Language in Society* 13 (2): 145–204.

Bell, A. 1991. *The Language of news media*. Oxford: Blackwell.

Bell, A. 1995. Review of Biber, D. and Finegan, E. 1994. *Language in Society* 24 (1): 265–70.

Bell, A. 1996. "Style: the neglected dimension." Paper presented at a workshop on style variation (sponsored by the National Science Foundation), University of Stanford.

Biber, D. 1988. *Variation across speech and writing*. Cambridge: Cambridge University Press.

Biber, D. 1995. *Dimensions of register variation*. Cambridge: Cambridge University Press.

Biber, D. and Finegan, E. 1994 (eds) *Sociolinguistic perspectives on register*. New York/Oxford: Oxford University Press.

Blanche-Benveniste, C. and Jeanjean, C. 1987. *Le français parlé: transcription et édition*. Paris: Didier.

Blom, J.-P. and Gumperz, J. 1972. "Social meaning in linguistic structure: code-switching in Norway." In *Directions in sociolinguistics*, Gumperz, J. and Hymes, D. (eds), 407–34. New York: Holt, Rhinehart and Wilson.

Boomer, D. S. 1978. "The phonemic clause: speech unit in human communication." In *Nonverbal behaviour and communication*, Siegman, A. W. and Feldstein, S. (eds), 245–62. Hillsdale, NJ: Lawrence Erlbaum Associates.

Bourdieu, P. 1982. *Ce que parler veut dire. L'économie des échanges linguistiques*. Paris: Fayard.

Bourdieu, P. and Passeron, J.-C. 1970. *La reproduction*. Paris: Editions de Minuit.

Boutet, J. 1994. *Construire le sens*. Bern: Peter Lang.

Bradac, J. J. 1990. "Language attitudes and impression formation." In Giles, H. and Robinson, W. P. (eds), *Handbook of language and social psychology*, 387–412. Chichester: John Wiley.

Brown, G. 1982. "The spoken language." In *Linguistics and the teacher*, Carter, R. (ed.), 75–87. London: Routledge and Kegan Paul.

Calvet, L.-J. 1994. *L'argot français*. Paris: Presses Universitaires de France.

Calvert, D. R. 1986. *Descriptive phonetics* (second edition). New York: Thieme.

Capon, A. J. E. 1963. *Avec ou sans liaison?* Oxford: Blackwell.

Carton, F., Rossi, M., Autesserre, D. and Léon, P. 1983. *Les accents des Français*. Paris: Hachette.

Cedergren, H. and Sankoff, D. 1974. "Variable rules: performance as a statistical reflection of competence." *Language* 50: 333–35.

Chambers, J. K. 1995. *Sociolinguistic theory*. Oxford: Blackwell.

Chambers, J. K., and Trudgill, P. 1998. *Dialectology* (second edition). Cambridge: Cambridge University Press.

Cheshire, J. 1982. *Variation in an English dialect*. Cambridge: Cambridge University Press.

Cheshire, J. 1997. "Syntactic variation and the concept of prominence". In *Speech past and present. Studies in English dialectology in memory of Ossi Ihalainen*, Klemola, J., Kytö, M. and Rissanen, M. (eds), 1–17. Bern: Peter Lang.

Clermont, J., and Cedergren, H. J. 1979. "Les 'R' de ma mère sont perdus dans l'air.". In *Le français parlé: études sociolinguistiques*, Thibault, P. (ed.), 13–28. Edmonton: Linguistic Research.

Corréard, M.-H. and Grundy, V. (eds) 1997. *The Oxford-Hachette French Dictionary*. Oxford/Paris: Oxford University Press/Hachette.

Coupland, N. 1980. "Style-shifting in a Cardiff work-setting." *Language in Society* 9: 1–12.

Coveney, A. B. 1990. "Variation in interrogatives in spoken French: a preliminary report." In Green, J. N. and Ayres-Bennett, W. (eds), 116–33.

Coveney, A. B. 1991. "Contemporary variation in the omission of *ne*." Paper presented at a Workshop on Historical Linguistics, University of Oxford.

Coveney, A. B. 1995. "The use of the QU-final interrogative structure in spoken French." *Journal of French Language Studies* 5 (2): 143–171.

Coveney, A. B. 1996. *Variability in spoken French. A sociolinguistic study of interrogation and negation.* Exeter: Elm Bank.

Coveney, A. B. 2000a. "Vestiges of *nous* and the 1st person plural verb in informal spoken French." *Language Sciences* 22: 447–81.

Coveney, A. B. 2000b. "Sociolinguistics." In AFLS (Association for French Language Studies) *Cahier* 6HS: *A Brief Guide to Research in French Language and Linguistics*, Lodge, R. A. (ed.), 37–8. Hull: University of Hull/AFLS. URL: www.unl.ac.uk/sals/afls/resguide.htm#Sociolinguistics

Crinson, J. 1997. *Standard English, the National Curriculum, and linguistic disadvantage: a sociolinguistic account of the careful speech of Tyneside adolescents.* PhD thesis, University of Newcastle upon Tyne.

Dannequin, C. 1977. *Les enfants bâillonnés.* Paris: CEDIL.

Dannequin, C. 1988. "Les enfants bâillonnés (gagged children): the teaching of French as mother tongue in elementary school." *Language and Education* 1: 15–31.

Dauncey, H. D. 1999. "Building the finals: facilities and infrastructure." In *France and the 1998 World Cup: the national impact of a world sporting event*, Dauncey, H. D. and Hare, G. E. (eds), 98–120. London: Frank Cass.

De Jong, D. 1988. "Sociolinguistic aspects of French liaison." PhD thesis, Free University of Amsterdam.

De Jong, D. 1991. "La liaison à Orléans (France) et à Montréal (Québec)." Mimeo of paper presented at the XIIth international congress of phonetic sciences, Aix-en Provence.

De Jong, D. 1993. "Sociophonological aspects of Montreal French liaison." In *Linguistic perspectives on the Romance languages 21*, Ashby, W., Mithun, M., Perissinotto G., and Raposo, E. (eds), 127–138. Amsterdam: Benjamins.

Delattre, P. 1956. "Les fréquences des liaisons facultatives en français." *French Review* 30 (1), 48–54.

Dell, F. 1980. *Generative phonology and French phonology.* Cambridge: Cambridge University Press.

Diller, A-M. 1983. "Subject NP structure and variable constraints; the case of *ne*-deletion." In *Variation in the form and use of language*, Fasold, R. (ed.), 167–75. Washington, DC: Georgetown University Press.

Duneton, C. 1984. *A hurler le soir au fond des collèges.* Paris: Seuil.

Eckert, P. 1989. "The whole woman: sex and gender differences in variation." *Language Variation and Change* 1: 245–67.

Emirkanian, L. and Sankoff, D. 1985. "Le futur simple et le futur périphrastique dans le français parlé." In *Les tendances dynamiques du français parlé à Montréal*, Lemieux, M. and Cedergren, H. (eds), tome 1, 189–204. Quebec: Office de la Langue Française. Also in *Actes du XVIIe Congrès International de Linguistique et Philologie Romanes*, vol. 4.

Encrevé, P. 1983. "La liaison sans enchaînement." *Actes de la recherche en sciences sociales, 46,* 39–66. Paris: Editions de Minuit.

Encrevé, P. 1988. *La liaison avec et sans enchaînement.* Paris: Seuil.

Fasold, R. 1978. "Language variation and linguistic competence." In Sankoff, D. (ed.), 85–96.

Finegan, E. and Biber, D. 1994. "Register and social dialect variation: an integrated approach." In Biber, D. and Finegan, E. (eds), 315–347.

Fónagy, I. and Magdics, K. 1960. "Speed of utterance in phrases of different lengths." *Language and Speech* 4: 179–92.

Foulkes, P. and Docherty, G. J. (eds) 1999a. *Urban voices: accent studies in the British Isles.* London: Arnold.

Foulkes, P. and Docherty, G. J. 1999b. "Urban Voices — an overview." In Foulkes, P. and Docherty, G. J. (eds), 1–24.

Gadet, F. 1997a. *Le français ordinaire* (second edition). Paris: Armand Colin.

Gadet, F. 1997b. "La variation, plus qu'une écume." *Langue Française* 115: 5–18.

Gadet, F. 1998a. "Des fortifs aux técis: persistances et discontinuités dans la langue populaire." In *Linguistic identities and policies in France and the French-speaking world,* Marley, D., Hintze, M.-A. and Parker, G. (eds), 11–26. London: AFLS/CILT.

Gadet, F. 1998b. "Cette dimension de variation que l'on ne sait nommer." *Sociolinguistica* 12: 53–71.

Garmadi, J. 1981. *La sociolinguistique.* Paris: Presses Universitaires de France.

George, K. 1993. "Alternative French." In Sanders, C. (ed.), 155–70.

Giles, H. 1970. "Evaluative reactions to accents." *Educational Review* 22: 211–27.

Giles, H. 1973. "Accent mobility: a model and some data." *Anthropological Linguistics* 15: 87–105.

Giles, H. 1992. "Attitudes to language." In *The Oxford International Encyclopedia of Linguistics* Volume 4, Bright, W. (ed.), 132–34. Oxford: Oxford University Press.

Giles, H. and Powesland, P. F. 1975. *Speech style and social evaluation.* London: Academic Press.

Giles, H. and St Clair, R. N. (eds) 1979. *Language and social psychology.* Oxford: Blackwell.

Gimson, A. C. 1989. *An introduction to the pronunciation of English.* (fourth edition, edited by Ramsaran, S.). London: Arnold.

Gósy, M. 1991. "The perception of tempo." In *Temporal factors in speech: a collection of papers,* Gósy, M. (ed.), 63–106. Budapest: Research Institute for Linguistics, Hungarian Academy of Sciences.

Green, J. N. and Ayres-Bennett, W. (eds) 1990. *Variation and Change in French.* London: Routledge.

Green, J. N. and Hintze, M.-A. 1990. "Variation and change in French linking phenomena." In Green, J. N. and Ayres-Bennett, W. (eds), 61–88.

Green, J. N. and Hintze, M.-A. 1992. "Gendered links: the sociolinguistics of phonological linkage in Modern French." Paper presented at the annual conference of the Association for French Language Studies, University of York.

Grevisse, M. 1986. *Le bon usage (12ème édition, refondue par A. Goosse).* Gembloux: Duculot.

Guy, G. 1980. "Variation in the group and the individual: the case of final stop deletion." In Labov, W. (ed.), 1–36.

Hansen, A. B. 1994. "Etude du E caduc — stabilisation en cours et variations lexicales", *Journal of French Language Studies*, 4 (1): 25–54.

Hansen, A. B. 1997. "Le nouveau [ə] prépausal dans le français parlé à Paris." In *Polyphonie pour Iván Fónagy: mélanges offerts en hommage à Iván Fónagy par un groupe de disciples, collègues et admirateurs*, Perrot, J. (ed.), 173–198. Paris: L'Harmattan.

Hansen, A. B. 1998. *Les voyelles nasales du français parisien moderne. Aspects linguistiques, sociolinguistiques et perceptuels des changements en cours*. Copenhagen: Museum Tusculanum.

Hansen, A. B. 2000. "Le E caduc interconsonantique en tant que variable sociolinguistique — une étude en région parisienne." *LINX (Revue des Linguistes de l'Université Paris-X Nanterre)* 42 (1): 45–58.

Hare, G. E. 1989. *Parlons Sciences-Po* (second edition). London: Arnold.

Harms, L. S., 1961. "Listener judgments of status cues in speech." *Quarterly Journal of Speech* 47: 164–8.

Harris, M. 1988. "French." In *The Romance languages*, Harris, M. and Vincent, N. (eds), 209–45. London: Croom Helm.

Hawkins, R. 1993. "Regional variation in France." In Sanders, C. (ed.), 55–84.

Hérail, R. J. and Lovatt, E. A. 1990. *Dictionary of modern colloquial French*, London: Routledge.

Hinskens, F. 1992. "Dialect levelling in Limburg. Structural and sociolinguistic aspects." PhD thesis, Katholieke Universiteit te Nijmegen, 1992.

Hobsbawm, E. J. 1977. *The age of revolution*. London: Abacus.

Holmes, J. 1997. "Women, language and identity." *Journal of Sociolinguistics* 2 (1): 195–223.

Hornsby, D. 1999. "Optional liaison in two French cities: some preliminary observations". Paper presented at the First French Variation Forum, London Guildhall University, July 1999.

Hudson, R. A. 1996. *Sociolinguistics* (second edition). Cambridge: Cambridge University Press.

Hume, E. 1988. "The realisation of /R/ in Canadian and standard European French." In *Linguistic change and contact: proceedings of the 16th annual conference on New Ways of Analysing Variation*, Ferrara, K. et al. (eds.), 143–51. Austin: University of Texas.

Jahangiri, N. 1980. "A sociolinguistic study of Tehrani Persian." PhD thesis, University of London.

Jahangiri, N. and Hudson, R. A. 1982. "Patterns of variation in Tehrani Persian." In *Sociolinguistic variation in speech communities*, Romaine, S. (ed.), 49–63. London: Arnold.

Jespersen, O. 1922. *Language: its nature, development and origin*. London: Allen & Unwin.

Johnston, P. 1983. "Irregular style variation patterns in Edinburgh speech." *Scottish Language* 2: 1–19.

Joos, M. 1961. *The five clocks*. New York: Harcourt.

Judge, A. 1993. "French: a planned language?" In Sanders, C. (ed.), 7–26.

Juillard, C., Moreau, M.-L., Ndao, P. A. and Thiam, N. 1994. "Leur Wolof dit-il qui ils sont?" *Langage et Société* 68: 36–62.

Kerswill, P. 1987. "Levels of linguistic variation in Durham". *Journal of Linguistics* 23: 25–49.

Kerswill, P. and Williams, A. 2000. "Creating a new town koine: children and language change in Milton Keynes". *Language in Society* 29 (1): 65–115.

Key, M. R. 1975. *Male/female language*. Metuchen, NJ: Scarecrow Press.

Kroch, A. 1978. "Toward a theory of social dialect variation." *Language in Society* 7: 17–36.

Kroch, A. and Small, C. 1978. "Grammatical ideology and its effect on speech." In Sankoff, D. (ed.), 45–55.

Laberge, S. 1970. "The changing distribution of indefinite pronouns in discourse." In *Variation in the form and use of language*, Fasold, R. (ed.), 248–60. Washington, DC: Georgetown University Press.

Labov, W. 1966. *The social stratification of English in New York City*. Washington, DC: Center for Applied Linguistics.

Labov, W. 1970. "Stages in the acquisition of standard English." In *English linguistics: an introductory reader*, Hungerford, H., Robinson, J. and Sledd, J. (eds), 274–303. Glenview, Ill: Scott Foresman.

Labov, W. 1972a. *Language in the inner city: studies in the Black English Vernacular*. Philadelphia: University of Pennsylvania Press.

Labov, W. 1972b. *Sociolinguistic patterns*. Philadelphia: University of Pennsylvania Press.

Labov, W. 1978. "Where does the sociolinguistic variable stop? A response to Beatriz Lavandera." *Working papers in sociolinguistics 44*, Austin, Texas: South-West Educational Development Laboratory, University of Texas.

Labov, W. (ed.) 1980. *Locating language in time and space*. New York: Academic Press.

Labov, W. 1990. "The intersection of sex and social class in the course of linguistic change." *Language Variation and Change* 2: 205–54.

Labov, W. 1994. *Principles of linguistic change*. Oxford: Oxford University Press.

Labov, W. and Harris, W. 1986. "De facto segregation of black and white vernaculars." In *Diversity and Diachrony*, Sankoff, D. (ed.), 1–24. Amsterdam: Benjamins.

Lakoff, R. 1975. *Language and women's place*. New York: Harper & Row.

Laks, B. 1977. "Contribution empirique à l'analyse socio-différentielle de la chute de /r/ dans les groupes consonantiques finales." *Langue Française* 34: 109–25.

Laks, B. 1983. "Langage et pratiques sociales. Etude sociolinguistique d'un groupe d'adolescents." *Actes de la recherche en sciences sociales* 46: 73–97. Paris: Editions de Minuit.

Landick, M. 1995. "The mid-vowels in figures: hard facts." *French Review* 69 (1): 88–103.

Lavandera, B. 1978. "Where does the sociolinguistic variable stop?" *Language in Society* 7: 171–82.

Lavandera, B. 1981. "Sociolinguistics." In *Trends in Romance linguistics and philology, Volume 2: Synchronic Romance linguistics*, Posner, R. and Green, J. N. (eds), 129–228. The Hague: Mouton.

Lass, R. 1984. *Phonology*. Cambridge: Cambridge University Press.

Laver, J. 1994. *Principles of phonetics*. Cambridge: Cambridge University Press.

Leech, G. 1981. *Semantics*. Penguin: Harmondsworth.

Lemieux, M. and Cedergren, H. (eds) 1985. *Les tendances dynamiques du français parlé à Montréal, Volume 2*. Québec: Office de la langue française.

Léon, P. (1993). *Précis de phonostylistique*. Paris: Nathan.

Lewis, C. S. 1967. *Studies in words* (second edition). Cambridge: Cambridge University Press.

Li, W. 1998. "The 'why' and 'how' questions in the analysis of conversational code-switching." In *Code-switching in conversation, Language, interaction and identity*, Auer, P. (ed.), 156–76. London: Routledge.

Lodge, R. A. 1989. "Speakers' perceptions of non-standard vocabulary in French." *Zeitschrift für Romanische Philologie* 105 (6): 427–44.

Lodge, R. A. 1993. *French: from dialect to standard*. London: Routledge.

Lodge, R. A., Armstrong, N., Ellis, Y. and Shelton, J. 1997. *Exploring the French language*. London: Edward Arnold.

Lucci, V. 1983. *Etude phonétique du français contemporain à travers la variation situationnelle*. Grenoble: Publications de l'Université de langue et lettres de Grenoble.

Macaulay, R. K. S. 1977. *Language, social class and education*. Edinburgh: Edinburgh University Press.

Mahl, G. F. 1972. "People talking when they can't hear their voices." In *Studies in dyadic communication*, Siegman, A. W. and Pope, B. (eds), 211–64. New York: Pergammon.

Malécot, H. 1975. "French liaison as a function of grammatical, phonetic and paralinguistic variables." *Phonetica* 32: 161–79.

Malécot, H. 1976. "The effect of linguistic and paralinguistic variables on the elision of the French mute-e." *Phonetica* 33: 93–112.

Martel, P. 1984. "Les variables lexicales sont-elles sociolinguistiquement intéressantes?" In *Sociolinguistique des langues romanes. Actes du XVIIème Congrès International de Linguistique et de Philologie Romanes vol. 5*, 181–93. Aix-en Provence: Université de Provence.

Martin, J. P. 1967. *The basal ganglia and posture*. London: Pitman Medical.

Martinet, A. 1945. *La prononciation du français contemporain*. Paris: Droz.

Martinet, A. 1962. *A functional view of language*. Oxford: Oxford University Press.

Martinet, A. 1974. *Le français sans fard*. Paris: Presses Universitaires de France.

Martinon, P. 1913. *Comment on prononce le français*. Paris: Larousse.

Matthews, P. 1981. *Syntax*. Cambridge: Cambridge University Press.

Mees, I. 1990. "Patterns of socio-phonetic variation in the speech of Cardiff schoolchildren." In *English in Wales*, Coupland, N. (ed.), 167–194. Clevedon: Multilingual Matters.

Meillet, A. 1912. "L'évolution des formes grammaticales." In *Linguistique historique et linguistique générale*, Meillet, A. (ed.), 131–48. Paris: Champion.

Merle, P. 1986. *Dictionnaire du français branché*, Paris: Seuil.

Milroy, J. 1992. *Linguistic variation and change*. Oxford: Blackwell.

Milroy, J. and Milroy, L. 1978. "Belfast: change and variation in an urban vernacular". In *Sociolinguistic patterns in British English*, Trudgill, P. (ed.), 19–36. London: Edward Arnold.

Milroy, J. and Milroy, L. 1985. "Linguistic change, social network and speaker innovation." *Journal of Linguistics* 21: 339–84.

Milroy, J. and Milroy, L. 1991. *Authority in language* (second edition). London: Routledge.

Milroy, J. and Milroy, L. 1992. "Social network and social class: toward an integrated sociolinguistic model." *Language in Society* 21: 1–26.

Milroy, L. 1987a. *Language and social networks* (second edition). Oxford: Blackwell.

Milroy, L. 1987b. *Observing and analysing natural language*. Oxford: Blackwell.

Milroy, L. 1992. "New perspectives in the analysis of sex differentiation in language." In *Sociolinguistics today: international perspectives*, Bolton, K. and Kwok, H. (eds), 163–79. London/New York: Routledge.

Milroy, J., Milroy, L., Hartley, S. and Walshaw, D. 1994. "Glottal stops and Tyneside glottalisation: competing patterns of variation and change in British English." *Language Variation and Change* 6: 327–57.

Milroy, J. 1996. "Gender difference as a factor in language change." Paper presented in the Department of Speech, University of Newcastle upon Tyne.

Moreau, M.-L. 1986. "Les séquences préformées: entre les combinaisons libres et les idiomatismes. Le cas de la négation avec et sans *ne.*" *Le Français Moderne* 54: 137–60.

Nadsadi, T. 1995. "Subject NP doubling, matching, and minority French." *Language Variation and Change* 7 (1): 1–14.

Neu, H. 1980. "Ranking of constraints on /t,d/-deletion in American English: a statistical analysis." In Labov, W. (ed.), 37–54.

Newbrook, M. 1986. *Sociolinguistic reflexes of dialect interference in West Wirral.* Bern: Peter Lang.

Nicholson, G. G. 1909. *A practical introduction to French phonetics.* London: Macmillan.

Nicolson, H. G. 1955. *Good behaviour: being a study of certain types of civility.* London: Constable.

Opie, I. and Opie, P. 1959. *The lore and language of schoolchildren.* Oxford: Oxford University Press.

Paltridge, J. and Giles, H. 1984. "Attitudes towards speakers of regional accents of French: effects of regionality, age and sex of listeners." *Linguistiche Berichte* 90: 71–85.

Pohl, J. 1975. "L'omission de NE dans le français parlé contemporain." *Le français dans le monde* 111: 17–23.

Pooley, T. 1996. *Chtimi: the urban vernaculars of northern France.* Clevedon: Multilingual Matters.

Poplack, S. (1989) The care and handling of a mega-corpus: the case of the Ottawa-Hull French project. In: *Language change and variation*, Fasold, R. W. and Schiffrin, D. (eds.), 411–51. Amsterdam: Benjamins.

Powell, A. 1966. *The soldier's art.* London: Heinemann.

Preston, D. 1991. "Sorting out the variables in sociolinguistic theory." *American Speech* 66 (1): 33–56.

Price, G. 1984. *The French language: present and past* (second edition). London: Grant & Cutler.

Rey, A. and Rey-Debove, J. (eds) 1986. *Le Petit Robert: dictionnaire alphabétique et analogique de la langue française.* Paris: Les Dictionnaires Robert.

Rey, A. and Rey-Debove, J. (eds) 1995. *Le Nouveau Petit Robert: dictionnaire alphabétique et analogique de la langue française,* Paris: Les Dictionnaires Robert.

Rickard, P. 1993. Review of Lodge, R. A. 1993. *Journal of French Language Studies* 3 (2): 243–4.

Roach, P. 1999. "Some languages are spoken more quickly than others." In *Language myths*, Bauer, L. and Trudgill, P. (eds), 150–8. Harmondsworth: Penguin.

Romaine, S. 1979. "Postvocalic /r/ in Scottish English: sound change in progress?" In *Sociolinguistic Patterns in British English*, Trudgill, P. (ed.), 144–57. London: Arnold.

Romaine, S. 1981. "On the problem of syntactic variation: a reply to B. Lavandera and W. Labov." *Working papers in sociolinguistics 82*, Austin, Texas: South-West Educational Development Laboratory, University of Texas.

Romaine, S. 1984. *The language of children and adolescents.* Oxford: Blackwell.

Sacks, O. 1985. *The man who mistook his wife for a hat.* London: Picador.

Sanders, C. (ed.) 1993a. *French today. Language in its social context.* Cambridge: Cambridge University Press.

Sanders, C. 1993b. "Sociosituational variation." In Sanders, C. (ed.), 27–54.

Sankoff, D. (ed.) 1978. *Linguistic variation: models and methods.* New York: Academic Press.

Sankoff, D. 1988. "Sociolinguistics and syntactic variation." In *Linguistics: the Cambridge survey. Volume IV Language: the socio-cultural context*, Newmeyer, F. J. (ed.), 140–61. Cambridge: Cambridge University Press.

Sankoff, D. and Laberge, S. 1978. "The linguistic market and the statistical explanation of variability." In Sankoff, D. (ed.), 239–50.

Sankoff, D., Thibault, P. and Bérubé, H. 1978. "Semantic field variability." In Sankoff, D. (ed.), 23–43.

Sankoff, G. 1973. "Above and beyond phonology in variable rules." In *New ways of analyzing variation in English*, Bailey, C.-J. N. and Shuy, R. (eds), 81–93. Washington: Georgetown University Press. Also in Sankoff, G. (ed.) (1980).

Sankoff, G. (ed.) 1980b. *The social life of language.* Philadelphia: University of Pennsylvania Press.

Sankoff, G. and Cedergren, H. 1971. "Some results of a sociolinguistic study of Montreal French." In *Linguistic diversity in Canadian society*, Darnell, R. (ed.), 61–87. Edmonton: Linguistic Research.

Sankoff, G. and Cedergren, H. 1976. "Les contraintes linguistiques et sociales de l'élision du *l* chez les Montréalais." In *Proceedings of the XIII international congress of Romance linguistics and philology*, Boudreault, M., Moehren, F. and Moehren, M. (eds), 1101–16. Quebec: Presses de l'Université Laval.

Sankoff, G. and Thibault, P. 1980. "The alternation between the auxiliaries *avoir* and *être* in Montreal French." In Sankoff, G. (ed.), 311–45.

Sankoff, G. and Vincent, D. 1980. "The productive use in *ne* in spoken Montreal French." In Sankoff, G. (ed.), 295–310.

Schenk-van Witsen, R. 1981. "Les différences sexuelles dans le français parlé: une étude-pilote des différences lexicales entre hommes et femmes." *Langage et Société* 17: 59–78.

Schiffrin, D. 1985. "Multiple constraints on discourse options: a quantitative analysis of causal sequences." *Discourse Processes* 8 (3): 281–303.

Schiffrin, D. 1987. *Discourse* markers. Cambridge: Cambridge University Press.

Siptár, P. 1991. "Fast-speech processes in Hungarian." In *Temporal factors in speech: a collection of papers*, Gósy, M. (ed.), 27–62. Budapest: Research Institute for Linguistics, Hungarian Academy of Sciences.

Smith, A. 1996. "A diachronic study of French variable liaison." MLitt dissertation, University of Newcastle upon Tyne.

Smith, A. 1998. "French variable liaison: a proposed simplification." *Francophonie* 17: 11–14.

Smith, A. 2000. "Linguistic change on British and French public service radio." PhD thesis, University of Newcastle upon Tyne.

Tagliamonte, S. 1998. "*Was/were* across the generations: view from the city of York." *Language Variation and Change* 10: 153–91.

Traugott, E. C. 1989. "On the rise of epistemic meanings in English: an example of subjectivication in semantic change." *Language* 65: 31–55.

Trudgill, P. 1972. "Sex, covert prestige and linguistic change in the urban British English of Norwich." *Language in Society* 1: 179–95.

Trudgill, P. 1974. *The social differentiation of English in Norwich.* Cambridge: Cambridge University Press.

Trudgill, P. 1975. *Accent, dialect and the school.* London: Edward Arnold.

Trudgill, P. 1986. *Dialects in contact.* Oxford: Blackwell.

Trudgill, P. 1988. "Norwich revisited: recent changes in an urban English dialect." *English Worldwide* 9: 39–49.

Trudgill, P. 1995. *Sociolinguistics: an introduction to language and society* (third edition). Harmondsworth: Penguin.

Trudgill, P. 1997. "Language contact and inherent variability: the absence of hypercorrection in East Anglian present-tense verb forms." In *Speech past and present. Studies in English dialectology in memory of Ossi Ihalainen*, Klemola, J., Kytö, M. and Rissanen, M. (eds), 412–26. Bern: Peter Lang.

Trudgill, P. 1999a. "New-dialect formation and dedialectalisation: embryonic and vestigial variants." *Journal of English Linguistics* 27 (4): 319–27.

Trudgill, P. 1999b. "Norwich: endogenous and exogenous linguistic change." In Foulkes, P. and Docherty, G. J. (eds), 124–40.

Ullmann, S. 1975. *Principles of semantics.* Glasgow: University of Glasgow Press.

Valdman, A. 1982. "Français standard et français populaire: sociolectes ou fictions?" *French Review* 56 (2): 218–27.

Walter, H. 1976. *La dynamique des phonèmes dans le lexique français comtemporain.* Geneva: Droz.

Walter, H. 1982. *Enquête phonologique et variétés régionales du français.* Paris: France Expansion.

Walter, H. 1988. *Le français dans tous les sens.* Paris: Robert Laffont.

von Wartburg, W. 1967. *Evolution et structure de la langue française* (sixth edition). Bern: Francke.

Watt, D. and Milroy, L. 1999. Patterns of variation and change in three Newcastle vowels: is this dialect leveling?" In Foulkes, P. and Docherty, G. J. (eds), 25–46.

Weinreich, U., Labov, W. and Herzog, M. I. 1968. "Empirical foundations for a theory of language change." In *Directions for historical linguistics: a symposium*, Lehmann, W. P. and Malkiel, Y. (eds), 95–188. Austin: University of Texas Press.

Wheeler, M. W. 1995. "'Politeness', sociolinguistic theory and language change." *Folia Linguistica Historica* 15: 149–74.

Williams, A. and Kerswill, P. 1999. "Dialect leveling: change and continuity in Milton Keynes, Reading and Hull." In Foulkes, P. and Docherty, G. J. (eds), 141–62.

Wioland, F. 1991. *Prononcer les mots du français.* Paris: Hachette.

Wolfram, W. 1969. *A sociolinguistic description of Detroit Negro speech.* Washington: Center for Applied Linguistics.

Woods, H. B. 1979. "A socio-dialectology survey of the English spoken in Ottawa: a study of sociological and stylistic variation in Canadian English." PhD thesis, University of British Columbia, Vancouver.

Wright, S. 1989. "The effects of style and speaking rate on /l/-vocalisation in local Cambridge English." *York papers in linguistics* 13: 355–65.

Wyld, H. C. 1906. *The historical study of the mother tongue.* New York: Dutton.

Yaeger-Dror, M. 1993. "Linguistic analysis of dialect 'correction' and its interaction with cognitive salience." *Language Variation and Change* 5: 189–230.

Index

The deletable French variables that are principally of interest here, schwa, /l/, /r/ and *ne*, are listed under *deletion*, as *deletion of /l/*, etc. These headings include references to insertion or non-deletion phenomena. Other French variables are listed alphabetically; either generally, as *grammatical*, or specifically, as *interrogatives*, *lexical*, *liaison*, etc. Topics considered at some length are listed in the table of contents as well as the index.